THE SOURCES OF HISTORY:
STUDIES IN THE USES OF HISTORICAL EVIDENCE

GENERAL EDITOR: G. R. ELTON

In the Same Series

The Sources of History:
Studies in the Uses of Historical Evidence

The United States
1789–1890

by
WILLIAM R. BROCK

CORNELL UNIVERSITY PRESS
Ithaca, New York

First published 1975 by Cornell University Press

This edition is not for sale in the United Kingdom, the British Commonwealth excluding Canada, or Europe.

International Standard Book Number 0-8014-0723-0
Library of Congress Catalog Card Number 72-2460

Printed in Great Britain

Contents

The United States 1789–1890

PART IV
THE AMERICAN MIND

General Editor's Introduction

By what right do historians claim that their reconstructions of the past are true, or at least on the road to truth? How much of the past can they hope to recover: are there areas that will remain for ever dark, questions that will never receive an answer? These are problems which should and do engage not only the scholar and student but every serious reader of history. In the debates on the nature of history, however, attention commonly concentrates on philosophic doubts about the nature of historical knowledge and explanation, or on the progress that might be made by adopting supposedly new methods of analysis. The disputants hardly ever turn to consider the materials with which historians work and which must always lie at the foundation of their structures. Yet, whatever theories or methods the scholar may embrace, unless he knows his sources and rests upon them he will not deserve the name of historian. The bulk of historical evidence is much larger and more complex than most laymen and some professionals seem to know, and a proper acquaintance with it tends to prove both exhilarating and sobering—exhilarating because it opens the road to unending enquiry, and sobering because it reduces the inspiring theory and the new method to their proper subordinate place in the scheme of things. It is the purpose of this series to bring this fact to notice by showing what we have and how it may be used.

G. R. ELTON

Preface

This book is not a guide to American archives but a personal survey of the sources upon which the edifice of American history rests. If there are points at which the handling of sources is criticised, and others at which gaps in existing historiography are suggested, the background is one of enormous respect for the achievement of American historians. Indeed there is no field in which more has been done or in which there is more lively speculation about future developments. If the quality of American professional history had been commended wherever praise were due this book would have become a sustained eulogy rather than a study in the use of historical evidence.

It seemed best, in this book, not to attempt a survey of the sources for frontier and western history; to have done so would either have extended it to inordinate length or imposed unwelcome restrictions upon the discussion of other aspects of American history. Moreover, many of the sources for western history introduce techniques and types of evidence which demand separate consideration. It was therefore decided to leave this important area of history for separate treatment in another volume of this series. For somewhat different reasons it was also decided to make only incidental reference to business history which could, more appropriately, be treated as an international study.

It would have been possible to ask colleagues who are experts in the fields surveyed to read and comment upon the various chapters. I am sure that I should have learnt much from their criticism, but the book would have turned into a committee report rather than a personal statement. I have, therefore, thought it best to let the book stand, with all its omissions and idiosyncrasies, as the reflections of one scholar upon the sources of American history.

Glasgow   W. R. BROCK

GENERAL INTRODUCTION
Purpose and Principles

The proliferation of historical literature makes it increasingly difficult to see the broad perspectives that the study of history is supposed to reveal. Historical studies become fragmented, specialisation replaces generalisation, and it is a bold man who ventures far from the field in which his authority is recognised. There are thousands of volumes which neatly package great chunks of history for the educational supermarkets, but it is uncommon for historians to contemplate the production of the multi-volume histories which were once regarded as the supreme achievement of historical craft. The accumulation of specialised literature makes it almost as difficult for the historian as it is for the scientist to keep abreast of studies outside his chosen field; there is even developing a professional etiquette which discourages trespassing and demands that scholars continue to travel along the channels marked out by their first research.

Specialisation proceeds by period and by topic. It may not be precisely true that one rich and great university maintains a full professor for each decade of American history, but it is not far from the ideal to which many universities aspire. The Revolutionary period, the 'early national' period, Jacksonian America, the era of the Civil War, Reconstruction, and so on, have each produced their high priests, their rites, and their ritual controversies. The history of the South tends to become segregated from the history of the United States; so does the history of the West. The various branches of history develop their own internal processes so that they become unintelligible to outsiders, while economic history, which is normally separated administratively from Departments of History, becomes incomprehensible to fellow

13

historians. Traditional branches of study—constitutional history, political history, and intellectual history—strive to maintain their separate existence. Urban history has now staked out its claim for separate courses and a specialised literature. Black history is the newest and most vocal advocate for independence. As the demands for autonomy are recognised each study develops its own techniques, its own criteria, and its own concept of valid evidence; yet all are studying the same society.

For the student history tends to exist in two forms: the survey course in which complex issues are reduced to lucid but bland generalisation, and the specialist course in which he samples some source material and reads some professional literature. But even in the advanced course it is probable that much of the source material comes to him in a pre-digested form—in 'readers' along with some modern chapters or articles which are said to mark 'turning points' in historical interpretation. Frequently, in this palatable form, the footnote references in modern extracts have been removed by the editors, so that the student sees the argument without means of judging the evidence.

The panorama of historical studies may therefore be compared to a mountain landscape. In a survey the student can see the peaks but little of the valleys; he learns to appreciate the cold impersonality of the heights but knows little of those who toil on the lower slopes; nor does he know anything of the geology, the biology, the botany, or the materials of which his landscape is made. At the same time the men working in the valley or on the mountain side know little of life in other valleys or on other slopes.

The reading of history is not confined to students and professional scholars. There is an immense appetite, amongst educated people on both sides of the Atlantic, for works which reconstruct the past in a readable way. Professionals are apt to scorn 'popular history', but they ignore it at their peril. A scholar's reconstruction of the past, conveyed in closely written pages with dense documentation, may influence future generations as it percolates down through layers of the pedagogic world, but the successful popular historian may have an immediate impact. Some popular history is bad history in that it exploits the bizarre and sensational, selects what is striking or shocking, leaves aside what is dull but important, and is careless of evidence provided that an effect is produced. But not all widely read works of popular historians are like this and some are based on intensive research into the sources and a scrupulous respect for truth. Bruce Catton's books about the Civil War are 'popular' in the sense that they are vividly written and sell widely, but their literary elegance rests upon a solid foundation of knowledge. The difficulty is that the non-professional reader finds it impossible to distinguish between sound history and unsound history. Only if he knows something about the materials out of which a historical edifice must be built can he begin to assess the credibility of popular history.

This book has therefore several aims. It is not intended to tell the specialist anything about the sources of his own field; it may tell him something about the sources, and their problems, in other fields. It is intended to give the student some conception of the mass of evidence which lies beneath the survey, and suggest ways in which history is dependent upon sources. For the person who reads works of history for literary enjoyment, its message is that history is not easy; that the dramatic personality or the moving incident is part of a past society which can only be reconstructed carefully and professionally from the debris of information left by men who lived in another age.

In the following pages it will frequently be necessary to comment upon the limitations of particular kinds of source material, and to convey warnings against attempts to use a source for a purpose which it cannot serve. It may therefore, at this stage, be appropriate to indicate some general limitations upon all kinds of historical source material.

The first limitation is that, with a few exceptions, historical evidence consists of that which was written down, and its purpose was seldom to inform posterity. Laws were passed, documents were issued, letters were written because of needs which existed at the time. It is a major part of historical research to discover what these needs were, for evidence cannot be evaluated until one understands why it was committed to paper. The historian is often therefore arguing in circles: from cumulative evidence he builds up a picture of the environment which enables him to evaluate particular sources. This is a justifiable method provided that one realises its limitations; it can tell us a great deal but it cannot go beyond the range of the original evidence and we must continually beware of travelling too far into the realms of imagination or of piling hypothesis upon hypothesis.

Much evidence on which historians depend consists of ephemeral responses to particular problems. Even statistical evidence, so often regarded with greater respect than literary evidence, is often explained by the political need for information at a particular point in time. Historians may give figures a universal importance, but their original compilation was often the outcome of a specific question which had to be answered. The many gaps in quantitative evidence are readily explained, of one realises that the demand for information was not sufficiently urgent or important to put an official to the trouble of supplying it.

In historical sources one is therefore constantly dealing with human factors; not only do we see before us the handwriting of a long dead man, but we are looking at things written down because other men requested, prompted, or ordered these things to be done. It follows that there is always an element of chance; the information may have been lost or it may have never been recorded because no one thought of asking for it. In an era in which the sources are abundant we are apt to overlook this simple fact and to assume that everything can be known. In fact, of all the events that have ever happened only minute portions have been recorded, and of all the persons who have ever lived only a tiny minority have left records behind them. Even in a modern record-keeping society, which amasses a great deal of information about every individual—birth, marriage, children, employment, liability for tax, death, and social security number at the very least—the facts about his character and personality vanish for ever, unless he plays some part of note which he himself or others wish to explain.

Limitations upon the usefulness of evidence must be recognised, but the exercise also reveals the strength of what remains. The misuse of evidence results from a failure to understand the environment in which the evidence was produced and the circumstances under which it was collected or recorded; but when these things have been understood the sources become the foundations of an impressive edifice. Reflections upon the sources of history, and upon the way in which they can be used by trained minds, should therefore inspire confidence. A great deal of the history must be taken on trust, because only a few have the necessary knowledge, skill or access to sources to check the finished product; but it can be treated with respect when one understands the nature of the evidence upon which it rests.

It would be far too ambitious to perform this task for every aspect of the century of American history covered by this book, and it is necessary to select examples to demonstrate general propositions. Selection is necessarily a personal matter, and criticism will undoubtedly fasten upon what is not said as much as upon what is said. The choice has been guided by the topics which have engaged numbers of historians and provided the staple for survey histories: the growth of the nation, the government of the Union, the life of the people, and American ideas and attitudes. It is necessary to deal all too briefly with some important topics, and to deal with others in a somewhat selective way. There is, for instance, nothing on Indians or public lands (though it is hoped that something will be said on these topics in another volume in this series); there is not much on overseas trade, science, medicine, and technology. Economic history is treated so far as it enters (and must enter) the cognisance of general historians. These omissions and inadequacies are certain to cause some annoyance; but one can only reply that this book is intended as an essay upon the sources of American history, not as an encyclopedia of historical sciences, a manual of technique, or a union catalogue.

There are excellent reasons for beginning this study with the year 1789. The inauguration of the first President, and the meeting of the first Congress meant a new departure in the history of the United States. In the wider perspective of world history American events may have been overshadowed by those in France, but the balance may be redressed when one recalls that in the United States the world's oldest written constitution came into force, that the first successful experiment in federal government for a large nation was launched, and that, for the first time, an assembly elected by wide suffrage took its place at the centre of a modern government.

The historian has other reasons for regarding 1789 as the start of a new era, for the establishment of a new government meant the beginning of the great series of national records. The financial accounting of the national government began. The separation of powers meant regular and public communications between the Executive and Congress. The first reports from the Treasury appeared and the first census was taken in 1790. The reporting and publication of debates in the House of Representatives began, though in an incomplete and garbled form. Information of all kinds began to flow and to leave its mark on the record. Within a short time violent dissensions in Congress and in the country would produce a torrent of polemical literature, which would include profound controversy about the meaning of the American political system. For all these reasons 1789 is an appropriate year to begin a volume on the sources for United States history.

The end of the 'period' may appear to be more arbitrary. 1890 has been taken as a symbolic date to mark 'the closing of the frontier', but its significance can be exaggerated and is, in any case, not strictly relevant to the theme of this book. If 1890 does not symbolise 'the closing of the frontier' it could be argued that the year has no greater significance than 1877 or 1896 or 1901 and certainly less than 1917. Indeed 1890 has been chosen not because it marks a single event but because it stands in a cluster of events which together constitute a watershed; on this side lie the developments which dominate contemporary America, on the far side the issues which dominated the nineteenth century. Of course there is continuity, but in almost every field one finds some indication, round about the year 1890, that American civilisation was taking on a new shape.

The Interstate Commerce Act of 1887 marked the acceptance of new and far-reaching public responsibility; the Anti-Trust Act of 1890 laid the foundation of a new code of commercial ethics under the supervision of the Courts. The golden age of the small businessman was not quite over, but the age of the great corporation was definitely on the way. The rise of Populism in and after 1890 has been interpreted by some historians as a backward-looking peasant's revolt; but it can equally well be seen as the parent of a host of subsequent social, political and legal reforms. The prophets of imperialism were already being heard in 1890, though they would reap no harvest until 1898 when the acquisition of a colonial empire would mark a clear break with the traditions of the past. About 1890 the American Federation of Labor was establishing a new pattern of unionism which depended upon the tight organisation of the skilled and neglect of the unskilled. In 1890 the Republicans finally abandoned their attempt to enforce the fifteenth amendment in the South, and in 1896 the Supreme Court accepted 'separate but equal' as an acceptable interpretation of 'equal protection of the laws'. There are marked changes in immigration, with eastern Europe and the Mediterranean taking a long lead over northern Europe as the traditional source of 'new Americans'.

In the more prosaic field of administration far-reaching changes were occurring in both public and private fields. An increasing use of the typewriter meant that copies of 'out letters' could be made easily and as a matter of course. The telephone meant that the most important discussions might never be recorded, and that it would be necessary to read more and more between the lines of increasingly voluminous documentation. Men working together had always conferred in private, and the telephone was still far too expensive and erratic to take the place of letters over long distances; but the addition of a new means of communication would be of profound significance for the future. At the same time the increasing size of bureaucracies, both public and private, meant that administration became more impersonal and more dependent upon rules laid down for subordinates; this was a long-term trend but it is one of the features which separate the twentieth century from the simpler world of the past. In urban government the years after 1890 see more and more pressure for professional non-political administration. It may also be suggested that the last decade of the nineteenth century sees the final defeat of the lucid language in which public business had once been conducted and its replacement by prose which is neither elegant nor readily understood. Language comes to have three principal and separate purposes: the satisfaction of lawyers who wish to cover every contingency, the rhetorical appeal to emotion, and the concealment of meaning.

The first government under the Constitution was a simple affair though it confronted great problems. Small offices with a few clerks, messengers and cleaners sufficed, and departmental heads could meet face to face the humblest of their subordinates; a hundred years later government was not yet on its vast modern scale, but it was well on the way. The Civil War caused a surge forward in the size and range of government activity, but even before that—in an age which still paid lip-service to the ideal of 'wise and frugal government'—there had been a steady upward trend in the number of government employees and in the tasks which they performed. After the war, in a period when subsequent historians have diagnosed 'laissez faire' as the dominant mood of America, the upward trend continued. Between 1820 and 1890 the population increased by a factor of less than eight, but the number of Federal employees was multiplied by more than twenty-six. If records existed for business administration they would undoubtedly show growth of equal or greater magnitude. A growing army of subordinate officials and clerical workers was interposed between governors and governed, between the people making decisions and the people affected by them. The period covered by this volume is the formative age of modern government, and the change is evident in the accumulating number of sources available for the historian.

A modern society is a record-keeping society, and a modern government is dependent upon the possession of a vast range of information. Early in this century it could be said that

> Few persons realize how crowded with the richest material has been the brief record of the United States since it achieved its independence. The life of our society has made up in intensity what it has lacked in duration. So far are we from being destitute of materials for history that, in fact, for the time covered by our existence as an

independent nation, we possess them in an abundance that is quite unique.[1]

Today far more sources are known to exist than were then contemplated. Not all of these sources are officially compiled—and many private sources will be described in the later chapters of this book—but government has led the way and provided a backbone of evidence without which the other sources would appear impressionistic and insubstantial. It will be necessary to emphasise many weaknesses in the statistical apparatus of the earlier part of the period; yet from the outset it is evident that the age of statistics has dawned and that this makes an extraordinary difference to the historian's task of reconstructing the past. Again and again, where the historians of more distant periods and of less developed nations must fall back upon hypothesis, the study of nineteenth-century America can be brought down to the solid foundation of quantitative evidence.

The abundance of evidence does not rule out the necessity for imaginative hypothesis, but it does mean that historians need never venture too far from verifiable material and can devote more of their attention to personality, attitudes, and the inner springs of human conduct. Indeed the vast range of sources available does not make history less personal but gives greater scope for investigating what is erratic, irrational, or dependent upon assumptions which are accepted without investigation.

It is inevitable that many historians should spend a great deal of time upon the history of their own country. The combination, in the United States, of a large demand for university teachers, of the great mass of material still to be explored, and of challenging questions about the character of American civilisation, has produced an enormous volume of professional work upon nineteenth-century history. Some of this work has been too faithful to the creed of scientific history so that accumulation of material, and its orderly presentation, completes the historian's task. On the other hand the apparent urgency of questions about the meaning of American experience has produced some bold guess-work

[1] John Bates Clark in the Introduction to John R. Commons *et al.*, eds. *Documentary History of American Industrial Society* (New York, 1910).

21

which has cut too far adrift from the material. Between these two extremes lies the enormous bulk of productive work which has made nineteenth-century America one of the best cultivated fields of historical writing and research.

Major criticisms of all this work are its introspective character and emotional commitments. A good many historians, especially in the South, are still fighting the Civil War. A good many historians, especially in the North and West, accept uncritically the assumptions of American nationalism. And there is a frequent failure to see the history of America as a part of the civilisation which it shares with Europe. New movements in historiography have done little to correct these failings. The New Left historians restate old theses about the nature of American civilisation in a radical disguise. Black historians seem to narrow the vision still more and claim a separate history for their race. A good deal of history is still written with the tacit assumption that America stood alone in the world, though modern internationalism may dictate some passing references to external influences.

However, the best contemporary historians, who follow where their sources rather than their prejudices lead, are opening new and fascinating vistas. It would be impossible to categorise all the work now in progress, but much of the most interesting effort flows along one of five channels. There are studies dealing with major problems in national development which were little considered by early historians, amongst which can be listed administration, business, science, medicine, technology and urban history. These are often combined with new approaches to local history which have ceased to be merely descriptive and seek, by analytical techniques, to discover new dimensions in society. Differently orientated, though often using the same material, are studies of national issues through their local impact. Other historians accumulate evidence about popular attitudes and hitherto neglected social problems. Finally, there are fresh approaches to familiar controversies, with new questions and new ideas upon the materials from which to find answers. Included in this category are both mature political studies and the use of econometrics to discover new aspects of economic growth.

Compared with some of the bolder experiments in contemporary historiography this book is conservative in its approach; its structure is determined by the traditional fields of major interest for historians of the United States, and it considers sources which have provided their stock in trade. There is a centrifugal force in historical studies as scholars are impelled to adopt new and technically more sophisticated methods of research. Computers have come to the aid of historians, and even invaded the apparently conventional field of political history where modern scholars are as likely to be collecting data about voting behaviour as studying the papers of public men, the debates in legislative chambers, or administrative records. At the same time, if one wishes to reach the point at which decisions are made, there is much to be said for following what has hitherto been the main stream of historical writing and research. Indeed the demand for general history rather than specialised history still exists and must be satisfied if historians feel any sense of obligation to students and the educated public. If directors of graduate studies urge upon their students the importance of detailed local studies and of experimentation with new techniques, it will not be long before a publisher is urging the successful graduate to make a contribution to international, national, or at least to regional history.

It is also true that the huge bulk of the records in national depositories exercises a gravitational pull upon scholars. The Library of Congress, the National Archives, and the collections in various large libraries have absorbed the energies of countless scholars, but every reconnaissance comes back with the answer that more remains to be explored than early generations imagined. At the risk, therefore, of ignoring some local and detailed material, which excites the interest of many contemporary scholars, there is ample justification for a book which concentrates upon the more obvious sources for national history.

This kind of history is open to one telling criticism from radical scholars. Official documents, the records of political activity, the literary evidence in diaries and memoirs record an 'establishment' view. Even statistics are recorded officially because some part of the 'establishment' wished to use the information for a particular purpose. The criticism is valid but need not be exaggerated; once the point has been made, good historians will be aware of the difficulty. One cannot discover the thoughts of people who left no record, but this is no reason for neglecting those who did. Historians have always been aware of the need to discount partisan and class bias in their sources, and no one would now suggest that the whole history of a society is contained in the records of its rulers and writers. Indeed, in nineteenth-century America, there is comparatively little danger of mistaking 'the establishment' for 'the people'. There was no permanent national establishment, and the claims of the old Federalists to function as one were decisively rejected in 1800. Amongst white men, outside the South, there were few illiterates, and the habits of a democratic society opened the doors of public life to a wide range of men. The opportunities for expressing views were frequent. If America in the late eighteenth century was still a 'deferential' society, by the middle of the nineteenth foreign visitors were uncomfortably aware that Americans of every class felt free to express their opinions on every topic. Thus, if it is still difficult to penetrate the feelings of the great mass of the people, the historian of the United States can tap a wider variety of sources than those of most other nineteenth-century societies.

Ironically it is that part of America with the most meagre materials for investigating the life of the people that has received the closest scrutiny. The internal history of the old South has fascinated both friends and critics of southern institutions. By contrast the social history of northern cities, where the materials are abundant, remained relatively unexplored before the rise of a new generation of urban historians. Nearly everyone who has studied the coming of the Civil War knows that in 1860 there were little more than 300,000 slaveowners and that only a small minority owned more than ten slaves; but how many know anything about the distribution of wealth in northern cities? At one time it was fashionable, amongst some historians, to speak of the 'masters of capital', but no one made a survey or analysis of this mysterious class. Still largely neglected is the history of small towns in the North and West, though this was the background of a majority of politicians throughout the whole of the nineteenth century.

The contrast between the treatment of southern and northern society has some obvious explanations, but it is also indicative of the difficulties which arise in the study of a federal nation. Federal records will normally contain little material relating to subjects over which the President and Congress had no control. Until the twentieth century most questions affecting the daily lives of the people were the responsibility of the states, and it is to the state archives that one must look for much of the material on social history. In the British Public Record Office is preserved, principally in the Home Office papers, voluminous evidence about crime and punishment, protest and discontent, and economic affairs. The American National Archives contain very little about law and order (except during the Civil War and Reconstruction periods), and though there is a great deal about banks, currency, tariffs, and internal improvements, the responsibility for health, welfare, and most forms of business behaviour lay with the states. Even in immigration, which was of vital concern to the nation as a whole, the Federal Government did little more than keep a statistical record. Poverty, housing and disease left little imprint upon the Federal records. These circumstances, arising from federal structure, have tended to widen the gap between national and local history.

The separation of Church and State has had similar consequences for the history of religion. The Federal government had no responsibility for religion, a Federal court could only take cognisance of religion to enforce the first amendment, and Congress was prevented from debating any religious question. In European countries the problems of Church and State were at the heart of many political controversies; in America the question could arise only in the separate states and did so infrequently. The historian who spends most of his time with the national records has therefore no reason to consider religion except, peripherally, when religion inspired reform such as abolitionism. The sources for religious history lie scattered in the archives of many denominations, and though religion was at the forefront of many nineteenth-century minds its history has largely been left to specialists whose piety often exceeded their professional skill.

The examples of social and religious history illustrate a major influence in American historiography. The great size of the country, its federal structure, and the tendency of voluntary associations to adopt a federal organisation have all combined to make it difficult to bring together general and particular history. On the one hand the unifying concepts—the Union, the Constitution, nationalism versus sectionalism—are easy to grasp and can be studied in records which are either concentrated at the centre or found in a small number of readily identified libraries. On the other hand the sources for the history of many aspects of human behaviour lie widely scattered; local manifestations can be studied but a national synthesis tends to produce large, weak generalisations rather than precise statements. The most notorious was the attempt to explain American history in terms of a continuing conflict between 'agrarians' and 'capitalists' though neither category was ever described or defined. Another example was the attempt to treat 'the frontier' as the determinant in American history, though 'the frontier' itself remained an impressionistic generalisation rather than an account of what actually happened in the West.

The preceding pages have demonstrated that the abundance of materials, for the history of the United States during the nineteenth century, does not make the reconstruction of the past simple or straightforward. The historian must use his sources to serve a purpose for which they were never intended: the enlightenment of posterity. Other difficulties arise from the federal structure of the country, and from the contrast between the concentration of records dealing with a central but limited government, and the wide dispersion of records dealing with most aspects of the daily life of the people.

To some extent these difficulties have been offset by American curiosity about their own past, and by the need to explain national character through history. The writing of history is a dialogue between evidence derived from the sources and the desire of people to understand themselves. Conscious that their national existence began with a historic event—the Revolution—and was built around historical documents—the Declaration of Independence and the Constitution—Americans have been more assiduous than most peoples in collecting and preserving evidence from the past. Local historical societies appeared at a very early stage, and their number grew throughout the nineteenth century. Much of the work of these societies consisted in the collection and publication of material. The selection of material for publication and its editorship was often designed to demonstrate the importance of the state and its past leaders rather than inspired by a quest for impartial truth. Nevertheless the result has been an enormous collection of printed material in the proceedings of local historical societies, and if the modern scholar does not trust the editing he can at least be assured that he will find the original manuscripts in the archives of the society. If a local society is defunct he may have some difficulty in tracing its collections, but there is usually an easily discoverable solution to this problem.

In the first half of the nineteenth century the historical societies were concerned mainly with the records of the Revolution, and devoted comparatively little attention to what was then contemporary history. New areas west of the Appalachians showed, however, an early determination to collect sources relating to the foundation and development of their communities. The Civil War had an immediate effect upon historical activity, and both states and communities displayed considerable industry in the collection and preservation of material relating to their own part in the struggle. Innumerable regimental histories appeared in the years following the war, and as regiments were firmly identified with particular areas this was seen as an extension of local history. These regimental histories were often hagiographic; no regiment suffered a defeat which was not also a monument to its heroism; no soldier ever deserted or suffered court-martial; the dirt, disease, and bungling of war was transmuted into an epic of gallantry. Nevertheless the material collected by the regimental historians was often far superior to their judgment, and later historians have been able to use them as sources which can be valuable if used with discrimination.

The Civil War also produced the first acceptance, by the Federal Government, of a responsibility for collecting records and writing history. In 1865 an Archives Office was set up in the War Department; at first as a depository for captured Confederate records (with an eye to possible criminal prosecutions), but in 1866 Congress appropriated funds for writing 'the official history of the rebellion'. In the following years little was done except through pressure from local and regimental historians who frequently wrote with requests for official information. In 1880 the volumes of the official *War of the Rebellion* began publication. The delay proved to be fortunate for by then it was realised that the purpose of such a history should not be merely the celebration of Union triumphs but must cover all aspects of the war from both sides of the struggle. The result was the first multi-volume 'official' history in the English-speaking world, and it remains one of the most impressive. In the same spirit the *Century Magazine* published a series of articles, subsequently collected in the four volume *Battles and Leaders of the Civil War*, in which most of the accounts were written by participants and often by one of the commanding generals. In this way, therefore, the determination of Americans to record, while memory was still fresh, the great struggle added to the sources available to future historians.

The example of the official history of the *War of the Rebellion* may have helped to inspire later co-operative efforts in the collection of material. In the later nineteenth century and the early years of the twentieth, collections of the letters and papers of leading men in national history began to appear. Most of these early efforts fall far short of modern editorial standards, but at least they meant that historians had source material available in an easily accessible form. The second half of the twentieth century has seen mammoth collections launched for most major figures in American history prior to 1865, which aim to record and edit every letter or paper written by the subject, together with those received by him. The task of the editorial team in these great scholarly enterprises is enormous; not only have letters and papers to be located, but every event or person mentioned must be identified. Often the notes on a particular letter will prove to be minor essays involving meticulous research. When these collections are complete no nation will have a fuller or more accurate printed record of the past, and one can assume that the principle of collection will be extended to more and more public men and to leaders in the later years of the century.

A fundamental problem in the strategy of historical studies is the attitude to other work in other disciplines upon the problems of human society. Historians have to rely much upon statistics which they are not trained to compile and cannot check. At the same time the importance of quantitative evidence is pressed upon them, while many economic historians go beyond a simple claim for statistical evidence and demand the use of sophisticated mathematical techniques. Even political historians have become increasingly conscious that voting figures are susceptible to far more delicate analysis than was ever contemplated in the past. The good historian will demand to know the sources upon which calculations are based, but he may still be unable to follow the subsequent steps and is therefore in much the same position as a doctor who knows the use but could not construct a complicated piece of hospital equipment. Historians have long been familiar with one particular example of statistical evidence—the cost of living index—and probably know enough about the problems of weighting to realise that an index can be highly misleading if the compiler has not got an accurate idea of how people lived and how they chose to spend their money; but should a healthy scepticism prevent the use of all indexes of the cost of living?

This is one occasion of several on which historians may have to use sources which have been analysed by experts who cannot be checked. A certain amount of common sense will usually provide a guide to what can or cannot be accepted; but even here one moves into an area in which the traditional assumptions of a historian may be sorely tried. A majority of historians would reject any appeal to 'contrafacts', that is, to arguments based upon what would have happened if something else had not happened. Professional historians were aghast when Robert W. Fogel attempted to rewrite the economic history of the United States as it would have been if the railroads had never been built; yet Mr Fogel has pointed out in a vigorous argument that traditional historiography bristles with arguments based upon unacknowledged 'contrafacts'.[1] Indeed most examinations of individual motives carry the implication that if a decision had not been made in the way that it was made, some other consequence would have ensued, and cannot therefore be assessed without implicit consideration of the possible alternatives. The historian who claims that he is only concerned to record what happened is either untruthful or a poor historian; for the sources do not tell only what happened but also what possibilities lay open. One can record exactly what Hamilton proposed in 1790, or what happened when Lincoln decided to send provisions to Fort Sumter, or how the transcontinental railroads were built, or why Rutherford B. Hayes became President in 1877; but the significance of these events is apparent only when one is aware of other choices which might have been made. It is always necessary to bear in mind that contemporary writers were responding to a particular need, wrote in ignorance of the future, but were conscious of the alternatives.

Sociologists and psychologists provide arguments about society and personality, and some of these rest upon carefully observed evidence which is (or should be) partly historical in character. It is a matter of controversy amongst historians whether they should welcome and use these arguments or insist upon the 'autonomy' of history. In part the argument is unreal because any historian is the child of his age, and cannot resist the influence of ideas which form a part of the common currency of conversation amongst educated men. Nor is he likely to reject an explanation of behaviour, which seems convincing and may help his reconstruction of the past, whatever its origin. A case in point is the current interest of many American historians in the problem of

[1] Robert W. Fogel, 'Historiography and Retrospective Economics', *History and Theory*, ix (1970), 256–7.

'status'. Once the idea was grasped that anxiety about status might provide a clue to certain kinds of behaviour, otherwise difficult to explain, there seems to be an obvious case for examining the sources with this explanation in mind. The results may not have been wholly convincing but they have demonstrated the possibility of a new dimension in historical studies.

This book is not concerned with methodology, and the arguments in the preceding paragraphs have been introduced merely to insist that though sources are the basis of all historical study there is nothing mechanical about their use. What is required is not merely a knowledge of the sources but the wider knowledge which will see them in the context of their times and as a part of unfolding human experience. The historian reconstructs the past by using the sources, but his mind is a modern mind and cannot be divorced from its environment. As one identifies a source one also asks, how can this material be used to supplement *our* knowledge? To this extent a source is inseparable from the use that can be made of it, and it is certain that the manner in which a source is used today may become obsolescent and perhaps perverse before a few years are out.

The sources with which this book is principally concerned are written; but there exist other ways of gathering information about the past. The physical survivals are relatively less important in American than they are in European history, but they are nevertheless significant. The same care which led to the preservation of documentary evidence has led also to care for historic buildings; unfortunately they now exist in isolation, and it requires an effort of imagination to recreate their original environment. Some small New England towns retain their eighteenth- or early nineteenth-century appearance; so do a small number of the great houses of southern plantations. A few homes of great men are preserved with loving care, and the historian can gain some sense of contact with the past. Of no place is this truer than of Monticello where imaginative preservation succeeds in adding an important element to one's understanding of Thomas Jefferson. A visit to the city of Washington forcibly reminds one of the grandiose scale upon which a weak, scattered nation conceived its future.

State historical museums have done noble work in gathering relics of the past, and both Federal and state governments have accepted responsibility for historic sites. The battlefields of the Civil War are probably the best preserved, and the best presented, of any war in history; and the enthusiastic pilgrim can follow their armies through all their major engagements from Bull Run to Appomatox Court House. The physical survivals of the first age of technology are also easily found. The ships, locomotives, industrial and agricultural machinery from an earlier period make an immediate impact, but it requires wide knowledge of the past to realise their full significance. The general historian will look to them to confirm and deepen his understanding rather than as sources from which to begin his researches.

The nineteenth century was a great age of pictorial art, not indeed (so far as America was concerned) in quality but certainly in quantity. Cheap methods of lithography provided a popular record of personalities and events, and the Civil War first revealed the importance of photography. From that time onwards the pictorial record becomes more and more important, and by the end of the period it is possible to experience visually almost every aspect of American life. As with the written record one must remember that the photograph was normally taken with some immediate need in view, and consequently there are things which we should like to see which were never recorded. Nevertheless an enormous mass of photographic material survives, and more is constantly coming to light. Perhaps the urban historians have reaped the greatest benefit from this; from the business man boosting his city to the civic reformer looking for evidence to support his case, numerous people had reasons for making a photographic record of urban scenes.

The arrangement of this book is straightforward.[1] The first

[1] The massive nature of the sources, and the comparatively short period covered, has dictated a somewhat different arrangement to that adopted in other volumes of this series. The sources for different aspects of American

General Introduction

part deals with evidence for the growth of the nation; this is mainly statistical but towards the end of the section an important and controversial question—the relationship of the Civil War to growth and change—is discussed. Part II deals with the government of the Union; it covers the records of the national government, Congress, the courts, public men, external relations, and the armed forces. In Part III the sources for the life of the people are considered; this is a wide-ranging survey and includes subjects as diverse as farms and cities, business men and slaves, immigrants and the South. There follows a section on the mind of the people which includes the media of communication, religion and the intelligentsia.

Part IV is more speculative and takes up two main themes. The first is the nature of the material with which the American historian can analyse the problem of change. The second considers the extent to which the study of American history has been too introspective, and raises some questions about comparative history and the possibility of using foreign sources to test American experience and of using American sources towards a wider study of the Atlantic civilisation.

---

history are considered in separate chapters. At the same time it will be apparent that some classes of evidence underlie several different aspects. Thus, though the statistical framework is considered separately, quantification of one kind or another is an element in many aspects of social and political history. The evidence for government and political activity is considered in a separate Part, but American society is permeated by the assumptions and processes of democratic politics, so that they become an integral element in social and intellectual history. The arrangement of the material in the following pages is therefore dictated by convenience and does not imply a commitment to the departmentalisation of History.

PART I

The Records of National Growth

Introduction

All advanced nations of the modern world shared the experience of growth during the nineteenth century, but in America growth made the nation. Elsewhere growth occurred within existing institutional frameworks, but in the United States growth was the framework, and without it the results of the 'great experiment' could have been ephemeral; the permanent shape of American civilisation was determined by the continued expansion of population, prosperity and power.

The nation was born at the threshold of the age of statistics, and consequently some evidence for growth was recorded from the earliest years of the new government; but not until the later years of the nineteenth century was statistical information recorded for its own sake rather than in response to immediate needs as diagnosed by politicians. Consequently there are wide gaps in the record and the statistical series fail to provide much of the information which historians desire. In some instances gaps have been filled by modern research; in others the material has been lost beyond all hope of recovery.

Even with these qualifications one can say that there is an uncommon wealth of evidence for the growth fluctuations and major changes of direction in the United States. The official heirs of the earlier statisticians have put historians much in their debt by the magnificent *Historical Statistics of the United States.*[1] The first edition appeared in 1949 and took the record to 1940; the second in 1960 was greatly enlarged and took it to 1957. A majority of the series presented do not begin until after this period

---

[1] Published by the Bureau of Commerce; first issued in 1949 and again, with much revision and additional information, in 1960. The 1960 edition is hereinafter cited as *Historical Statistics*.

or in its closing years; but a number of important series go back to 1790 and others to the early years of the nineteenth century.

The simple injunction that historians should use quantitative data may prove to be more difficult to obey than one might suspect. The introduction to *Historical Statistics* expressed some of the difficulties in this way,

> Impediments to the use of historical statistics . . . include the initial difficulty of determining whether the data in fact exists, of identifying the public or private document in which the data may be found, of constructing time series where the data may not be arranged in suitable form, and of identifying and interpreting changes in concept and coverage. Definitions employed in published historical tables, moreover, may have to be sought in separate publications if, indeed, they have been published at all.[1]

It can readily be seen that the compilation of even comparatively simple tables may require a great deal of expertise and detailed knowledge. The general historian must take much of this on trust, while hoping to distinguish between material known to contemporaries and that compiled by statisticians. The distinction may not be significant in sketching long-term developments in broad terms, but may be of the first importance if one is seeking to reconstruct the information which the men of the past had about their world.

It is important for the general historan to know what figures can bear the weight of refined calculation. The 'new' economic history with its mathematical apparatus, its contrafacts, and its confident correction of established notions about economic growth, has many terrors for historians whose training forbids them to cross the threshold into this mysterious world; but practitioners of the new economic history are primarily concerned with history not with mathematics, and it is possible to meet them on common ground when one is investigating the sources upon which all knowledge of the past must depend. As a reviewer in the *Times Literary Supplement* observed,

Fogel and Fishlow, the terrible twins of the new economic history,

[1] *Historical Statistics*, Introduction, *x*.

are shown to be really in the Clapham tradition, using their abstruse mathematical techniques and their counterfactual hypotheses to ask 'How much? How large? How long? How often? How representative?' as Clapham advised us all to do.[1]

The writer went on to remark that however much their methods might have been criticised, they had made historians 'more aware of the need for measurement and more cautious in their use of such vague but overworked adjectives as "considerable", "important", and "significant".' On the other hand, the good historians amongst the econometricians know the limitations imposed by the data and, as their arch-priest has said,

> Some historical questions involve relationships that go beyond the set currently covered by mathematics. In other cases the equations system required to describe a given reality may be insoluble. Or it may be that, although one can define a model and solve it, the data required to estimate the parameters of the model are not available.[2]

The 'new' economic history does not therefore make claims which are vastly different from the old. 'The paucity of data has been as formidable an obstacle to the new work as to the old. Much of recent research has been based not on the measurement of the relevant parameters but on informed guesses as to their probable magnitude.'[3] The non-mathematical historian may not be able to follow the calculations but he can learn a good deal about the sources upon which they depend; he can discover the administrative conditions which made for accuracy or inaccuracy, learn something of the motives which led to the collection of statistical data, and say with some certainty which series or which

[1] *Times Literary Supplement*. No. 3,600. (26 Feb 1971), 245. Reviewing G. R. Hawke, *Railways and Economic Growth in England and Wales* (Oxford, 1970). The persons referred to are Sir John Clapham, often regarded as the father of descriptive economic history in Great Britain, Robert W. Fogel and Albert Fishlow (who have led the study of econometrics in American economic history).

[2] Robert W. Fogel, 'Historiography and Retrospective Economics', *History and Theory*, ix (1970), 247.

[3] Robert W. Fogel and Stanley L. Engerman, 'A Model for the Explanation of Industrial Expansion during the Nineteenth Century', *Journal of Political Economy*, lxxvii (1969), 307.

parts of what series should be treated with respect. In the following pages space forbids discussion of all the statistics which historians may be required to use, but the examples selected will indicate the questions which must be asked and answered before one can speak with assurance.

CHAPTER 1

The Growth of the People

The Constitution laid down that 'Representatives and direct taxes shall be apportioned among the several States which may be included within this Union, according to their respective numbers . . . the actual enumeration shall be made within three years after the first meeting of Congress of the United States, and within every subsequent term of ten years, in such manner as they shall by law direct'. The Federal census was thus decreed in direct response to the political need to ascertain the apportionment of representatives, but once launched on its course the decennial census proved to be a convenient way of discovering more and more about the people of the United States though the quest for new data was usually determined by contemporary political argument.[1]

As the first census was required merely to decide the number of representatives allocated to each state, precision in enumeration was unnecessary. The responsibility for the census lay at first with the Secretary of State and enumeration was the responsibility of Federal Marshals. The Marshals remained in charge until 1880 when Supervisors of the Census were appointed for each district. For the first census seventeen Marshals were employed and an estimated 650 assistants and enumerators; a hundred years later there were 300 district supervisors and 46,804 enumerators. The original intention—to provide the necessary figures for the

[1] Material used in the following paragraphs is drawn from Katharine H. Davidson and Charlotte M. Ashby, *Records of the Bureau of the Census* (National Archives, Preliminary Inventory No. 161: Washington, 1964); Carroll D. Wright, *History and Growth of the United States Census* (Washington, 1900); Senate Documents. 56th Congress. 1st Session. No. 194; House of Representatives Documents. 57th Congress. 1st Session. No. 262.

apportionment of Congressional seats—demanded neither accuracy nor a permanent organisation. A separate act of Congress was therefore necessary to authorise each census and until 1902 there was no permanent staff for the Bureau of the Census. The work on the census was not so sporadic as this might suggest, for preparation took a considerable period and the assessment and tabulation of data even longer; this meant that Superintendents of the Census were necessarily in office for some years. Even so, there were intermissions and even if the previous Superintendent were reappointed (as happened on several occasions) there was no continuity in administration.[1] The age of statistics had begun but was yet in its infancy.

The first census asked for heads of families, free white males over sixteen, free white males under sixteen, free white females, all other free persons, and slaves. In 1800 the enumerators were asked to include the county, city or township of residence, and to provide more detailed information about ages. In 1810 questions were added about manufacturers, and these were repeated (with increasing detail) in all subsequent censuses except 1830. In 1820 the age and sex of coloured persons, information about unnaturalised foreigners, and the occupations of all persons were required. In 1830 more details about ages were included and also information about white and coloured, deaf, dumb and blind. In 1830 printed schedules were issued for the first time in place of paper (often business ledgers) privately supplied and completed without uniformity in presentation. In 1840 still more questions were added about occupations, and for the first time about education, agriculture, fisheries, mines, commerce, and white and coloured idiots and insane; in this census too, for the first and only time, there was an enumeration of Revolutionary pensioners.

It will be seen that the needs of a growing nation were reflected

[1] The first to fifth censuses were directed by the Secretary of State, a Superintending Clerk was appointed for the sixth census (William A. Weaver), the seventh census came under the direction of the Secretary of the Interior and from that time onward a Superintendent of the Census was appointed. The post was held by J. C. G. Kennedy (May 1850–March 1853), J. B. D. De Bow (March 1853–Nov 1855), J. C. G. Kennedy (1859–65), Francis A. Walker (1870–81), Charles W. Seaton (1881–85), R. P. Porter (1889–93).

in the information required. By 1840 the purpose of the census had outgrown the original need for enumeration as a basis for apportionment, and embraced information about ages, the balance of sexes, health, economic life, and comparative statistics for white and coloured. Without additional questions the administrators of the census could also work out the statistics of mortality, the growth of towns, immigration, and the use of land. The census of 1850 can be regarded as the first modern census; under the able superintendence of Joseph C. G. Kennedy the information was systematised, further questions were added on dwellings, the value of real estate, the names of free persons, nativity, marriages during the year, paupers, convicts, slaves and mortality. From 1850 onwards there was a steady elaboration of the schedules and more and more facts about the life of the people were brought within range of the census, and it became a decennial review of the whole life of the nation so far as it could be tabulated. Even so, errors could occur and the census of 1870 later became notorious for having missed over a million persons in the southern states, though it was also the first to use mechanical aids for tabulation. A cynic might attribute the error to this innovation, but there were more charitable and probable explanations.[1] The year 1890 saw the dawn of the numerate age with the use of punch cards and electric tabulation.

All this meant more and more of the printed word. The first census occupied fifty-six pages, that of 1860 2,879 pages, and by 1900 it was 10,900. The report of 1880 was almost twice as long as that of 1870, and by 1890 it had almost doubled again. The main report became a multi-volume publication spread over a considerable period, but from 1840 onwards advance information was issued in a condensed form (variously called Preliminary Reports, Abstracts, Digests), and in normal controversy these

---

[1] The error was attributed to the number of former slaves without settled places of residence, but one may also surmise that southern officials had little incentive to co-operate with Federal authorities and were not assiduous in the quest for Negroes who had gone away from their former homes. The total given in the census was 38,558,371; most modern compilations give the revised estimate of 39,818,449.

handy compendia were probably studied more closely than the main reports; they serve historians well and provided the evidence from which most educated Americans derived information about the growth and diversity of their country. In addition to the printed reports the manuscript returns of the enumerators survive and recent research has made profitable use of them to build up composite pictures of areas where little literary evidence survives. It has, for instance, been possible to reconstruct a picture of life in the South away from the great plantations where there were few literate people and even fewer occasions to write.[1]

This brief survey of the history of the census in the nineteenth century illustrates the extent to which statistics depend not only upon administrative efficiency but also upon the needs of society and the willingness of legislators and executive officers to recognise them. With the census we can know what information was required, what tables can be compiled, and the date at which series can begin; with equal confidence we can say that before that time reliable information on the subject cannot exist. With much less precision we can say that experience and new methods gradually cut down the possibility of error. For many purposes the early census material will provide sufficient evidence about trends and growth, but we will learn to look with suspicion upon elaborate mathematical calculations based upon early sources, though with increasing respect at calculations based upon more recent data. The expert staff of the modern Bureau of the Census are constantly reworking the accumulated data about the past, and calculations issuing from that authoritative source can be treated with deference.

In 1798 Federalist apprehension over the arrival of Irish and others with revolutionary ideas caused the passage of an Act requiring reports on alien arrivals, but this lasted only until 1800 and there were no further immigration figures until 1819. In that year an Act required the captains of ships to deliver to the local collector of customs a list of his passengers. The list was to include

---

[1] There are many references in the following chapters to the use of manuscript schedules; they have become a mainstay for much economic and social history and are essential for most exercises in 'micro-history'.

the age, sex and occupation of each passenger, together with his or her country of origin. This information was transmitted periodically to the Secretary of State and the consolidated figures were included in his reports to Congress. In 1855 an Act required quarterly reports to the Secretary and annual reports to Congress.

There were several gaps and possibilities of error in this mode of collecting data about immigration. The accuracy depended in the first instance upon the honesty of ships' captains who might have reasons for rendering false returns and suppressing the number of deaths during the voyage.[1] There was no means of checking the ethnic background of immigrants; some captains might conscientiously examine their passengers, others might simply record the port of embarkation, and others might guess the answer from speech and appearance. Later attempts to use the information about ethnic origins are complicated by the changes in European geography; during the nineteenth century Poles might be classified as Russian, Austrian or German. Czechs, Slovaks, Slovenes and Northern Italians might be Austrians. No separate record was kept of Jews. Serious errors arose from the failure to keep continuous count of immigrants arriving from British North America; this was attempted in 1855 but was interrupted by the Civil War, and checks at the frontier were discontinued in 1885. No record was kept of immigrants who subsequently returned to their own countries, and between 1856 and 1867 temporary visitors (estimated at 1·5 per cent of the whole) were included in the totals.[2]

The occupation of groups of immigrants as given in the published tables are not very illuminating. In most years over half are described as of no occupation; but this is understandable as this category includes women and children. The other categories were 'professional', 'commercial', 'skilled', 'farmers', 'servants',

[1] *Historical Statistics*, Chapter C, pp. 48-9.

[2] Brinley Thomas, *Migration and Economic Growth* (Cambridge, 1954), p. 44. He stresses particularly the failure to account for immigration from British North America (which would include many who landed at British North American ports and proceeded directly to the United States).

'laborers', and miscellaneous. The original returns, in the National Archives, should, however, yield a great deal more information, as the instructions specified that descriptions under the general classification should be as precise as possible.

Attempts to compile a statistical record of internal migration began with the census of 1850. Non-white internal migration was not recorded until 1870. The difficulties in compiling an accurate record can be imagined: persons resident in states other than those in which they had been born were recorded but this took no count of migration within States or of intermediate movements between birth and residence at the time of the census. It is therefore difficult to distinguish between 'short jump' and 'long jump' migration, though the figures do record separately those who had been born in states contiguous and non-contiguous to the state of residence. Local evidence suggests that by far the most common form of internal migration was a move of two or three hundred miles, from an established farm to a new farm, or from an old town to a new town and those who changed region, occupation, and social environment in one move may have been rare. There is, however, enough evidence to correct some of the more extravagant statements about geographical mobility. In every census from 1850 over 75 per cent of the whites were residing in the states where they had been born, and from 87 per cent to 89 per cent were still living in the region of their birth. In the censuses of 1870, 1880 and 1890, 81 per cent, 84 per cent and 84·5 per cent of non-whites were living in the states where they had been born and 96·4 per cent, 96·5 per cent and 95·5 per cent in the same region.[1]

Some of the difficulties in using the census figures have been indicated above; yet allowing for their deficiencies the statistics collected by the census—in growing volume over the years—provide a backbone for any account of the growth of the nation. Without the census the historian would often be floundering in the dark; with it he has the material for innumerable comparisons, contrasts and generalisations. State by state, district by district, and city by city he can study the development of the country so

[1] *Historical Statistics*, Chapter C, p. 39. Series C, 1–24.

far as it is possible to do so from statistical evidence. The existence of the census places quantitative evidence at the heart of the national story, and no historian can afford to ignore it.

Most historical enquiries involve some use of census material. In addition to the information already mentioned, the censuses record the distribution of population, the advance of settlement, the growth of towns, the location of industry, the value of property, and the economic development from census to census. Enough has been said to indicate some of the difficulties which arise from the omission of information in early censuses, and from the lack of consistency from census to census. Information is sometimes sporadic, sometimes presented in different forms in succeeding censuses, and sometimes incomplete because the questions asked were inadequate or poorly devised. Even so, the census, especially from 1850 onwards, provides a great deal of information about social life which can be obtained from no other source. There are figures for newspapers and their circulation; schools, attendance and illiteracy; hospitals and disease. There is abundant information about the churches, religious denominations and congregations. Essential for demographers are the figures for the age structure of the population, mortality, marriages and the expectation of life. The ethnic composition of the population, as a whole and district by district, provides basic evidence for the students of migration, assimilation, and cultural influences. The existence of the census also stimulated private statistical enquiries, which in turn influenced the conduct of the census, its accuracy, and the information requested. The great improvement in and after 1850 was, for instance, closely connected with the foundation of the American Statistical Association in 1840 and with the growing frequency of consultation between census officials and statisticians. J. C. G. Kennedy, who was superintendent of the census 1850–1853 and 1859–1865, was an innovator in this respect, and Francis A. Walker who superintended the censuses of 1870 and 1880 was a highly qualified economist and statistician.

The great strength of the census need not conceal certain weaknesses. The lack of a permanent staff was a major handicap, and though some with experience might be available, many had to be trained quickly for a highly technical job. Errors sometimes occurred in transcribing information from the manuscript schedules, and though unlikely to affect the overall picture, they can be of great significance in the study of a single district, ethnic group or occupation. A more striking example of error—which had political repercussions—occurred in the census of 1840. For reasons not unconnected with the southern response to abolitionism, information was requested about the number of insane by race, with results which were highly satisfactory to defenders of slavery and showing an abnormally high rate of insanity amongst free Negroes in the North and an extraordinarily low rate amongst southern slaves. These figures were frequently referred to in the debate over slavery, and were given world-wide prominence by John C. Calhoun in his celebrated letter to Pakenham during the Texas controversy. In 1851 the *American Journal of Insanity* referred to the 1840 census to substantiate the proposition that one out of every fourteen Negroes in Maine was insane. In fact the figures were almost entirely bogus and were exposed by a contemporary statistician, Dr Edward Jarvis. Some northern towns had been credited with insane Negroes though no Negro inhabitants were recorded. One town in Maine was credited with three Negro inhabitants but with six insane Negroes. Worcester, Massachusetts, was credited with 133 coloured insane; in fact this was the total number of inmates—white and coloured—in the State Hospital for Insane situated in the town. The low rate of insanity recorded in the South could be accounted for by the lack of institutional facilities, the reluctance of those that existed to accept Negro patients, and the tendency to keep slaves, who were mentally deficient but not dangerous, engaged in low-grade tasks. In 1844 John Quincy Adams requested an enquiry into these figures; Calhoun, the Secretary of State, requested William A. Weaver, who had been Superintending Clerk of the Census, to conduct an investigation, and subsequently reported that there was no reason to doubt the accuracy of the figures. No reference was made to the discrepancies revealed by Jarvis.[1]

[1] A. Deutsch, 'The First United States Census of the Insane and its use as

In 1854 J. B. D. De Bow reprinted the 1840 figures for insanity without comment in his *Statistical View of the United States* (a compendium of the seventh census). A comparison between the 1840 and 1850 figures might have produced some surprise if the former figures had not already won a secure place in political controversy. Some of the more striking discrepancies, abstracted from De Bow's compendium, are illustrated in the following table:

State	Ratio of white insane and idiotic to total white.		Ratio of coloured insane and idiotic to total coloured.	
	1840 as I to	1850 as I to	1840 as I to	1850 as I to
Alabama	1,445	784	2,045	2,091
Connecticut	606	486	185	769
Georgia	1,387	645	2,117	2,149
Illinois	2,217	1,417	49	1,359
Kentucky	742	588	1,053	1,625
Maine	932	514	14	195
Mississippi	1,554	1,227	2,397	2,825
New Hampshire	584	436	28	520
Massachusetts	605	403	137	378
Michigan	5,425	1,242	27	646
New York	1,108	738	258	892
South Carolina	689	580	2,447	3,117
Virginia	706	509	1,299	1,327

Apparently the proportion of white insanity had doubled or almost doubled in Alabama, Georgia, Maine, New York and Illinois, and had increased in Michigan by a factor of 4·5. One knows that the 1840s were trying times for Americans but it is improbable that so many were driven to the madhouse. On the other hand the incidence of insanity amongst the free coloured in northern states showed dramatic improvements. The figure for insanity amongst slaves was still suspiciously low in the southern states; but the ratio of insane amongst the free coloured population in Connecticut, Michigan and New York now

Pro-Slavery Propaganda' (*Bulletin of the History of Medicine*), 15 (1944), pp. 469–482, and Leon Litwack, *North of Slavery* (Chicago, 1961), pp. 40–46.

appeared to be better than that of the white population in Georgia, South Carolina and Virginia.

The figures for insanity in 1840 are notorious because they were widely used by southern speakers and writers, but their examination compels one to ask how much reliance can be placed on other figures which attracted less comment. De Bow himself showed more critical spirit when dealing with crop returns than with insanity amongst Negroes. He observed that,

> Corrections have been made in the cotton and sugar returns . . . pounds having been intended by the enumerators in many cases, where they returned bales or hogsheads. It is impossible to reconcile the hemp and flax returns of 1840 and 1850. No doubt in both cases tons and pounds have often been confounded. In a few of the States, such as Indiana and Illinois, the returns of 1850 were rejected altogether for insufficiency. Letters from Kentucky entitled to high credit, state the water-rotted hemp for that year to be not a third as much as the census gives.[1]

On manufacturers De Bow cautiously and correctly observed that 'It will be very long before any country can expect entire accuracy in such reports', and, though he believed that the figures giving the number of hands employed and the value of annual product were 'no doubt entirely correct', the ratio of profits in the several states presented anomalies which could not be reconciled. On the question of urban and rural population, he observed that in many parts of the South and the West the population of urban places was not distinguished from that of the county in which they were situated, while in New England and some other northern states the returns for 'towns' often included large rural districts. He suggested that in future 'all places having an aggregation of over fifty or a hundred persons, with a store, tavern, blacksmith shop or school house and post office, or some or all of these' should be separately enumerated.

The existence of errors, inconsistencies, and incomplete returns does not destroy, or seriously weaken, the historical value of the census. In most cases it is the essential basis for the whole structure

[1] *Statistical View of the United States: a Compendium of the Seventh Census* (Washington, 1854), p. 170.

of quantitative evidence about the American past, and few countries can show so much over so long a period. Moreover, as statisticians used and criticised the various series, their accuracy and range improved with each successive census. However, figures are never more than the answer to a question, often framed by someone without statistical skill, and answered by a man who was untrained, hurried, and inadequately supervised. Somewhere on the ground floor of many statistical series there may well be men who failed to define what was meant by a 'town', confused pounds, bales and hogsheads, or accepted wild estimates of profits made from producers who had no knowledge of accountancy.

CHAPTER 2

Economic Growth

The historian who enters upon the treacherous ground of economic growth does so at his peril. Complex and highly technical problems abound, and practitioners are not agreed amongst themselves. Early figures are scanty and often suspect, and there are constant temptations to exaggerate the importance of those which exist, whilst forgetting that lost evidence might put that which survives in a quite different light.

The first Congress ordered that the records of foreign trade should be collected and preserved. Acutely aware of America's economic weakness, and conscious of the need to stimulate commerce by united action, legislators felt a need for information; and in the newly established Treasury and revenue service there existed an agency capable of collecting and recording the data. Unfortunately in the early days there can be no guarantee of either accuracy or comprehensiveness. The figures for imports which paid duty depended upon the accuracy and honesty of the individuals concerned; for imports which paid no duty there were either no figures at all or vague estimates; exports depended upon the declarations of bulk and value made by merchants, and as these were not dutiable there was no particular need to check them. A further complication was that some goods paid specific duties (i.e., fixed duties irrespective of price) and others ad valorem duties (i.e., a percentage of the declared value). As with early population figures the trade statistics indicate general trends but cannot be taken as the basis for elaborate calculations to which great significance is attached. Leading authorities have summarised the situation as follows:

The United States may be said to have had an adequate set of import and export statistics only since about 1821. Prior to that time no information was compiled on the amount of imports of articles which

52

were free of duty upon importation into the United States. No value figures were compiled on imports subject to specific rates of duty and the dollar value for imports subject to ad valorem rates of duty, though apparently accurate, was compiled only as a total with no information on how much of each commodity was imported. Existing figures on the total dollar value of imports during the years 1795 to 1801 were apparently estimated at the time by the Secretary of the Treasury, and the figures for 1790–94 and from 1802–20 were apparently estimated many years later.[1]

With goods liable to specific duties a customs house official had only to verify their description and quantity; with those liable to ad valorem duties he would have to check invoices and compare the declared value with current prices. Figures for specific duties therefore provide a fairly accurate record of the volume of imports, but ad valorem duties were not only affected by prevailing prices but also by the ability of importers to get undervalued goods through the customs. Undoubtedly many importers found it worth their while to cultivate good relations with the clerks in the custom house, and these underpaid officials depended a good deal upon what they could make on the side. In the 1840s a further complication was introduced with a requirement for home valuation when the custom house official would estimate the value with reference to home prices for similar goods; this tended to produce a much higher figure, as it not only eliminated undervaluation on invoices but also reflected the higher prices obtainable in America for many articles in common use. As home valuation tended, in this way, to cut the importers' margin of profit upon duty-paid goods, there was an even greater incentive for bribery.

In 1820 the contemporary controversies over the tariff stimulated a demand for more accurate figures, and Congress set up a Division of Commerce and Navigation in the office of the Register of the Treasury, and required collectors of customs to submit annual reports showing in detail the trade with foreign countries and the shipping employed. From 1821 these reports provided

[1] R. G. D. Allen and J. Edward Ely, *International Trade Statistics* (New York, 1953), 269.

the data for the annual *Commerce and Navigation of the United States*, and from that time the trade statistics can be used with much greater confidence, though there were recurrent difficulties in estimating the overland trade to Canada, and the difficulties over the valuation of imports described in the preceding paragraph persisted.

In 1866 Congress established the Bureau of Statistics and required the collection of figures in much greater detail than heretofore. This perhaps marks the first positive recognition of the fact that statistical information, recorded with accuracy and classified in as much detail as possible, is an essential tool for modern government. Though the act of 1866 may have been influenced to some extent by current controversies over the tariff and the currency, it accepted the principle that the collection of statistical information was a continuing responsibility of government and should be divorced from the consideration of particular policies. No statistical series is perfect, and the historian may still wish to know more than the figures can tell him about methods of compilation; but from 1867 onwards he can be confident that the trade figures were compiled with as much accuracy as could be obtained and that the questions asked, the consolidation of data, and calculations based upon the raw material were all the responsibility of experts whose aim was to provide as full a picture as possible without reference to the political conclusions which might be drawn from it.

The earliest trade figures in 1790 give merely the total value of exports and imports (and showed an adverse balance of trade of $3 million); in the second year exports were separated from re-exports so that one can trace the rise and decline of the re-exports, from the outbreak of war in Europe until catastrophe (in the shape of non-intercourse and war with Great Britain) hit the business. At first domestic exports were described simply as 'merchandize', though there are some separate and unreliable figures for tobacco, cotton and wheat. The early figures give the destination of exports only for the United Kingdom and European countries; from 1821 British North America, Cuba, Mexico, Brazil, other American countries and China were added. Until 1821 there was no breakdown of imports by country of origin; thereafter they were classified in the same way as exports. It is possible in some cases to supplement the American figures with figures produced by other countries—especially Great Britain and Canada—on their trade with the United States. The British series begins in 1831 and the Canadian in 1850.

Over the whole of this period calculations of the balance of payments depend upon private investigations. In the early years these do not pretend to offer more than an informed guess; in later years the accumulation of more and more statistical information relating not only to trade and shipping but also to banking, commercial services and investment give greater and greater solidity to the estimates.[1]

The evidence from official sources for industrial growth, during the first half of the nineteenth century, is scanty. The first enumeration of manufactures was included in the census of 1810 and describes the position in 1809. Thereafter a decennial census of manufacturers was taken except in 1829. The basic information provided by the census was the number of manufacturing 'establishments'. An establishment was defined as 'a geographically isolated manufacturing unit maintaining independent book-keeping records'. The enumeration of 'establishments' therefore gives no indication of their size or complexity and small workshops were included as well as factories. In addition there are separate figures for certain manufacturing processes, but these are incomplete and of doubtful validity. For instance, the figures for the production of pig-iron come from the censuses of 1810, 1840, and 1850; there are no figures for 1811-19, 1821-27, 1833-39, 1841, 1843-45, 1851 or 1853. Figures for other years during this period are said to be 'largely estimates by early statisticians'. From 1854 the figures for production were collected by the American Iron and Steel Association. Even if the figures before 1854 were complete, one might still have serious doubts about

[1] The principal authorities in this difficult field are Douglass North ('The United States Balance of Payments 1790-1860') and Matthew Simon ('The United States Balance of Payments 1861-1900') in *Studies in Income and Wealth of the National Bureau of Economic Research*, xxiv (Princeton, 1960).

their accuracy; the census figures depended upon the willingness or ability of producers to give returns, and upon the efficiency of enumerators in verifying the information received. Even if these doubts were satisfied one would still have to ascertain the extent to which the production of pig-iron was a true indication of iron production as a whole.

There are early annual figures for the mining of Pennsylvania anthracite (from 1809) and for bituminous coal (from 1800). From 1850 there are decennial figures for the net value of all coal shipments. The records of railroad miles in operation, and miles completed during the year, begin in 1830. It is not always clear whether the miles built during the year refer to the completion of whole lines, or whether to lines still in progress of construction; nor is it possible to distinguish between work on trunk routes and on branch lines. With these qualifications the railroad figures— especially if used in conjunction with contemporary railroad maps—provide a reliable indication of the development of communications.

From 1860 information about manufacturers begins to accumulate. Figures for wheat flour milled, sugar refined, and cotton used in textile manufactures appear in 1860. By 1870 there are figures for steel, beer, spirits, tobacco and cigarettes; by 1890 these have been joined by figures for canned foods, silk, constructional materials, bricks, locomotives, freight and passenger cars. From 1879 there are figures for the capital engaged in the principal branches of manufactures.

The involvement of banking in politics led to the collection and publication of a large amount of official information. The Treasury, the state governments, and the First and Second Banks of the United States all collected statistics about banking, and so, from time to time, did Congressional committees. It was not, however, until 1863, with the establishment of the National Banking system that the Comptroller of the Currency was given responsibility for collecting and compiling all the data necessary, and even after that officials in the separate states remained responsible (as directed by state laws) for information on banks chartered by the states and outside the national system. In 1873 the need for comprehensive information was recognised and the Comptroller was required to obtain statistics from the states; but even after that the lack of uniform procedures in the states introduces an element of doubt. It can be seen from this that through all the great debates on banking policy, from 1790 to 1863, neither Congress nor the Treasury ever had comprehensive information about the banking system as a whole. Indeed the confident assertions of politicians often betrayed ignorance of the way in which the banking system worked, and of the true relationship between the Bank of the United States (or the Independent Treasury), the great private banks of the eastern cities, and the multitude of small banks. The historian need not be quite so ignorant, but too often the political rhetoric of the day has been used as the basis for generalisation, without realising or acknowledging the inadequacy of quantitative data.

Considering how many Americans were engaged in agriculture, statistical information is surprisingly late in its appearance. Before 1850 there was some attempt to include agricultural statistics. In 1840 there were inventories of domestic animals, poultry, dairy and wool production. In 1850 there was an enumeration of farms and farmland, but little was done about production. A change began in 1862 with the establishment of the Department of Agriculture. Though called a Department its functions were rather those of a Bureau in the Department of Interior; but it did have the specific task of collecting and disseminating information, and was a product of a period which saw the Homestead Act, Land Grant Colleges, and the first Pacific Railroad Act. From 1866 onwards the reports of the Department contained a growing volume of information about crops and conditions, and in later years officials of the Department pieced together a good deal of information about earlier production.

The weakness of official statistics in the pre-war years, and the lack of tables for illustrating national trends, do not, however, complete the story. A good deal of evidence has been resurrected, and probably still more lies buried. The archives of the Departments contain a good deal of unpublished economic material, and so do the reports and papers of Congressional committees.

Some material is in print, in early State and Congressional Papers, but covers only a short run of years. Much of this can be put into shape by skilled investigation. For instance, working mainly from census materials, officials were able to make estimates of the 'value added by manufacture' from 1849. There is also source material in local archives, newspapers, market reports and business records. As America has always been engaged in international trade, it is also possible to derive knowledge of the economy from foreign sources. The inadequacy of early statistical material need not, therefore, deprive us of all knowledge of economic growth in the first seventy years of national existence.

Once one gets away from reliable figures collected by contemporaries, one has to rely more and more upon the historian's skill in generalising from insufficient data and in filling gaps by calculation. The calculations of economic historians are enormously valuable, but they are always open to criticism in a way that a census figure or a figure for government revenue is not. We can insist that there may be a margin of inaccuracy in the official figure—because it was inaccurately recorded or inadequately checked at the time of collection, or because the questions asked were not comprehensive—but this is criticism of a different order from that directed against a statistical historian for weighting his material badly, making untenable assumptions as the base of his calculation or failing to take all the relevant data into account. Every account of economic growth includes criticisms of this kind levelled at men who have previously trod the same path, and differing views are inevitable when one is generalising from information covering a brief span or a single market or a single economic factor in a single district and dependent, perhaps, upon amateur interest rather than official responsibility. One can, indeed, admire the ingenuity of the quantitative historian who has extracted a convincing hypothesis from scanty data, and the way in which he has discovered fresh evidence to support his argument; but fragmentary evidence, however skilfully used, can never be a substitute for full statistics, and one must always discount the speculative element in a hypothesis.

The relationship between sources and hypothesis is admirably illustrated by *The Economic Growth of the United States 1790 to 1860*, by Douglas C. North and first published in 1961. It is doubtful whether this book could have been written without reasonably reliable figures for exports, re-exports and imports from 1820 onwards. It is fortunate, too, that the major thesis of the book was that the timing and pace of an economy's development is determined by the success of its export sector, the characteristics of the export industry, and the disposition of income received from export earnings; for this is a thesis which can command a great deal of support from the census and trade figures. Even so, it is instructive to notice how far the argument has to be buttressed by evidence which is fragmentary, local in character, or restricted in time. North uses an elaborate calculation of his own on the United States balance of payments, an export price index also calculated by himself, British figures on freight rates (partly from a reckoning made by the Ship-Owners Society in 1807 and partly from a Parliamentary paper of 1835), the value of the exports of certain commodities from Timothy Pitkin, *A Statistical View of the United States*, published in 1817, figures for the value of cotton exported 1791–1815 compiled by Matthew B. Hammond in 1897, a modern estimate of the remittances by immigrants to the United Kingdom 1847–1863, and an index of wholesale prices 1720–1920 compiled by G. F. Warren and F. A. Pearson in 1932. Each modern table used has its own source history which may range from an informed guess to Warren and Pearson's voluminous collections of wholesale prices of various commodities, in various markets, for varying periods of time. For inter-regional trade North uses figures from American State Papers XXI (published 1834) of tonnage passing through the locks on the Potomac, 1800–15; tonnage engaged in internal and coastwise trade, 1790–1815, from official sources; value of produce received at New Orleans, 1815–60, from a House of Representatives report of 1888; tonnage passing through the Erie Canal, 1836–60, from a Senate Report of 1908; tonnage in the Lake Trade, 1816–60, from a Senate Document, 1864; receipts on Ohio Canals, 1827–1860, from a monograph published in 1924; receipts of flour and grain at Buffalo, 1836–60, from a Senate document of 1864; tonnage in the coasting trade, 1816–60, from statistics compiled by the Bureau of Commerce in 1936; Californian gold production and exports, 1848–60, from a Californian State document; an index of Western State's terms of trade, 1816–40, from a study made in 1943; an article of 1927 on the sale of public lands; issues, 1820–60, of the *New York Shipping and Commercial List* and *New Orleans Prices Current*; a 1948 account of annual incorporations in Ohio, 1803–51; cotton prices at Charleston from a study made in 1958; the Report of the Secretary of the Treasury in 1863. This by no means exhausts the sources necessary for this one book, because each of the modern studies depended upon the compilation, tabulation and weighting of original figures revealed by research.

The example of one scholarly book has been cited at length to demonstrate how, before the age of comprehensive official statistics, the historian has to range over a wide field—utilising official sources, old contemporary sources, modern studies, figures supplied by government departments, figures surviving (more or less at random) from local markets and canals, and tables compiled by private statisticians of long ago. Thus this excellent study demonstrates the nature of the sources and shows the extent to which even quantitative history must depend upon calculation, hypothesis, and the chance survival of scattered data. The historian who attempts the same task for the latter part of this period will not find his calculations easier, but will be able to work from a much larger range of figures compiled with something approaching modern standards of accuracy.

An interesting footnote upon economic growth is provided by the record of patents issued by the Federal government. The first patents on inventions were isussed in 1790, and the practice was regulated under an Act of 1793. From that year until 1836 patents were issued upon application and payment of a $30 fee, but no investigation was made. In 1836 the examination of patents for novelty and other requirements was begun, and each year a number of applications were rejected. Patents issued in the early years are therefore comparable with the applications filed rather than with the patents issued from 1836. As the years went on and the range and complexity of inventions increased, the investigation became more elaborate, more thorough and more scientific. The records of the Patent Office therefore cover a vast amount of information about the history of technology and science. Botanical plants could also be patented, so there is also information on agriculture and horticulture.

In 1790 three patents were issued; from 1796 to 1801 the average yearly issue was over forty; an upward trend, with some fluctuations, then set in with peaks in 1803 (97), 1812 (238), 1825 (304) and 1835 (752). The effects of investigation are shown in sharp divergences between applications field and patents issued, but the gap between the two varies in a puzzling way. For instance, in 1840 458 out of 765 applications were accepted but in 1847 only 495 out of 1,531. The average seems to have been acceptance of a little over half. By 1860 the number issued had risen to 4,357; the onset of war caused a drop to under 4,000 in the next three years, but 1864 saw a recovery to 4,630 and a sharp rise to over 12,000 in 1867. This proved to be a plateau until 1881 when a further rise began. The year 1890 saw a peak with 25,313 patents issued while 14,571 applications were rejected.[1]

There has been considerable debate amongst historians upon the role of government in the economy. This is a complex and technical problem and the immediate intention is merely to indicate the statistical information which bears upon this problem. In 1792 the expenditure of the Federal government was $5,080,000, of which $1,101,000 went to the Army and $3,202,000 to interest on the national debt. There was a slow rise in subsequent years and the war of 1812–14 raised the annual expenditure to over $30,000,000. From the end of the war to 1831 there was a downward trend to $15,248,000; an upward trend then commenced with peaks in 1837 ($37,243,000) but slackened again in the 1840s until the Mexican War brought it to $57,281,000

[1] *Historical Statistics*, Chapter W. Introduction, 63–4. Series W 66–76. A brief history of the patent system and its relationship to invention is given in S. C. Gilfillan. *Invention and the Patent System* (88th Congress, 2nd Session. Joint Economic Committee, Washington, 1964).

in 1847. The next peak was $74,185,000 in 1857. It is an interesting comment upon the relationship between rhetoric and reality that the two interludes of Whig rule (1841–45 and 1849–53) were comparatively low periods of public expenditure, while the sharpest rises took place during the ascendancy of the party dedicated to 'wise and frugal government'. In 1858 the expenditure upon defence totalled $39,500,000 and interest on the public debt had fallen to the very low figure of $1,567,000, but the expenses of civilian government were $33,148,000.[1]

As might be expected the expenses of government rose very steeply during the Civil War, though depreciation of the Greenback means that the figures are not strictly comparable. In the years from 1867 to 1890 expenditure remained fairly stable, moving between $235,000,000 and a little over $350,000,000; but if one looks at the expenses of civilian government alone there is a generally upward trend from $87,000,000 to over $215,000,000. Debt charges were very high immediately after the war, but gradually sank to under $40,000,000 by 1890. In other words, the comparative stability of government expenditure is deceptive; falls took place in defence and debt charges, but the expenditure of government for other purposes more than doubled during the age of laissez-faire.

A similar picture emerges from the record of Federal employees. In 1816 there were 535 in Washington; on the eve of the Civil War there were 2,199; in 1871 there were 6,222, 13,124 in 1881, and 20,834 in 1891. Outside Washington the figures were 4,302 in 1816, 34,473 in 1861, 44,798 in 1871, 86,896 in 1881, and 136,608 in 1891. The Post Office accounted for the majority of Federal employees in all these years; but even allowing for increases necessitated by more territory and more people there is a significant rise in the number of other executive employees outside Washington from 4,891 in 1861 to 34,834.[2] Thus in both expenditure and staff the growth of the Federal government ran far ahead of the growth in population.

Another indicator of governmental activity is the number of

---

[1] *Historical Statistics*, Chapter Y. Series 350–356.
[2] *Ibid.* Series Y, 241–250.

Acts passed, and in reckoning the influence of government upon economic life the number of private Bills is significant. The first Congress passed ninety-four public Acts and eight private Acts; the last complete Congress before the Civil War (1857–59) passed 100 public Acts and 174 private Acts. There was a tremendous upsurge in legislation during the war to 318 and 79 in the thirty-eighth Congress (1863–65). There was only a temporary easement after the war and the fifty-first Congress (1889–91) passed 531 public Acts and 1,633 private Acts.[1]

Far more research is, of course, necessary before one can venture any statements about the relationship between economic growth and government activity, but the figures cited above indicate the wisdom of looking at quantitative evidence before accepting familiar generalisation. In text-book after text-book the federal governments of nineteenth-century America are represented as examples of minimal government activity; restrained in the first half of the century by respect for Jeffersonian principles and in the second by a dogmatic devotion to laissez-faire. Yet the evidence of the figures alone demonstrates the continually increasing volume of expenditure and legislation throughout the century. At all times the Federal government was the largest spender and the largest employer in the country and thus was *a priori* a major influence upon economic activity even before one has considered the functions performed.

A very important aspect of the government's role in economic growth was the disposal of public lands. Large land grants to railroads began in the 1850s. Grants totalling 3,752,000 acres were recorded in 1851, and 14,085,000 acres in 1856. There were some sharp fluctuations from year to year but the peaks were very high: 30,877,000 acres in 1863, 41,452,000 in 1865, and 23,535,000 in 1867. Many lands granted to the states were for the building and support of schools, bridges and other internal improvements. Here too there were very sharp variations from year to year. There was an extraordinary peak in 1850 with a grant of 55,401,000 acres, but this was the outcome of territorial arrangements agreed under the Compromise laws of that year, and especially

[1] *Ibid.* Series Y, 129–138.

the admission of California. More typical peaks were recorded in 1841 (7,807,000 acres), 1849 (9,491,000), 1862 (9,420,000). From 1863 the history of the public lands is dominated by the Homestead Law. Entries began at 8,223 and climbed sharply after the war. As one might expect the number of entries was closely linked with economic fluctuations; thus there were 39,768 in 1871 and 38,742 in 1872, followed by a steady fall to 18,675 in 1877. An upward trend was then resumed to a peak of 61,638 in 1886 while 1890 with 40,244 was a comparatively low year. The further history of the Homestead policy lies beyond the chronological confines of this book, but it is perhaps worth noting that, in spite of everything that has been written about the deficiencies of the law, there were more entries in nearly every year between 1890 and 1916 than in most years before that period. It should, however, be noted that both before and after 1890 the number of final entries seldom exceeded more than half the original entries; in other words, a great deal of land claimed was either abandoned or not taken up. This qualification does not, however, seriously affect the massive consequences for economic growth of Federal land policy.[1]

Whatever qualifications can be made, the facts of economic growth are plain and easy to read; argument centres upon the pace of growth, the role of railways or manufacturers as leaders in growth, and the distribution of increased wealth between sections and classes. It has not been difficult to establish the general pattern of trade cycles, though there may be some disagreement over the dating of turning points. Price data, banking statistics, trade figures, bankruptcies and interest rates can all be employed to reinforce the literary evidence for booms, panics and depressions. A closer study of regional data is necessary to establish the relative incidence of prosperity or depression upon agriculture, industry or commerce, and upon different parts of the country. Still greater difficulties are encountered when an American cycle is set in its international context. It is worth remembering that all the abundant data available did not enable contemporaries to

[1] *Ibid.* Series J, 10–18.

agree upon whether the events of 1929 to 1933 were primarily of domestic or foreign origin, and that more recent analysts, while eliminating some possibilities, have not reached a consensus of judgment upon this question. The scantier material for nineteenth-century booms and depressions makes diagnosis difficult. Something may be achieved by a close empirical study of the sequence of events on both sides of the Atlantic, supplemented by information derived from records of Baring Brothers, and their American correspondents, and this may be more productive than a purely theoretical approach.

Superimposed upon the study of economic fluctuations is the effect of political decisions and war upon economic growth. What were the long-term consequences of establishing the first and second Banks of the United States, of the withdrawal of government deposits in 1833, of the 'Independent Treasury', and of the creation of the National Banking system? Here were issues which aroused the passions of men and became questions of acute political controversy; yet their economic implications remain almost as cloudy as they were to contemporaries. The long controversy over the tariff and protection—which extends over the whole of this period—may offer more opportunities for measurement. One can calculate the immediate consequences for the prices of certain products of alterations in the tariff; and from this go on to some more speculative statements about the probable effects upon production, profits, wages and investment.

In earlier generations two generalisations about war and the economy seemed likely to stand the test of time. The first was that the war of 1812 was crucial in stimulating manufactures and economic nationalism, and the second that the Civil War accelerated industrialisation. The first may well require some qualification but has not, so far, been seriously challenged. The second has been so seriously undermined that some economic historians will assert that the Civil War retarded industrialisation. The evidence for this rests upon comparatively sparse data, and there seems to have been a reluctance to define 'industrialisation'.[1]

[1] The argument over the economic effects of the Civil War was opened by

There is also an incipient confusion between short- and long-term causes. It is established that the production of some manufacturers —especially pig-iron—was not accelerated sharply during the war; but two weak years (1861 and 1862) seems insufficient evidence on which to base a theory. If one takes a broader view one can see the manufacturing 'establishments' increasing from 140,433 in 1859 to 252,148 in 1869; and the 'value added' rising from $854,257,000 to $1,395,119,000. The figures tell one nothing about the organisation of industry, which may be crucial when discussing industrialisation. Nor do they help to establish the relationship between pre-war expansion and the great upward surge after the war reaching a figure of $4,102,301,000 'value added' by 1889. It is quite right to point out that the existing figures do not support the thesis that industrial production increased sharply during the war, and that they do suggest that the two preceding decades were characterised by considerable growth. But having raised the question it seems impossible to deduce from the figures alone any valid conclusions about the relationship of the war to industrialisation. Indeed the whole argument illustrates the limitation which the nature of the source places upon historical reconstruction. The real economic history of the Civil War remains to be written and its materials are to be sought in government documents, business records, individual biographies, and in a careful assessment of the abundant evidence

---

Thomas C. Cochran in 'Did the Civil War Retard Industrialization?' *Mississippi Valley Historical Review* 48 (Sept, 1961), 191–120. Cochran's argument was criticised by Pershing Vartanian. 'The Cochran Thesis: a critique in Statistical Analysis,' *Journal of American History*, 51 (June, 1964), 77–89 and Stephen Salsbury. 'The Effects of the Civil War on American Industrial Development' in Ralph Andreano, ed., *The Economic Impact of the American Civil War* (Cambridge, Mass, 1962), 161–8. An article by Stanley L. Engerman, 'The Economic Impact of the Civil War' in *Explorations in Entrepreneurial History*, Second Series, 3 (1966), has been reprinted in Robert W. Fogel and Stanley L. Engerman, eds., *The Reinterpretation of American Economic History* (New York, 1971), so it is presumably regarded by the editors as the latest if not the last word. To an outsider it seems that some confusion persists between short- and long-term effects, and the effect of war upon business behaviour and organisation has still to be taken into account.

for feverish economic activity during the Civil War. Only then will it be possible to construct valid observations about the continuity or discontinuity of economic growth during the nineteenth century.

CHAPTER 3

The Transformation of Life

Quantitative evidence bears massive testimony to changes in American society during the period covered by this volume. Every series demonstrates sustained expansion; further statistical information could elaborate the picture, but no further emphasis is required to make the principal point. There are, however, more elusive consequences of growth which raise difficult problems for historical enquiry.

Without accepting or rejecting dogmatic assertions of economic determinism one can readily agree that every aspect of life—social, intellectual, and psychological—will be profoundly influenced by economic changes of this magnitude. Many scholars have been concerned with the diagnosis of what was distinctive about American history, with what made 'this new man, this American'; but American development is also a part of the history of advanced societies everywhere, so that one may expect to find universal characteristics of such societies alongside others which were peculiarly American. Indeed, it is sometimes salutary to forget the unique characteristics, or to allow them to merge into the larger picture of developments shared by several nations of the Atlantic world.

The difficulty is that, whether we are looking introspectively for clues to American character or extrovertly for the features of modern advanced societies, much of our reasoning is subjective and speculative rather than objective and based upon verifiable evidence. Garbled versions of the past have been produced by historians who confused conscious motives, unconscious conditioning, and decisions which seem to fly in the face of interest or convention. A policy may have promised immediate gain to individuals, or speculative profits to others, but its adoption may well have depended upon convincing others that it was for the 'good' of society. It can be argued that apparent altruism is determined by the environment; but this cannot be proved. The impulse behind a decision may be elusive, and frequently the motives are inferred from the results; but this may exaggerate the rationality behind success while failure leaves few traces upon the record. It is too easy to move the men of the past into a rational world when they were, in fact, bewildered, misled or incapable of calculating the material consequences of their acts. And what does one make of decisions to found hospitals, museums, or schools? Determinists are usually tempted to ignore philanthropy, but its consequences are more easily measurable than those of many decisions taken by the strict canon of profitability.

There is, then, a wide gap separating quantifiable evidence from the mainsprings of human activity. Even in the area where figures reign, their implication cannot be grasped without imaginative analysis. Many years ago W. Stull Holt speculated upon the consequences of a falling birth-rate.[1] From 1790 to 1830 the number of live births per thousand was in the fifties, from 1830 to 1860 in the forties, and by 1900 had dropped to thirty. This was 'a revolution of the first magnitude, with consequences affecting every phase of American history'. Amongst the many possible lines of enquiry Stull Holt drew attention to three: the increased proportion of older people in the population, the psychological effect of growing up in smaller families, and the growing freedom of women, who had to spend less and less of their lives in bearing and breeding children. Some consequences of the first effect can be documented from available sources. The average age of leaders rose—in 1825 the median age of the House of Representatives was 41·81 and of the Senate 46·5; by 1875 it was 47·48 and 51·5, and was to rise still further. As a result 'America is no longer remarkable for the youthfulness of its leaders, as it was to European observers in the first part of the nineteenth century'. This effect was doubtless due to increased

[1] 'Some Consequences of the Urban Movement in American History', *Pacific Historical Review*, xxii (Nov, 1953), 337–51.

longevity, secured by improvements in medicine, so that older men retained positions of leadership for longer. There are all kinds of other ramifications of falling birth-rates and increased longevity, which affect not only obvious areas such as the increased expenditure on pensions and care of the old, but in more obscure social and psychological by-products. It may even be that this has had an important effect in weakening the position of theistic religion—for the possibility of early death has always been a strong stimulus for supernatural belief—and in shifting the social emphasis from faith to works, from prayer to welfare. These are important and profound speculations and 'we who study and write history must take cognizance of this meaningful change even though we must go to unaccustomed sources for our evidence'.

A more familiar strain of speculation is generated by the social consequences of the railroads. In broad terms there is ample evidence of their impact, and the geography of many nineteenth-century cities can be explained by their useful but destructive presence. It was no accident that 'the wrong side of the track' became identified with poverty and poor breeding. The railroads brought in new goods and helped to destroy less efficient local manufacturers; on the one hand they broke down isolation, on the other they facilitated settlement in yet more remote regions; they were greeted with enthusiasm but later became synonymous with impersonal monopoly. A good many of these consequences of railroad building can be fully documented and underpinned with quantitative evidence; but if one wishes to understand the total effects of the railroads upon society, one must introduce all kinds of other evidence.

Private letters, diaries, newspapers and literary productions can help to build up the other evidence required. The value and limitations of some of these sources are discussed in subsequent chapters; in the present context it is enough to say that they tend to be both selective and unconscious of long-term trends. In the nature of things there will be much evidence on exceptional impact and little on what was normal and expected. Dozens of sources will spring to life when there is a disaster to describe and discuss, but the historian who wishes to reconstruct a picture of humdrum normal life may have to rely on scraps and unrelated fragments. Yet many of the most significant forces of history can be understood only by tracing the currents of change in ordinary life.

This calls in question the extent to which historians should or must call the concepts of other disciplines to their aid. Must the historian turn anthropologist, psychologist, sociologist, or political scientist in order to understand the transformation of life? The prosposition will be stoutly resisted by many historians, and it is easy to give examples of bad history which has succumbed too readily to the temptation of a psychological or sociological short-cut. Yet if the theorists in these other disciplines have revealed universals in human society, their concepts are a necessary part of the historian's equipment. There is, too, some inconsistency amongst conservative historians who will readily borrow from classical economists a concept such as 'diminishing returns' or use biological analogies without realising that they are doing so. A good many historians will go on talking confidently about 'class' while refusing to hear what sociologists have to say about one of the central preoccupations of their discipline, while analyses of individual motives bristle with psychological assumptions made by men who would indignantly exile professional psychologists from the territory of history.

American historians have normally employed certain sociological or psychological concepts to explain the transformation of their society. They have taken, as points areas of reference, from European civilisation from which the Americans separated and the civilisation of the Atlantic seaboard from which modern America has evolved. Many attempts have been made to express the relationship between the United States and the parent culture of Europe, and concepts such as 'rejection', 'assimilation', 'cultural dependence and independence', have dominated the argument. The relationship between the Atlantic and the interior has been analysed mainly in terms of economic tension and conflict, of revolt against eastern élites, and of struggle against control by the metropolis. The characteristics of American society have been explained by 'social mobility', 'internal migration', 'the safety valve', a 'classless society', and the lack of a feudal past. It can readily be seen that these words, phrases, and themes—which have become commonplace—draw upon complex and debatable theories of human relationships. One moves rapidly from the contemplation of quantitative evidence about population, distribution, trade, manufactures and agricultural production to descriptions of the transformation of life in terms which are subjective though often presented as simple statements of fact. As these concepts have been so generally used, it is necessary to ask what evidence can be produced for their validity. Is there an easy road from the relatively firm ground of quantitative evidence to the less secure heights of social analysis? Historians cannot send out questionnaires, nor can they do field work amongst the people whom they study; they can only work with the sources which have survived and which were not compiled with the purpose of answering their questions.

It has been a persistent claim amongst Americans that individual mobility has had a major part in the transformation of life. There was a comforting belief in nineteenth-century America that a man could rise in the social scale as high as his initiative and talents would take him. This was coupled with the assertion that men who found their road blocked in one locality could move to another. It was generally assumed that a man who moved to another locality entered the new society at a point where his ambition was more likely to be satisfied. No one, of course, was so dogmatic as to claim that all mobility was beneficial, but it was generally assumed that the overall effect was to reward not only the fortunate few but also the great mass of individuals who were prepared to work hard and risk a little.

It goes without saying that in a rapidly expanding society some places at the top would be filled by men who had started at the bottom; but a secure social base was a much better starting-point than the shifting sands of poverty. A successful man was more likely to have begun life as the son of a small property owner, minister, teacher or lawyer; than as a member of a penniless immigrant family. It is possible to verify this by individual biographies in a large number of cases, but it must be realised that the man who reaches the point at which he can be identified and the details of his career discovered is, by definition, untypical. The evidence does not exist to make a systematic survey of the great American middle-class—moderately successful and moderately well-to-do—and still less of the great mass of men in the lower echelons of white-collar employment or engaged in manual labour. It is possible to collect evidence about success, but there is little hope of gathering sufficient material to construct general theories about modest achievement or failure.

It is possible that patient work upon the manuscript census returns can go a little way towards bridging this gap. By comparing the returns made by individuals over three or four decennial periods, there is some hope of constructing a picture of social mobility in single localities; but the other great American phenomenon—geographical mobility—will, then however, distort the results. In European rural communities it has been possible to trace families over several generations, and migration out of the community more frequently took younger sons than whole families. The relatively static nature of the European population opens up further possibilities of investigation through church records, wills, title deeds, and court records. The greater geographic mobility of American society in the nineteenth century (and today) makes this kind of evidence of social change and structure far less useful.

One area in which this kind of study has been productive is the old South. Using the census and various local records it has been possible to reconstruct the life of the 'plain people', in districts remote from the plantations where little literary evidence survives. Here it has been possible to follow individuals and families through successive censuses, to trace changes in their real estate, in their holdings of slaves, and to estimate their personal property. It should be possible to conduct similar studies in New England; large numbers migrated to other parts of the United States, but the family farms tended to remain in the same hands over long periods. Neither type of community is, however, likely to yield much evidence for solving general problems of social mobility.

There is a superficial ease in establishing facts of physical mobility. The census recorded the country or state of birth, and a comparison with earlier censuses can show how many newcomers have moved in and how many former inhabitants have left. The difficulty arises in tracing the previous history of newcomers and the subsequent history of persons leaving the community. Undoubtedly many did improve their situation by movement; but it seems equally probable that more moved from one failure to another, or at best from defeat to minimal security. Theoretically, and with the help of computers, it should be possible to trace the life histories of thousands of persons from birth to death, and, with habitual migrants, to catch them for an instant every ten years. It would be idle to anticipate the findings of such a study, but a close student of urban history has deduced that many who moved from town to town were shiftless, inadequate or improvident people, moving hopefully but fruitlessly from place to place until overtaken by old age or chronic illness.[1] Particularly, it would seem, very few of those who moved into the cities, from European peasant societies or from rural America, climbed to material success in one or even two generations. The myths of a land of opportunity may have to be qualified but it remains true that there was more opportunity in urban and industrial America than in most other parts of the civilised world. The path of upward social mobility may have been hard and

[1] Stephan Thernstein, *Urbanization, Migration and Social Mobility in Late Nineteenth-Century America* (in Barton J. Bernstein, ed., *Towards a New Past: Dissenting Essays in American History* (New York, 1968), 158–72). Drawing mainly upon his detailed research on Newburyport, Mass., Mr Thernstein concludes that 'many ordinary working people on the move owned no property, had no savings accounts, had acquired no special skills, and were most likely to leave when they were unemployed'. In a more speculative vein he suggests that 'one reason that a permanent proletariat envisaged by Marx did not develop . . . is perhaps that few Americans *stayed* in one place, one workplace, or even one city long enough to discover a sense of common identity and common grievance'. There is a possible confusion here; in any country the unsuccessful working men were unlikely to form a permanent proletariat; if Mr Thernstein means that the successful as well as the unsuccessful moved he is back to the old proposition that mobility was the safety valve which averted class conflict.

narrow, but it was a better road than in Europe, the old South, or even the rural areas of the eastern United States. The prospects were best for migrants from New England, old England, Scotland, or Northern Ireland; encountering no barriers of language or religion, they contributed most examples to demonstrate the truth of the great American success story, but even so, the achievement of the majority was modest.

Most recent analyses of the available sources have therefore tended to question mobility as it was presented in the conventional 'model' constructed from American rhetoric. Another favourite theme—the 'melting pot'—has similarly drawn criticisms and requires substantial qualification. The major impact of Mediterranean and Slav immigration lies beyond the scope of this volume, but before 1890 there is already enough evidence to question views of assimilation derived from the experience of early years when the majority of immigrants were North Europeans and Protestant. An Englishman, a Lowland Scot, or an Ulster Protestant found little difficulty in assimilation or acceptance; a Highlander or a Welshman found little more, though the latter tended to concentrate in a few areas. Germans, though predominantly Protestant in the early years, tended to cluster together and to maintain their own language and culture, so that even in the early national period the operation of the melting pot was limited. The mass immigration of Catholic Irish and Germans in the middle years of the century introduced elements which not only regarded themselves as alien but were so regarded by Americans of the 'old stock' (many of them belonging to families which had been barely established for a quarter century on American soil). The picture of universal Americanism begins to dissolve under scrutiny and in its place emerges a complicate mosaic of custom and racial or religious particularism.

This critical approach should encourage the historian to look with a candid eye upon the social rationalisations of our own age. If the 'models' of an earlier era are modified or discarded, there may be equally good reasons for questioning the latter-day 'models' of social scientists. There is this difference: the earlier accounts were admittedly and unashamedly expressions of faith, but contemporary theories claim the validity of empirical observation. The good historian should be familiar with the method and with the kind of evidence used by social scientists, but he alone can bring time and change into the picture. Historians, who have rashly borrowed modern concepts of 'class' and 'status', and used them as keys to the past, have not contributed much to understanding. These descriptive concepts have evolved in response to contemporary needs and did not exist as ideas in the past; but the forces that they now represent existed in former times and are subjects for historical investigation. In other words, the social scientists may present historians with new questions which must be answered historically.

The conclusion is, therefore, that historians should not ignore social science, and must be aware, at all times, that social scientists may be presenting new tools of analysis; at the same time, historians should treat their concepts with a healthy dose of critical relativism. What is true now may not have been true in the past, and it is certain to be qualified if not corrected in the future. It is probable that each new attempt to analyse present reality will provide some new clues for an understanding of the past; but an analytical tool must be sharply distinguished from a theory which analysis must confirm. It is, perhaps, a good rule to take source material at its face value, to understand it as it was understood by those who committed it to paper, and not to assume that greater wisdom entitles us to say that they should have understood it in a different way. But this is not to say that a historian is a slave of his sources; he is a modern man with modern questions to ask, and even within the walls of the past he has a wider vision than any contemporary could have had. To assume that men of the past (to cite one example) were dominated by anxieties about status is to import into the past the code of a modern middle-class suburb; but this is not to deny that a phenomenon, which we now define as 'status', could have had an influence on their lives. The danger begins when we substitute 'status' for the fears or hopes which they expressed for themselves. There are hidden forces in human history, but we cannot take a short cut to their discovery by assuming that what men said for themselves should be ignored.

American historiography has been particularly rich in such attempts. There is a false but persuasive illusion of 'realism' in disregarding what was on the surface of argument. American intellectuals have often been impelled to react against the shallow rhetoric of public life and patriotic education, so that a great deal of history has been written on the assumption that men did not mean what they said and that the mainsprings for action must be sought elsewhere. Too often the result has been to by-pass the sources, or to use them merely to provide evidence for a pre-determined theory. It should be added that admirers of the more fashionable social theories are not the only sinners; the fashion was set by Jefferson, who looked behind what Federalists said to discover the supposed influence of anglomen and monocrats, and later by historians of the old South, who worked upon the assumption that economics and envy were sufficient explanations for northern actions. The defenders of the old South have not found it difficult to join forces with more sophisticated expo-nents of modern social analysis; neither help us much to under-stand how real men faced their real problems.

Psychology offers a somewhat different challenge to historians. Modern discourse has become so impregnated with the language of psychiatry that it is used unconsciously as a descriptive and analytical tool. Modern historical writing is full of 'images'; individuals or groups become 'alienated' or 'withdraw from reality'; men 'play roles' or regulate their activity by negative or positive 'reference points'. An influential book discusses 'the paranoid style' in American history, and the possibilities of schizophrenia or monomania are always before us.[1] A biographer may not commit himself to a psychoanalytical diagnosis of his subject's personality, but he is likely to emphasise the early environment and to infer its importance for the future. Historians

[1] Richard Hofstadter, *The Paranoid Style in American Politics* (New York, 1965). For an example of an attempt to apply psychoanalytical concepts to the coming of the Civil War see my *Character of American History* (2nd ed., London, 1965), 130–32.

have been justly suspicious of attempts to 'explain' actions by psychoanalysis, but time and again they assume that the language of psychiatry contributes something important to our understanding of the past. In an absolute sense this must be true. Human personality lies at the heart of every historical enquiry and the characteristics of the human mind must be a basic 'source' of history.

Even before the age of modern psychiatry the influential frontier thesis assumed that the response of individuals to environment was important and uniform. Special characteristics, attitudes, and assumptions were not innate but the product of circumstances. From the earliest period of national history Jeffersonians assumed that life in cities would have distinct effects upon personality and behaviour, and subsequent studies of ethnic minorities in the cities have frequently stressed the psychological importance of living in an alien world. In another field pro-slavery advocates built elaborate defences of the institution upon what they believed to be the ineradicable characteristics of Negro personality; abolitionists argued that this personality was the result of slavery, not its justification, while Stanley M. Elkins has sought to prove that the qualities of the 'good nigger' were themselves the inevitable products of a closed authoritarian system. Thus historians who have paid the closest attention to the importance of environment have gone furthest in using, consciously or unconsciously, the 'facts' of psychology to 'explain' personality.

Nineteenth-century America is rich in opportunities for the use of these techniques. Living in an environment which was changing with unprecedented rapidity, 'adjustment', 'tension' and the need to compensate for 'frustration' became a part of the common experience of mankind. Living in a changing society with weak traditional institutions, men constructed 'myths' to substitute for fixed relationships. Sectional conflict and the Civil War have prompted much speculation along these lines; when conclusions seem irrational, it is tempting to seek comfort in psychic explanations. The sturdy empiricist who relies upon 'fact' finds himself portraying a world in which the decision for war is inexplicable, and, to avoid the introduction of moral issues, flies to sociological or psychological concepts. It is a curious phenomenon in American historiography that the men who have been the most 'professional' in their methods and have claimed most for historical 'science', have also most readily borrowed concepts which they have not been trained to evaluate. The importance of psychology for historical understanding is undeniable, but the language of psychiatry is no substitute for knowledge of the sources—any more than the sources can tell us everything about the men who were once here and now are gone.

The chapters which follow will examine the sources for many aspects of American history during the period covered by this volume. It is impossible to be comprehensive, because the range of enquiry and the discovery of evidence is constantly ahead of all attempts to define what history is; and it is important to remember that sources exist in time and change. When one has taken the quantitative evidence, and attempted to weigh the literary evidence, one is left with the qualitative problems of how societies change, how men react to change, and how their reactions modify ideas, institutions, and human relationships.

The bridge from quantitative evidence to socio-historical theory may often seem to cover too wide a span. Subsequent chapters in this book will deal with many kinds of other evidence: the history of government, of ideas, and of social life. It would clearly be wrong to approach all these sources of evidence with a ready-made theory of growth and transformation, to which the sources are expected to supply supporting evidence. Much bad history has been produced in this way. But it is improbable that any historian will approach his evidence without some broad concepts to guide his steps and to suggest the questions which should be asked. There can be no firm rule, but it may be suggested that the general historian can put his task in perspective by making himself familiar with the kind of specialised history which seldom appears in history syllabuses; with the history of science and technology, of medicine and public health, of art and architecture, and even of such by-ways as costume, cookery, and interior decoration. The histories of particular institutions such as churches, schools, universities, voluntary societies, or corporations are more familiar, but are usually relegated to secondary roles except when they become involved in national political crises. Yet the more the general historian knows about these fields, and about the sources on which they depend, the more aware will he be that the transformation of life spreads across the whole spectrum of society. It seems unlikely that any single concept can explain all these manifold changes, and the more one knows about the sources of information for the history of social development, the more reluctant one may be to accept single concepts as adequate explanations. There must be a general theory of social change, but a close acquaintance with the sources of history should foster a due humility and a realisation that working historians may be more adept at undermining the confidence of social theorists than at constructing their own philosophy of life.

PART II

Government and the Law

Introduction

Governments accumulate records as a necessary part of their activities. As raising and spending money is the heart of the governmental process it has been traditional to preserve exact accounts of what has been done, and in constitutional governments this need is reinforced by the requirement of public accountability. Men who administer government can use their discretion only within the limits set by law and convention, and it is therefore necessary to preserve records of precedents, rules, and past practice. Modern government accepts, as a first principle, that justice must be done to individuals; it is therefore necessary to preserve full records of every transaction which affects life, liberty or property. In democratic societies it is also an accepted principle that the Executive Departments may be required at any time to render account of their actions to the representatives of the people, and their records must therefore be ready for public investigation at any time. Legislative bodies must keep records of their own activities and decisions, both for their own information and for the public. For these and other reasons it is imperative that every branch of government should accumulate and preserve records of everything that is done. The weight of material that accumulates is sometimes seen as evidence of bureaucratic proliferation; but it has been well-said that 'Government documents, as they are often called, are the living records of the efforts of a people to govern themselves'.[1]

[1] Laurence F. Schmeckebier and Roy B. Eastin, *Government Publications and their Use* (Washington, 1960). Introduction, 1.

CHAPTER 4

The Federal Government

The sheer bulk of Federal archives bears witness to the industry and interest of a record-keeping society. Even before the close of the nineteenth century the mass—though dwarfed by subsequent additions—had reached a formidable size. Early in the new century the leading authority on the Federal archives wrote,

> The mere mass of these records of the government is well-nigh appalling. It is impossible to form an estimate of the aggregate space occupied by them: in a single office of the Treasury Department, for example, they cover ten miles of shelving; the volumes of diplomatic and consular correspondence in the State Department are to be numbered by thousands; in a few years the Adjutant-General reported that in addition to several tons of Confederate records . . . there were over ten tons of books and papers, the character of which had not as yet been ascertained. In some departments entire buildings are rented for no other purpose than that of filling them from cellar to attic with records and files that are not in immediate demand in the prosecution of current work.[1]

Most of these archives are now housed in the National Archives, or accessible from there, and the endless task of cataloguing has progressed a long way since 1900. It is a safe generalisation that today the searcher can locate the departmental papers which he wishes to consult provided that these deal with the more important questions of departmental business. Minor matters, or items which found their way rarely into a department and did not constitute a normal part of its responsibilities may still be very difficult to identify.[2]

[1] C. H. Van Tyne and Waldo G. Leland, *Guide to the Archives of the Government in Washington* (Washington, 1904), Preface, iv.

[2] The National Archives are publishing preliminary inventories of the federal records. A very useful account of the archives is Laurence F. Schmecke-

The ever-increasing scale of government activity during the nineteenth century has already been emphasised, and greater awareness of administrative needs also ensured that the records of what had been transacted became more and more comprehensive. There is therefore not only an increasing number of things recorded, but each is also recorded more voluminously. If one is studying the administration of government it is also necessary to consult the personal letters of departmental heads, both because they are more likely to divulge the politics behind the policy and because nineteenth-century secretaries often retained official papers after leaving office. There are also papers emanating from Washington now found in state and local archives (though the practice of keeping copies in the departments was established at an early date). Congressional debates and documents enable one to assess how much of the material in the departments was made available to the public.

Much of the manuscript material in the departmental records is dreary stuff, but the excellence of a historian often consists in divining the existence of a seam of precious metal amid the great slag-heaps of administrative archives. For instance, in recent years some unexpectedly lively social history has depended for its major source upon the manuscript census returns. It is also axiomatic that in order to use the records of government one must understand the working of governmental institutions. So much of the value of information depends upon knowing how it was collected, for what purpose, and with what competence. Yet the student of nineteenth-century America is often compelled to take the intention for the deed, and to take the material relevant to his particular enquiry without embarking upon the years of research which would be necessary to describe and analyse the institutions of government. Fame if not fortune awaits the scholar

bier and Roy B. Eastin, *Government Publications and their Use* (Brookings Institution, Washington; rev. ed., 1960). Kenneth W. Munden and Henry P. Beers, *Guide to the Federal Archives Relating to the Civil War* (National Archives, Washington, 1962) gives retrospective accounts of the history of the departments, and the classification provides a complete guide to records of government in the mid-nineteenth century.

who will produce an administrative history which is sufficiently detailed to serve the scholar while readable enough to carry the conviction that the organisation and growth of central government is a vital aspect of the history of modern society.[1]

The oldest of the great departments is the State Department which was established on 27 July, 1789, as the Department of Foreign Affairs.[2] When Congress had completed the task of establishing the other departments, and defining their responsibilities, there remained a number of domestic duties unassigned and these were given to the renamed Department of State. Over the years these minor domestic responsibilities tended to expand and were hived off into new departments or separate bureaux operating under one of the existing departments. The Department of State is thus the parent of the Department of the Interior, the Bureau of the Census and the Bureau of Patents. During the nineteenth century the Department of State was responsible for the Territories, corresponded with the governors of state on many official matters, received the constitutions of proposed new states and transmitted them to Congress, and sent proposed constitutional amendments to the states and reported to Congress when the requisite number of states had ratified. The historian will therefore find much material on domestic history in the archives of the State Department; but it was not responsible for police (except in the Territories) and had only an indirect responsibility for public order. Moreover, many of the department's domestic duties were strictly bound by rule which even the secretary could not vary. The domestic records of the Department of State are therefore in no way comparable to those of the

---

[1] The standard history of the administrative system of the United States is provided by Leonard D. White's four volumes (*The Federalists*, 1948, *The Jeffersonians*, 1951, *The Jacksonians*, 1956, *The Republicans*, 1958). These contain some references to archival material but is based mainly upon contemporary published sources and secondary works. The administrative history of the Civil War is omitted and the preceding fifteen years are treated somewhat cursorily.

[2] See Daniel T. Goggin and H. Stephen Helton, *General Records of the Department of State* (National Archives Preliminary Inventory, Washington, 1963), and Graham H. Stuart, *The Department of State: a history of its organization, procedure and personnel* (New York, 1949).

British Home Office, which bear witness to the continuous oversight of public order under a departmental head who had the power to act and to decide.

By contrast the papers relating to foreign affairs contain the living record of the nation's external relations. This does not necessarily mean that the record is comprehensive for, as the most authoritative work on diplomatic records observes,

> Diplomacy is a business where things can be done and have been done orally or even by gestures, traces of which speedily evaporate. In the name of diplomacy, too, things have been done—let us use the perfect—of which, without documents, only the angels in heaven are witness.[1]

With qualification this might be said of many branches of public administration, but in diplomacy the unrecorded can be more significant and more tantalising than in most. One has also to recognise that important documents—or portions of documents—may have been lost and occasionally deliberately lost. However, the history of diplomacy would be a dry game if it did not record the actions of fallible human beings whose omissions or falsifications force upon historians the need to guess.

The papers accumulating in the Department of State are of several kinds. There are letters out, sometimes with copies of enclosures. There are letters in, and the searcher will have to look carefully for a note of the date received (often of major importance). There are drafts and fair copies of instructions to representatives abroad, and signed despatches (often several copies) from diplomatic agents in foreign countries. The inward despatches will often include enclosures which help to reconstruct the picture, formed in Washington, of conditions in other countries. There are notes from the secretary to the diplomatic representatives of other countries and vice versa. There are memoranda—ranging from informal jottings to formal statements—dealing with conversations and policy, and the records of

[1] Samuel Flagg Bemis and Grace Gordon Griffin, *Guide to the Diplomatic History of the United States* (Washington, 1935—reprint by Peter Smith, Gloucester, Mass., 1963), 786.

the Secret Service or other forms of Intelligence. There is correspondence with other departments, and official correspondence with other countries; amongst the latter the department kept separate files for letters from heads of state which can be very important during a period when European monarchs kept a close control over foreign policy. Another category of the records deals with treaties and international congresses or conferences. A huge mass of consular papers are found in the archives of the Department of State. Before diplomatic relations are established with a country the consular letters may include important material for foreign relations, but thereafter they tend to be confined to citizens abroad, American ships, and commercial information. Their utility for diplomatic history thus sharply diminishes, though the patient historian of trade may be rewarded after laborious search.

The Department of State was frequently called upon by Congress to communicate papers, and every treaty sent to the Senate would normally be accompanied by supporting correspondence and other evidence. Most of this material was printed, in the first instance for the use of Congress and subsequently for the public. Papers sent to the Senate with treaties were confidential, but in most instances they subsequently became public. There is therefore an unusual amount of State Department material in print (when one compares the record with that of other countries), but it is always necessary to recall that the selection of treaty papers lay with the secretary, who was naturally concerned to place his handiwork in a favourable light. It is estimated that between 1789 and 1828 about a quarter of the diplomatic correspondence found its way into print and the choice could be selective and slanted; in later years, and especially since the Civil War, one expects to find that the selection printed is fairly representative of the whole; but it is never safe to assume this.[1] Finally, it is always necessary to remember that the records of one country tell only a part of the story. 'To know the whole

[1] A. C. McLaughlin estimated that not more than one fourth of the material found its way into *State Papers, Foreign Relations, 1789–1828* (*Diplomatic Archives of the United States*, Washington, 1906).

history of the game, the historian must seek to turn up the cards of all the players who sat at the table, not of one player alone.'[1]

In one respect the diplomatic correspondence of the United States displays more variety than that of other nations. The ministers of other powers were usually career diplomats or men of high rank with long experience of public life, and their secretaries were younger men of the same breed. Their correspondence was largely conducted in a recognisable and uniform official style, and they tended to move—in foreign countries—in a comparatively small circle. American ministers abroad were of many different types and backgrounds, often with little official training; this may have handicapped them as diplomats, but it lent variety and interest to their correspondence. For instance, between 1841 and 1850 the United States was represented at London by Edward Everett, a brilliant intellectual turned politician, who became a celebrated orator, Louis M'Lane, who had been President of the Baltimore and Ohio Railroad, George Bancroft, the most noted American historian of his period, and Abbot Lawrence, the great Boston textile magnate. The principal secretaries were normally young protégés of the minister and displayed a similar variety of background; during the Civil War Charles Francis Adams, in London, employed his famous son, Henry. Even consuls could be surprising people; Nathaniel Hawthorne was consul at Liverpool during the presidency of Franklin Pierce. The personal relations of these amateur diplomats also covered a wide range: Everett made it his business to accept large numbers of speaking invitations and penetrated deeper into the world of the urban middle class than any previous diplomat, while Bancroft gathered British intellectuals for weekly 'historical breakfasts'. Thus the archives of the State Department can reveal flashes of personality and social experience which would have been lacking in a more professional service.

What diplomatic correspondence seldom reveals, or reveals inadequately, is the pressure behind politics. The official men with whom the diplomat deals will be at pains to conceal the fact that they and their government have only a limited control over the

[1] Bemis and Griffin, *op. cit.*, 805.

situation and may have to consider many different groups and opinions. The diplomat lacks the knowledge to interpret what he reads in the newspapers and fails to understand the numerous currents moving in a political world. The historian who turns hopefully to the despatches of British ministers at Washington to find information upon the American scene will find plenty of reporting but almost all of it partial, misleading, and poorly informed. Conversely American correspondence from foreign capitals (apart from the personal touches mentioned above) gives little but garbled and inaccurate information. There was considerable improvement during the Civil War because Charles Francis Adams was an exceptionally able and persistent man, and because it was desperately important for the United States to know how British opinion was moving; but the general conclusion can only point to the poverty of the information upon which the policy-makers in Washington were forced to depend. When one remembers that most nineteenth-century Presidents and Secretaries of State were little-travelled men, who had spent most of their lives moving in a circumscribed world of politics, one can only be thankful for the comparatively small number of crises in external relations which they had to confront between 1814 and 1890.

The records of the Treasury contain sources for much of the statistical information described in the preceding chapter.[1] As with the other great departments much of the most important material found its way into print via reports to Congress, but somewhere there must be in existence (so far unexplored) a great body of exchanges with the Ways and Means Committee of the House. It was extremely important for all Secretaries of the Treasury to ensure that the men responsible for the first draft of revenue Bills and appropriations had all relevant information. Another large and little used body of materials is the correspondence between the Treasury and the Bank of the United States, private banks, and individual financiers. Much of the information yielded by the Treasury records must, of necessity, be highly tech-

[1] For an excellent account of the mid-nineteenth-century Department of the Treasury, see Munden and Beers, *op. cit.*

nical or of little interest save to students of fiscal administration. The Treasury was also one of the great patronage departments, and the records should yield a wealth of material illustrating the inner working of the political system. In a broader context, however, the Treasury archives (which have received far less attention than those of the State Department) must yield a wealth of information about the growth of the nation and its transformation from a simple rural society with a few commercial centres into a modern industrial and urbanised nation. The political history of the United States is littered with economic controversies, and throughout its history the Treasury has administered (and often initiated) policies which men believed—correctly or incorrectly—to be of vital importance to the nation. Since the days of Alexander Hamilton the Treasury was also in the vanguard of efficient administration, and, despite some notable scandals, the collection of revenue was too important to permit chronic inefficiency. Collectorships, and other high offices in the revenue service, were lucrative, influential and much in the public eye. Several minor political crises were precipitated over the appointment of collectors. The Treasury records should therefore provide a great deal of information about a highly sensitive and largely concealed area of public life. The 'spoils system' has been studied mainly through the eyes of civil service reformers and public debates on the issues raised, and there remains much to discover from the insider's view of how patronage and rotation in office really worked. Presidential papers sometimes give agonising glimpses of frustration and irritation of men who had to wrestle with the knotty task of staffing the public administration. There was no surer way of making political enemies or of bringing discredit upon a party.

General historians are most likely to turn to the records of the Post Office for further information about patronage. The Post Office has, of course, its own important history, but for most nineteenth-century Americans the Post Office meant the Post-master. He was, indeed, the only Federal official whom many of them ever met, and in an intimate way he stood locally for the party to which he belonged and for the President who had appointed him. Party regulars deserved their just rewards but a Postmaster who was unpopular or incompetent did no one any good. The difficulty lay in assessing the merits of men who had to present no formal qualifications for office, and there was little alternative to accepting the men proposed by local party organisations or by individual Senators or Representatives. The official business of the Post Office touched the life of the nation at many points, for communications were of the first importance to scattered people straggling over half a continent. The efficiency of the mail affected politics and commerce, the dissemination of news, and contact with foreign countries. The Post Office was responsible for designating postal routes and it could request Congress to establish post roads (this power played a persistent though minor part in the interminable controversy over Federal aid for internal improvements). The Post Office was also responsible for mail contracts with the shipping lines, stage coach companies, and railroads; a great deal of social history therefore lies buried in its routine records.

The early records of the Army and Navy deal mainly with professional matters; commissions, promotions, training, discipline and equipment have obvious relevance for military and naval historians, but historians who are interested in political issues have been reluctant to embark upon the uncharted seas of Army and Navy records, even when relevant to their major themes. The history of the War of 1812, and of the events preceding it, has been written with little reference to these sources, and only limited use has been made of them for the Mexican War. The picture changes dramatically with the Civil War. Volume after volume of official records fill one or two shelves in most large libraries; the Confederate War Records were transferred to Washington at the end of the war, and the bulk of them have also been published. Innumerable local and regimental histories have drawn upon the Washington archives for materials.

In 1860 the entire military force of the United States consisted of 16,215 regular troops, the Navy of 9,942, and the Marines of 1,801. During the war the quotas charged against the states totalled 2,759,049, and at the close of the war there were over a million men in the Army, 58,296 in the Navy, and 3,860 in the Marines. During the war 364,511 men were killed (140,414 in battle) and 281,881 were wounded. It can readily be imagined that this expansion in numbers, together with all the incidental duties of fighting arduous campaigns, supplying the armies, and providing medical services all brought about a vast enlargement in administration. When Gideon Welles became Secretary of the Navy his office contained a chief clerk, a register clerk, nine correspondence clerks, a warrant clerk and two messengers; there were also a number of small bureaux dealing with different aspects of naval administration. The highest pre-war expenditure on the Navy (in 1859) had been $14,643,000; by 1865 it was $122,613,000 (though some allowance should be made for depreciation of the greenback dollar). The Army expenditure was $25,485,000 in 1858—the highest pre-war year of peace (in 1847 the Mexican War raised it to $38,306,000); in 1865 the expenditure was $1,031,323,000. In addition to specifically military duties the War Department became responsible for the military government of occupied areas, for military tribunals set up to try disloyal persons, for fugitive slaves and freedmen. In March 1865 responsibility for former slaves was given to the Freedmen's Bureau, but it remained under the Secretary for War. The War Department also operated, at different times during the war, forty railroads in the South, and in Pennsylvania Army engineers built lines where existing communications were inadequate. After the war the War Department had far-reaching responsibility in the South, which continued until the withdrawal of Federal troops in 1877.

The records of the War Department thus became those of a government within a government; and expansion and improvisation took place under the continuous demands of war and, not unnaturally, under special scrutiny by Congress. In no area was the change more striking, or more illustrative of the clash between new and old, than the office of the Surgeon General, traditionally headed by very old men promoted for long service rather than for medical or military skill. From April 1862 to

August 1864 a dynamic Surgeon General, William A. Hammond, carried out a heroic task of reorganisation and administration; this was continued under his successor, Joseph K. Barnes. The Army medical service came to work in close co-operation (despite frequent friction) with the voluntarily organised Sanitary Commission which raised funds for medical facilities and vigorously investigated hygiene, health and amenities in Army camps. In addition to records kept at Washington during the war the National Archives house the files of correspondence and papers kept at the various headquarters in the field; so that it is possible to go down from the top level of strategy, supply and national policy to the immediate details of campaigns, camp life, and soldiers' grievances.

Historians have much reason to be grateful to the War Department during and after the war for one particular service already noted in the general introduction. In 1862 a small Records Office was established to act as a repository for captured Confederate records (partly to preserve evidence which might be required in future trials of 'rebels'). Later the records of the various Union armies and military operations were transferred to Washington and housed in the Records Office and in 1880 publication of these voluminous materials began with money appropriated by Congress. The general title of the series was *The War of the Rebellion*—a description which does not commend itself to Southerners—but in other respects this first major project in 'official history' achieved a remarkable degree of impartiality.

Until recently the archives of the War Department, apart from the Freedmen's Bureau, had hardly been touched by historians of Reconstruction. The omission has now been remedied by a general study, but there is probably still scope for a great deal of work on detailed problems.[1] The Freedmen's Bureau has not been ignored, but its records have still much to offer as a source of social history in the South. Responsible for relief, resettlement, vocational training, education and medical services it was the

[1] James E. Sefton, *The United States Army and Reconstruction* (Baton Rouge, 1967). This work is particularly useful for the attention paid to the papers of Army commands to the South.

largest experiment in social administration ever undertaken by any government up to that time. The most voluminous and most revealing records are not those of the Bureau's Washington office but of papers deposited, after the Bureau had been wound up in 1869, from the local headquarters of the Assistant Commissioners. More recently the importance of the Army in the administration of the South during the Reconstruction period has been recognised, and studies of the Freedmen's Bureau must use the Army records. Once this crucial period has passed, the accumulating records of the armed services are, for the most part, untroubled by historians.

The usefulness of the Civil War Army records is not confined to the history of campaigns and military units. In the draft the Army dealt with a great political innovation which touched society at many levels, and the records contain many sidelights upon living conditions, law enforcement, and popular protest. The Army and Navy were much concerned with equipment, supply, invention, and communications. It is one of the surprises of the war to discover how little it seems to have brought about technical innovation and improvement; but even so, the records of the Army and Navy must contain a great deal of information about the technological foundations of modern American society.

Some aspects of Civil War history will take us back once more to the State Department, for during the conflict the domestic responsibilities of the Secretary were greatly enlarged; partly because W. H. Seward—so often underrated by contemporaries and subsequent historians—was by far the ablest and safest man in Lincoln's cabinet. Acting through United States marshals and other officials he ordered the arrest of nearly a thousand persons suspected of disloyalty in the early days of the war and held them in military custody. Until February 1862, when these duties were transferred to the War Department, the Secretary of State was responsible for all political prisoners and set up a commission to examine those held in custody. Thus, at a crucial period in American history, the Department of State acted as a ministry of internal security.

The records of the Attorney-General have not been much used by historians. This is, in part, explained by the nature of its functions. The Attorney-General was the legal adviser to the United States government, but the work was mainly technical and professional and most of the important opinions of the Attorneys-General are more easily found in the archives of other departments. Though one of the original offices established in 1789, the Attorney-General was not a member of the cabinet, and the Department of Justice was not created until 1870. In 1859 the authorised staff consisted of an Assistant Attorney-General and five clerks. The records of the department should, however, yield considerable information about the way in which legal opinion was formed and consulted by the government; there is also a great deal of valuable information about judicial appointments. The processes by which Presidents were led to make nominations for the Federal judiciary, and especially for the Supreme Court, have yet to be chronicled and analysed. Clearly there must be a long process of evolution between the early years, when all Federal judges were drawn from a comparatively narrow circle and were personally known before appointment, if not to the President himself at least to his close associates, to the modern conditions in which judges must be drawn from all parts of the country, from political life and law schools as well as from practising lawyers, and when not only legal reputation but political pressures and social philosophy must be consulted. However, it is not until the close of the period covered by this volume that the Anti-Trust Act of 1890 conferred important new responsibilities upon the Attorney-General and made him the guardian of corporation ethics. But even in the nineteenth century the archives of the Attorney-General contain a wealth of information on international relations, maritime law, the extradition of criminals, fugitive slaves, and claims against the government, as well as the central areas of constitutional interpretation and relations between the Federal government and the states. In the years after the Civil War successive Attorneys-General had the difficult and delicate task of advising the Executive upon the interpretation and implications of the thirteenth, fourteenth and fifteenth amendments and of Congressional legislation during the Reconstruction period.[1]

The Department of the Interior was established in March 1849 to take over from the Department of State all matters relating to the public domain. The department soon tended to collect other duties not readily assignable to other departments. Thus the 1860 Census was placed under the direction of the Secretary of the Interior, and (somewhat incongruously) he was also made responsible for the suppression of the international slave trade and the colonisation of free Negroes. The latter function became important in April 1862 when the Act emancipating slaves in the District of Columbia included an appropriation for emigration to Liberia or Haiti. In July a similar appropriation was made available for the colonisation of slaves who were freed by confiscation or by escape from rebel masters, and Lincoln's personal interest in the possibilities of colonisation ensured that the prospects were actively pursued. There therefore exists in the archives of the Interior a good deal of correspondence about Negro emigration to Liberia, Ile à Vache (Haiti) and Chinqui (Panama).[2] At the same period the land grant to the Pacific Railroad brought the department into direct contact with railroad promotion; much correspondence in later years dealt with land grants and the conditions, the appointment of government directors, inspection by Federal commissioners, the approval of routes, and the withdrawal of public land from sale.

In its turn the Department of the Interior was the parent of two further government agencies: the Department of Agriculture (1862) and the Department of Labor (first organised in 1885 as a Bureau of Labour Statistics and in 1888 as an independent

[1] One Attorney-General, Edward Bates, left a Diary which has been published and edited by H. K. Beale, *American Historical Association. Annual Report, 1930* (Washington, 1933). Unfortunately Bates was not very illuminating on his official duties even though many crucial questions arose during his tenure concerning the legal authority of the Federal government. The Department of Justice publishes *Official Opinions of the Attorney General of the United States . . . since 1791*, a continuing series which began publication in 1852. A digest prepared by A. J. Bentley was published in 1885.

[2] Cf. Munden and Beers, *op. cit.*, 499 ff.

department). In its first years the Department of Agriculture was really a bureau, under a commissioner who was not a member of the cabinet. In 1889 it became a real department under a secretary. Its duties from its foundation consisted in the collection of agricultural statistics, the distribution of information, and the oversight of practical or scientific experiments. Beginning in July 1863 it ussued monthly agricultural reports (including meteorological tables supplied by the Smithsonian), and these are a prime source of information about conditions and changes in agriculture. The archives of the department supply further information, and contain much correspondence in agricultural matters. In consequence the historian of agriculture is well served in the later years of the century. The Department of Labor appears at the very close of the period covered by this volume, but its archives contain a few materials relating to earlier years; it will be more appropriate to consider these in the chapter on labour history.

Readers who are familiar with the extent and functions of the modern White House staff will be surprised to find how few official records remain of the nineteenth-century Presidency in action. The President's secretaries were his personal assistants, and apart from appropriations for their salaries, there was no legislative definition of their functions. They submitted no reports to Congress or to the departments, and at the end of a President's term there was no reason to preserve his personal files. Some did, of course, survive and found their way into the collected papers of the President; many more were destroyed or lost, so that for most Presidents we have very little information in the records of the way in which they ordered their days, maintained personal contacts with politicians and executive heads (in these matters it is often the scribbled memoranda of secretaries which are revealing), or arranged the social life of the White House. One of the several reasons why we know so much about the details of Lincoln's Presidency is that his principal secretaries—Nicolay and Hay— became his first biographers and went on to public careers of distinction. At the other end of the scale President Polk provides an interesting example: we know a good deal about the day-today life of the President in office because he himself kept a detailed diary, but if he had not done so we would know practically nothing. The two major Presidential diaries—Polk and Hayes—are therefore exceptions which prove the rule that one knows extraordinarily little about the inner life of the Executive, and the official records of the Federal government will not normally pierce the darkness.

One will consult the Federal archives, in the first instance, for information on subjects which lie within the sphere of the departments concerned; but there is a wider sense in which the records of the Federal government bear witness to many aspects of government and self-government in a democratic society. It is possible to trace the transition from the élitist views inherent in early Federalist administration to administration as the servant of the people, which meant, too often, administration under the domination of politicians. The influence of pressure groups, the demands of patronage, and the delicate balance between political needs and administrative efficiency, are all documented. The correspondence between Washington and officials in other parts of the country furnishes materials for studying the structure of a federal society. Not only the sinews of government but a whole anatomy of private and public enterprise should be exposed to view. The possibilities are endless and remain unexplored and uncharted.

Somewhat different criteria apply to the judicial branch of the Federal government. While all streams of national life flow into and through the Executive Department, the Supreme Court navigates upon a single broad river; its function is not to govern but to examine, interpret, and preserve the instrument of government itself. It has become a truism that the Court is, and always has been, a political agency of the national government; so much so that it is often necessary to remind oneself that it is primarily a court of law. It acts only when there is a case before it, and it accepts only those cases which require an examination of the Constitution for their decision. With a few exceptions, named in the Constitution, it is an appellate court and the cases before it have already been considered by two, three or more inferior courts. By the time the Supreme Court hears arguments, the essential points of law have been clearly defined, the constitutional quintessence of a case has been extracted, and it is this that the court is asked to consider. It is true that, in several celebrated cases, the Supreme Court has refused to confine itself to the narrow front but has taken the occasion to open and decide a large and controversial issue; but though these cases make constitutional history, the normal process is less dramatic.[1]

One must, therefore, expect the records of the court to be limited in range though important in content. This does not mean that the topics considered are limited in number—for, sooner or later, the Constitution touches most activities in American society—but that their presentation will be directed to a single purpose: the establishment of a constitutional point and its application to a specific dispute. It is sometimes forgotten that briefs prepared for the Supreme Court must not only argue their client's case but also convince the justices that right cannot be done without settling a constitutional issue. The dual task of arguing in favour of an interpretation of the Constitution, and maintaining that justice cannot be done to an individual without establishing the constitutional point, determines the character of the court archives.

The Supreme Court began its existence with two annual sessions, beginning on the first Mondays in February and August; this was altered to June and December in 1801; in the following year the earlier dates were restored, but in August purely routine business was transacted. There was, therefore, no session at which opinions were delivered between December 1801 and February 1803, and John Marshall had plenty of time to reflect upon the implications of Republican electoral victory. In 1827 the annual session was fixed for the second Monday in January, in 1843 for the first Monday in December, and in 1873 for the second Monday in October. Until 1869 the Justices of the Supreme Court

[1] Cf. James R. Browning and Bess Glenn, 'The Supreme Court Collection at the National Archives' in *American Journal of Legal History*, 4 July 1960, 241–56.

were also members of Circuit Courts, sitting with Federal District Judges; in that year Circuit Judges were appointed for each circuit, but the members of the Supreme Court were still required to attend one term of the Circuit Court in each district of his circuit not less than once every two years. In 1891 the Court of Appeals was established and justices of the Supreme Court sat as members of the Court of Appeals in their circuits, but ceased to attend Circuit Courts.

Congress has always had the power to decide the number of the Supreme Court justices and the appellate jurisdiction of the court. Despite this provision of the Constitution, Americans have tended to assume that the composition and powers of the court are fixed, and have vigorously protested against the 'unconstitutionality' of any increase or decrease in size or amendment of the court's appellate jurisdiction. The original court consisted of the Chief Justice and five Associate Justices; three more associates were added in 1837 and another one in 1863; in 1869 the court was fixed at its present size of a Chief Justice and eight associates. The most notable alteration in its appellate jurisdiction was made during the Reconstruction period, when it was forbidden to accept appeals from military courts in 'rebel' territory.

As a judge the Chief Justice is merely *primus inter pares* with only a single vote to cast; his authority and influence is exercised behind closed doors and leaves little written evidence of manner or method. Perhaps the subsequent prestige of the Chief Justice owed more to the personality and longevity of John Marshall and Roger B. Taney than to any institutional authority. The Chief Justice organises the business of the court, decides the timetable, and assigns to members of the court the duty of writing opinions. He cannot prevent any justice from writing a dissenting opinion or an opinion which concurs with the finding but not with the argument. He may normally have a dominant voice in deciding which cases shall be accepted by the Court, and may have considerable influence in deciding which cases demand an extended argument and which can be settled largely on technical grounds. Marshall was certainly responsible in 1803 for claiming the right to void a Federal Statute, but Taney in the Dred Scott case may have been forced by circumstances rather than inclination to exercise this power. After the Civil War, and with the increasing number of cases which brought Federal Statutes into question, the Chief Justice must normally have had a decisive voice in arguing for or against the validity of a law, and during the nineteenth century no Federal Statute was found to be unconstitutional without the concurrence of the head of the court. The influence of the Chief Justice must, however, remain a matter of inference rather than proof; equally the influence of any individual Associate must be guessed rather than demonstrated.

One knows the judges of the Supreme Court through their written opinions, and though their appointments have normally been politically inspired, they have ceased to be partisan on the bench. Their private lives became private, and with few exceptions Americans have respected this privacy as they have not that of other men. There is little correspondence about the cases that came before the Court, and none which questioned the wisdom or integrity of their fellow justices. Some judges have continued to nourish political ambitions—John McLean and Salmon P. Chase are notable examples—but they kept their political correspondence strictly apart from their judicial function. The right to record a dissenting opinion was a sufficient safety valve for injured feelings or strong emotions, and apart from this, personality disappears from the record; but if, in their official capacities, the justices ceased to be political men, they did not cease to hold political opinions. Since the wording of the Constitution has so often been susceptible to different interpretations, that selected by a judge can usually be explained by his basic political philosophy; but this was operating at a deep level of understanding and not at the superficial level of manoeuvre.

The *Reports* of the Supreme Court are basic documents for the history of the court and principal documents for the history of the nation.[1] The fame and importance of the celebrated cases which

---

[1] The *Reports* are not official documents but are published commercially by the reporter to the court. Since 1875 they have been known as *United States Reports*, prior to that date they were known by the name of the reporter and are referred to as Dallas (1790–1800, 4 vols), Cranch (1801–15, 9 vols), Wheaton

are the landmarks in constitutional history have tended to obscure the continuous and far-reaching work of the court in interpreting the legal implications of a Federal Constitution. The vast majority of cases deal with technical problems in interstate relations, the interpretation of Federal statutes, and more rarely treaties, maritime law, and the law of nations. The Supreme Court is also a court of appeal from the courts in the District of Columbia, and this has produced many decisions of more than local interest; suits in the Federal capital have included claims against Federal officers, titles to public domain, the disbursement of Congressional appropriations; during the Civil War a number of cases were also commenced in the courts of the District concerning aid to the enemy, enticement to desert, and treason. There were also a number of Fugitive Slave cases, especially from 1862 to 1864 when slavery had been abolished in the District but continued in Maryland. Only a small number of the District cases reached the Supreme Court, and the majority were ended in the Supreme Court of the District of Columbia, which thus became a kind of ancillary court for the settlement of national cases with records stored in the National Archives.

The unpublished records of the Supreme Court contain much routine material, minutes and indexes, but the case files include material of wider interest including petitions, transcripts of records, briefs, and depositions. Unfortunately the arguments before the court are often missing (though the arguments in important cases were occasionally reported in the Washington or New York newspapers); doubtless the justices kept their own notes of the arguments presented, but amongst the case records one is more likely to find notes on the arguments in lower courts than on those before the Supreme Court itself. The Engrossed Dockets are another class of documents of some general interest; they give the official history of each case including the title, the lower court from which appealed, lists of documents and proceedings, and usually the names of the attorneys. It has been said

---

(1816–27, 12 vols), Peter (1828–42, 16 **vols**), Howard (1843–60, 24 vols), Black (1861–62, 2 vols), and Wallace (1863–74, 23 vols).

that the case files 'constitute an important source not only for constitutional history but also for social, economic, local and maritime history and for biography'.[1]

If the records of the Supreme Court are to be used for purposes other than legal history, there are obvious difficulties to be overcome. Provided that the historian begins his search with the knowledge that a certain case touched upon his field of interest, he will know where to look, but if he attempts to pursue a more generalised field of enquiry through the case files, he may have a more arduous and less rewarding experience. It should, however, be possible to work from the printed *Reports*, to identify cases which may have some possible bearing upon the topic under investigation, and to pursue this clue in the National Archives. A further *caveat* is, however, necessary. As with all other sources one must remember the purpose for which the record was compiled and the people whom it was meant to inform. The court was a court of law, and its records are composed of material selected to bring out the legal problems raised by the case and to be decided by the court. It was compiled to inform judges, not social or economic investigators. For the general historian the most valuable evidence may be found in the prefatory statement with which most opinions begin, describing the background and circumstances of the case; but even this is a condensed statement abstracted from a mass of evidence and includes only so much as is necessary to set the stage for the opinion which follows. The supporting material in the case files may be fuller, but it will still be formal and abstract. In other words, the records of the court, both published and unpublished, have passed through the mill of rigorous selection by professional lawyers, writing for professional lawyers, and rejecting all information which seems to be redundant or irrelevant to the case in hand. Administrative records have undergone a similar process of selection and refining, but the process is normally less rigorous than in the preparation of material for courts of law; and the higher one rises up the judicial ladder, the barer the circumstantial bones and the further removed from the life of society. There are, however, valuable

[1] Munden and Beers, *op. cit.*, 82.

insights into the working of the American legal mind and the importance of the law in politics and business makes this evidence of considerable value in revealing the inner springs of national life.

CHAPTER 5

Congress

The records of the legislative branch have not accumulated at quite so rapid a rate, and a much higher proportion are to be found in print; nevertheless the constant increase in their volume bears mute witness to the growing complexity of government and the increasing responsibilities of Congress in an age which is popularly supposed to have been dominated by the maxim that the best government was that which governed least. The records of the first Congress—perhaps the most important in American history—fill two volumes, and they included the journals, Bills originating in the two houses, committee reports and papers, petitions, memorials, and reports from executive departments. By the eleventh Congress (1809–11) the journal alone filled four volumes, and presidential messages three; eleven important committees submitted reports and there were a large number of select committees reporting on minor matters. In the thirty-sixth Congress (the last before the outbreak of the Civil War) there were three volumes of journals, twelve of presidential messages, forty-five volumes of reports and communications, and reports and papers from twenty-eight committees. The fiftieth Congress (1887–89) produced ten volumes of minutes and journals, and the reports and papers from forty-six committees filled sixty-one volumes.[1] In addition to the records of legislative and committee work, Congress received, and usually printed, a very large number of executive papers, diplomatic papers, petitions, and miscellaneous documents. These form a record of activity even though many of these documents had no subsequent effect upon legisla-

[1] The figures are from Buford Rowland, Handy B. Fant and Harold E. Hufford, *Records of the House of Representatives* (National Archives Preliminary Inventory).

tion or politics. At the beginning these documents were collected in the series *American State Papers*, but from the fifteenth Congress (1817–18) they were published in separate volumes. The first session of the fifteenth Congress issued eight volumes containing 202 documents; the second session also issued eight volumes containing 150 documents. The first session of the thirty-sixth Congress (1859–1860) issued 52 volumes for 406 Senate Documents and 994 House Documents. The first session of the fifty-first Congress (1889–90) issued 137 volumes with 1,530 Senate and 3,443 House Documents; even this gives an incomplete picture of the expansion as several of the Documents bearing a single number consisted of a number of separate parts. For instance, in 1889–90, House Document No. 1 (Executive Documents) comprised eight separate parts.[1]

This profusion of documentation means that the most important records of the legislative branch are in print, but no class of record illustrates more surely the truth that one must know not only the source but also the history of the source. The debates of the first seventeen Congresses (1789–1824) were not published until 1824 when Gales and Seaton brought out *The Annals of Congress* (or, in a slightly variant edition, *The History of Congress*). What we have, therefore, is not a verbatim account of debates but a gallant attempt to preserve for posterity what might otherwise have been lost. The volumes were compiled from newspaper reports (after 1800 mainly from *The National Intelligencer*), so one is dependent upon the accuracy of the original reporters, the judgment of newspaper editors, and the accuracy of Gales and Seaton in making their compilation. The original reports were abstracts rather than full accounts of debates; the appendices to the records of each Congress included the text of laws passed (or the titles in the case of minor pieces of legislation) and some executive reports but not the corrected versions of speeches delivered. While Gales and Seaton were collecting and editing materials for the *Annals* they were also publishing the *Register of Debates*, which consisted of contemporary but not

[1] The figures are from *Check List of United States Documents, 1799–1909*, 3rd ed. (Washington, 1911—reprint by Kraus, 1962).

verbatim reports of debates from the second session of the eighteenth Congress (1824). The *Register* continued until 1837 but from 1833 it overlapped with the *Congressional Globe* which gave fuller accounts of debates and continued publication until 1873 when, with the *Congressional Record*, Congress assumed official responsibility for printing and publishing debates.

The *Globe* began as a précis of speeches using the third person for the speaker, but from 1851 an increasing number of speeches are published using the first person and apparently verbatim. A comparison between the *Globe* and newspaper reports will, however, reveal numerous discrepancies. These arose mainly because members were allowed to correct their speeches before publication in the *Globe*, and because the newspapers often included personal exchanges between members which were judged to be too frivolous by the editors of the *Globe*. For the individual member what appeared in the *Globe* was much more important than what appeared in a Washington or New York newspaper, and the requirements of accurate reporting were often sacrificed to the necessity of not giving offence. The importance of the *Globe* reports is indicated by the growing habit of members to refuse permission for immediate publication but to send in carefully revised versions for publication in the Appendix. Occasionally a speech appears in two forms, one in the text of the debates and one in the Appendix published some months later; more frequently a note in the text of the debates informs the reader that a missing speech will be found in the Appendix. Apart from the desire of members to present their wisdom in the most attractive literary form, publication in the appendix meant that the speech could be sent to constituents and other interested persons in a handy form.[1] The situation was complicated still further by the growing habit in later years of obtaining permission from the House to print in the record of debates speeches that were not delivered through lack of time. Thus the *Globe* does not give a verbatim account of debates, prints some speeches out of context and many in a form that was supposed by their authors to be a

[1] Information about the history of Congressional Reporting is summarised in Schmeckebier and Eastin, *op. cit.*

superior version to that actually delivered, and prints without explanation some 'speeches' that were never delivered at all.

The *Congressional Record* was official rather than semi-official and was intended to be verbatim and complete; but good intentions could not deprive members of the right to revise, of requesting permission to print undelivered speeches, and, with greater frequency as the years went on, to print as a part of their undelivered speeches material which never would have been delivered. It was easy flattery for a politician to incorporate the remarks of a divine, professor or businessman in the record of the national legislature. To complicate matters still further, the *Record* was published daily, bi-weekly and for a whole session. In the daily *Record* undelivered speeches and others withheld for revision were not printed; some might be included in the bi-weekly edition, while the sessional publication would print them at the appropriate point in debate, whether delivered or not. In justice to the *Record* it must be added that the standard of its reporting was higher than that of the *Globe* (particularly when compared with the latter's earlier years); unfortunately increased accuracy also meant increased bulk so that the collective wisdom of Congress came to be submerged beneath an intolerable weight of words.

The deficiencies of the *Globe* and the *Record* as accurate accounts of the legislative process diminish their reliability on points of detail but leave them unchallenged as a record of legislative controversy. Indeed the fact that they so often recorded what a politician thought he ought to have said rather than what he did say can itself be instructive. When a politician has taken the trouble to revise a speech (and probably to circulate it) one can be assured that he attaches value to it, and that the final version presents something to which he wishes to give publicity. In other words, though the *Globe* and *Record* give an inadequate account of what went on in the halls of Congress, they give a very good picture of the 'image' which legislators wished to present to the country. A careful study of revised speeches will therefore provide useful inferences about the opinions which a politician sought to express, the interests which he wished to serve, and the way in which he sought to increase his reputation as a public man.

More serious deficiencies of the debates are revealed as soon as one attempts to trace any measure through its various legislative stages. Sometimes one can find the text of Bills under discussion, but neither amendments nor the final form of the Bill can be located. Many minor Bills get a brief reference on one reading but one can find no further record of their progress through Congress; a large number of minor and private Bills are not noticed at all. The obvious remedy is to turn to the *Journals* of the two houses; these were the official working records of what had been done and for obvious reasons they were scrutinised for accuracy. Even so the numbering and nomenclature of Bills, particularly when similar or identical Bills were introduced simultaneously in the House and Senate can create unexpected problems. At some stage in the legislative process one or the other would be dropped but (for the sake of example) the House version might be so amended in the Senate that it became virtually the Senate Bill, though continuing to carry its House number. The *Journals* may also fail to provide information about the House or Senate rules, and legislators would themselves have been forced to consult contemporary manuals.[1]

For legislative history one must therefore use the *Journals* as well as the *Globe* or *Record*, but unfortunately it is far less common to find copies in institutional or public libraries. The *Globe* and the *Record* were widely circulated and many series are in existence, but the *Journals* were of limited interest for contemporaries who wanted to study oratory and catch the spirit of public controversy. One comes back therefore to the essential character of the printed debates as public information about what went on in Congress, designed to serve the interests of newspapers, people concerned

[1] The *House Manual* (originally Jefferson's Manual) was published in alternate years; it gives the rules and their current interpretation. The *Senate Manual* gives the rules but not their interpretation. For the House a convenient work of reference is Asher C. Hinds, *Precedents of the House of Representatives of the United States* (Washington, various editions). Hinds was Clerk at the Speaker's Table for many years.

with political controversy, and, of course, the legislators themselves. They were designed to inform people about what Congressmen considered important and the way in which they presented
their arguments; they aimed to present both the gladiatorial aspect
of politics and the considered judgment of politicians; they were
not intended to record the minutiae of Congressional business nor
for use in courts of law as documents of precise authority or exact
witness.

It is important, when using Congressional debates as a source,
to ask oneself why a speech was made and to what audience was
it addressed. A large number of speeches—including the shortest
and many of the most informative—were the natural outcome of
legislative business. They were given because a committee chairman had to make a report, because a Bill required an introduction,
because an amendment had to be moved and explained, or because the sponsor of the Bill felt obliged to comment immediately
upon a point which had been made. These contributions to the
legislative work of Congress are important if one wishes to understand individual measures, and to appreciate the atmosphere of a
serious and normally sober body. They do not make for lively
reading, though occasionally interjections, questions, and procedural manoeuvres enable one to glimpse the emotions which
could lie behind routine business. A second type of speech was
intended as an exercise in persuasion. When party lines were not
hard and fast, and when there was genuine doubt about the
wisdom of a policy, an effective speech could win votes. In the
House waverers might be brought over by an emotional appeal;
the Senate was likely to be influenced by a more judicial statement
of the case. A good many speeches were really delivered to
constituents; using his franking privilege a Congressman could
send out numbers of copies, and might even persuade a publisher
to reprint his speech as a pamphlet. This included those speeches,
referred to above, which were never delivered to Congress, but
printed in the *Globe* or *Record*. In the middle years of the nineteenth century it was customary, in the House, to let young
members try out their oratorical wings in a debate on general
policies and problems rather than specific measures.

Finally, there was the great set piece. It was mainly the privilege of Senators to indulge in this form of publicity. In the House, by 1840, the rules limited speeches to one hour's duration; this could be extended by unanimous consent (which was frequently given) but no Representative could deliberately plan an extended oratorical effort on the assumption that he would be given time to complete it. In the Senate, however, no rules checked the freedom of debate, and no Senator who had the floor could be silenced until he himself chose to sit down. Thus a Senator could plan and prepare for efforts which might last for several hours and contain a huge mass of material and argument. With the connivance of other Senators, he could probably arrange to give his speech on a day announced in advance, and a notable speaker was sure of a full Senate and a crowded gallery. Naturally speeches of this calibre were intended for the country as well as for Congress; they would certainly be reprinted in pamphlet form and widely distributed. All such occasions were important in the careers of the Senators concerned; sometimes they mark an important stage in national history. Daniel Webster's reply to Hayne in 1830 and his speech on 7th March 1850 on the Compromise were recognised at the time as important events which were not only an expression of individual opinion but also caught and expressed a body of opinion which was forming in the country.

For historians it is of particular importance that constituents wanted to know how their Representatives and Senators voted. Hence the large number of division lists printed in the *Globe* and *Record* (and less frequently in the earlier *Annals* and *Register*). One can also appreciate the fact that a demand to divide the House was a recognised means of gaining time or obstructing so that in addition to votes on the principal stages in the passage of important Bills one often finds votes on procedural questions. These can be particularly important because a minority within a party will often be prepared to oppose the leadership on a procedural question though feel obliged to close ranks when the main question is put. The analysis of division lists is extremely important for all political historians, and a close scrutiny will often reveal unexpected results. Without this tedious but useful exercise it is too easy to fall into avoidable errors, and unfortunately earlier writers, less numerate than the present generation, perpetuated misconceptions which are hard to overtake. It was, for instance, a familiar generalisation that the Whigs, between 1835 and 1852, had little cohesion as a party, yet an analysis of division lists over this period indicates that their party regularity was considerably superior to that of most modern parties.[1] Nor is it enough to be content with figures without scrutinising names; there is a familiar observation that Congress voted with only one dissent-ient voice for the Johnson-Crittenden resolutions in 1861; in fact the resolutions were divided with some conservative Democrats refusing to vote on the first resolution which declared that seces-sion was the cause of the war, and a group of Republicans ab-staining on the second that the restoration of the Union was its only objective. From the division lists it is possible to classify members by party, to demonstrate not only the extent of their party regularity but to classify the extent of their deviation; regional opinion can be studied through the votes of their representatives; the influence of particular groups on legislation can be surmised if not accurately measured. On the other hand, there is always a danger in relying too much upon figures, and though votes can check unsupported generalisations, that cannot replace an understanding of the men, their constituencies, and the controversies of the day.[2]

[1] Cf. Joel H. Silbey, *The Shrine of Party: Congressional Voting Behavior, 1841–52* (Pittsburgh, 1967). See especially the Statistical Tables and Chapter 11. Similar conclusions emerge from *Sectional Stress and Party Strength*, by Thomas B. Alexander (Nashville, 1967), which can also be cited as a case study in the analysis of Congressional voting patterns.

[2] Voting records must be used in conjunction with available biographical information. Since 1809 a *Congressional Directory* has been published for each Congress (published privately until 1847 and since then an official publication); it gave biographical information about senators, representatives, principal executive officers, and governors of states and territories. In the majority of cases the information must have been provided by the individuals themselves. *The Biographical Directory of the American Congress 1774–1949* uses information from the separate directories together with material on subsequent careers and information on members of Congress prior to 1809. It gives a complete list of all members of all Congresses with vacancies and replacements; the list of

The reports of Congressional committees cover a wide range of questions. They range from reports upon petitions from individuals (often dealing with claims or pensions) to lengthy documents dealing with major controversies. At the beginning of the period the two houses were small, leadership was clearly concentrated in a few hands, and committees were the servants of Congress with strictly defined tasks of investigation. At this stage they were primarily fact-finding bodies while legislation was initiated on the floor of the House. By the end of the period committees had become the masters of Congress (as Woodrow Wilson described it in *Congressional Government*). The normal procedure was for all legislative proposals to be referred to the appropriate standing committee, and it was the committee which decided whether to kill the measure, rewrite it, or allow it to be discussed on the floor of the House. Parties who were interested in the outcome of legislative proposals naturally concentrated their attention upon the committee which had charge of it, so that the committees were not only the channels through which all proposals were forced to pass but also the channels through which information and propaganda on a vast range of commercial and social matters reached Congress. Between the fact-finding committees of the early days and the rule of committees at the end of the period, committees had been used to investigate and recommend on policies which lay at the heart of national evolution. The Senate Committee of Thirteen which recommended the

---

members given in the *Annals, Globe* and *Record* is not always complete and subsequent changes may be difficult to follow without reference to the *Biographical Directory*. It may be difficult to identify the districts of Representatives; this is not normally noted in the *Globe* or *Record*, or in the list given in the *Biographical Directory*; it will be found in the original *Congressional Directory* and usually in the biographical entry of the *Biographical Directory*. Lists of members in the *Globe* and *Record* often included their postal addresses. The geographical area of Congressional Districts are often difficult to establish; The *Congressional Directories* include maps, but this may not help with small divisions of populous towns or counties, but the wards, precincts, or townships in each district precede the biographical entry. Party affiliations are sometimes given in the *Biographical Directory*, but they can only be ascertained with confidence from a study of voting lists.

Compromise measures of 1850, the Joint Committee on Reconstruction of 1866–72, and the various committees between 1869 and 1876 on the affairs of the South, took large problems, formulated policy, proposed measures, and subsequently provided legislative leadership in Congress. The Committee on the Conduct of the War during the Civil War tried to get control of policy, and though outflanked by Lincoln it succeeded in bringing before Congress a great deal of information about the war, and if some of its investigations were mistimed, their general effect may have been salutary.

The records of all this intense activity, growing and evolving throughout the century, vary enormously in bulk and importance. Many volumes of Congressional papers are filled with brief reports on routine matters; at the other end of the scale come the reports on disorders in the South during Reconstruction, each filling several volumes with evidence and recommendations. On the other hand, the Senate Committee of Thirteen in 1850 heard no evidence and made no formal report; it was, in effect, a negotiating committee between politicians, and its proposals were made verbally to the Senate by Henry Clay. On every occasion it has been within the competence of the committee to decide what evidence is heard, whether it is published, and if so, in extenso or by abstract or summary. On major questions party issues have usually played a great part in deciding how the committee should carry out its business. Though committees were always bi-partisan, the majority party looked upon their task as the presentation of evidence to support a policy already agreed in its main objectives; this governed the choice of witnesses, the way in which they were examined, and, of course, the recommendations of the majority report. The majority of Congressmen have always been lawyers, and they have tended to treat their committee functions in the same spirit as they would gather evidence to support a client's case. The minority could cross-examine, might occasionally be allowed to call witnesses, and had the right to submit a dissenting opinion. This procedure was a perfectly proper one when dealing with non-controversial and routine investigations, nor is it objectionable in policy matters provided that one realises what is being done. Congressional committees were not set up to conduct impartial enquiries, and one would no more expect the majority report to be non-partisan than one would expect the front bench in a British parliament to depart from party policy.

One result of this procedure is that the published reports of committees represent only a small portion of the vast amount of paper seen by committees during the course of their work. Minutes, correspondence, communications with the executive branch, and unpublished evidence accumulated in vast masses; but as nineteenth-century committees seldom had permanent secretaries and never had much office assistance, the filing of material and its subsequent preservation was erratic and unpredictable. A great deal of research is required even to ascertain the location and extent of unpublished materials left by Congressional committees; and the papers of some of the great investigatory committees, which should be magnificent sources for the problems they surveyed, have proved disappointing. For instance, a committee of such essential importance as the Joint Committee on the Conduct of the War left incomplete records of testimony, and complete papers have not been found in the records of either House or Senate. The papers of the Joint Committee on Reconstruction are far from complete, and only the chance discovery of its Minute Book provided an essential source for the study of Congressional policy in this controversial and perplexing era.[1] On the other hand, the papers of standing committees, especially in the later part of the nineteenth century when they established their ascendancy in Congress, have an importance that need not be emphasised.[2]

Until 1911 the House committees were appointed by the Speaker and the first-named member was chairman; normally

[1] B. B. Kendrick, *Journal of the Committee of Fifteen on Reconstruction* (New York, 1914). The detective work which led to the discovery of the Journal is given in Introduction, 18–22.

[2] There is a collection of *Committee Reports 1815–1887* by T. H. McKee. This is rarely found, even in large libraries, and it is thought that no complete set exists outside Washington.

some continuity in membership was preserved, but a member who had displeased the party leadership might be dropped; there was no seniority rule in selecting the chairmen, and as a result the committees, unlike their present-day successors, were working bodies appointed by party leaders to carry out party purposes. Control of the party rested with a Congressional in-group, but men became chairmen of committees because they were members of the group and could be deposed at the discretion of the Speaker. The Senate, with continuity of membership and, in theory, perpetual existence, had something much closer to the system that now prevails in both Houses. Committee members continued from session to session and normally lapsed only when a Senator resigned, did not seek re-election, or was defeated. However, the President *Pro Tempore* of the Senate (elected, like the Speaker, for each Congress on a party vote) appointed chairmen, and could remove awkward members of his party from committees at the beginning of a session.

House committees were therefore reliable indicators of party sentiment (at least as it was interpreted by the party in-group), and Senate committees, though somewhat more independent, were susceptible to party pressure. Things were changing towards the end of the period, as powerful committee chairmen developed an immunity which made it exceedingly difficult to remove them; nevertheless this system might have produced something much closer to party government than the system which now prevails. The Age of Reform would discover it impossible to attack the leadership without changing the system, with the result that committee members became irremovable, chairmanships went with seniority, and Congress moved towards the present system which gives disproportionate power to elderly chairmen with long service from safe constituencies. The nineteenth century did not go so far in weighting the scales against youth and coherent party policy.

The relations between the Executive and the Legislature, and consequently the delicate question of where and how policy is initiated, can be studied in a wide range of documents. First and foremost are the *Messages of the President*, edited in many volumes by James D. Richardson.[1] The presidential messages include inaugural addresses, annual messages, veto messages, and a very large number of messages in response to requests from Congress for information, conveying executive requests, and giving unsolicited information which was deemed worthy of urgent consideration. In addition to the presidential messages there are a very large number of reports from the executive departments, of which some are purely factual and statistical, a few argumentative, and a still smaller number major enunciations of policy. Most of these reports are buried in the voluminuous printed papers of Congress; presumably most of them also exist in the manuscript records of the departments from which they originated; in either case they are beyond the range of students who have no access to major libraries, and a selection from them by one of the reprint companies would be a service to scholars.

This and the preceding chapter have made reference to several areas in which the records of the Federal government still have much to reveal; it may be worth while to close with a brief review of the subjects which will not be covered, or touched upon only indirectly. The commerce clause gave Congress the power to regulate trade among the states, yet this was used sparingly; though the doctrine of Gibbons *v.* Ogden forecast the modern broad interpretation of Congressional power over commerce, it was treated with restraint by nineteenth-century governments. There was no dispute over the regulation of coastal shipping (which carried much of the commerce 'among' the states before the coming of the railroads), but the main intention of the commerce clause was to prevent the states from erecting obstacles to each other's trade, and this required no positive action on the part of the Federal government. It was not until the very

[1] 10 vols (Washington, 1896–99); supplementary volumes took the series to the Presidency of Calvin Coolidge. A useful collection is Fred L. Israel (ed), *The State of the Union Messages of the Presidents 1790–1966* (Introduction by A. M. Schlesinger, jr.), 3 vols (New York, 1967). The phrase 'State of the Union Message' was first used in 1945, but Presidents have, of course, been required by the Constitution to report to Congress annually, and the collection therefore forms a yearly account of the affairs, problems, duties and policies of the United States since 1790.

last years of this period that Congress used the commerce clause as the legal basis for establishing the Interstate Commerce commission, and the records of this and later regulatory commissions lie outside the chronological scope of this book. In Congressional debates and in Congressional papers discussions and proposals for railroad legislation left their mark before this date, but no law was passed which called for judicial notice or executive action. Nor did Congress attempt to regulate trade within the states which had only indirect effects upon interstate commerce; still less did it attempt to regulate manufacturers, wages or conditions of work. However, the government could and did act where it was the direct employer of labour in dockyards, military and naval installations, and construction works undertaken by the services or the Post Office. The record of the United States government as an employer must be amply documented in the records of the various departments and would be worth investigation.

Despite the long controversies over Federal aid to internal improvements—and the resistance of the Democratic party to expenditure of this kind—there was an upward trend (interrupted by some sharp checks) in appropriations for these purposes. There was a constitutional power to improve harbour and coastal navigation, and it did not require great ingenuity to extend this to the Great Lakes and the navigation of the great inland rivers. The Federal government could also construct post roads and communications necessary for defence; in the later part of the period it was also making land grants for long-distance railroads. In most of these operations the Federal government played a passive role; that is, the money was appropriated by Congress and paid out by the Treasury, but there was no active planning or supervision.

Law and order was the primary responsibility of the states, and from the Whiskey rebellion of 1794 to the Civil War the Federal government was not called upon to act save in rare instances when Federal laws were broken; the great field of crime, punishment, police and the protection of property lay in the domain of the separate states; nor did the Federal government have any responsibility for education or welfare (save where these services were ancillary to the Army or Navy). The Civil War and the amendments to the Constitution brought Congress cautiously and reluctantly to protect civil and voting rights, and at various times from 1877 onwards the President responded to calls from governors to deal with disorders resulting from labour disputes; but when the period closed, what the Federal government might do was still largely a matter of debate and hypothesis. If some men were anxious to nail the responsibility for dealing with industrial violence upon the Federal government, others clung tenaciously to the rights and duties of states.

From 1789 to 1890 the Federal government grew almost continuously; its responsibilities increased and its employees multiplied; the Civil War brought almost an explosion in government activity; yet even at the end of this period American society was hardly within sight of big government on the contemporary pattern. The records remain those of a government of limited powers, sharing sovereignty with the states, and cautious in the exercise even of those powers which were clearly conferred upon it by the Constitution.

CHAPTER 6

Public Men and Public Servants

The public man is the man who plays a role under the public scrutiny. The early interest of many Americans in the preservation of materials derived from the Colonial and Revolutionary eras made their public men peculiarly conscious of their place in history, and the assiduous activity of local historical societies in the collection of historical materials could hardly fail to impress upon public men the importance of preserving their papers for the enlightenment of posterity. And if public men themselves failed to recognise this duty, there was a strong possibility that there would be someone on hand to remind them of it. This consciousness of the importance of letters and papers has resulted in vast accumulations and an extraordinarily rich documentation for the official life of thousands upon thousands of men who played a greater or lesser part in the life of the country. The collections range from a few boxes containing the surviving papers of local politicians to the vast collections of the papers of Jefferson or Lincoln. The majority of the papers of the most important national figures are found in the Library of Congress; but some collections of the first importance are to be found in other repositories. The Massachusetts Historical Society claims the Adams family and Charles Sumner; William H. Seward's papers are to be found at the University of Rochester, and to consult the major collection of the papers of John C. Calhoun it is necessary to visit Columbia, South Carolina.

The papers of some public men were never collected in a single repository. A leading example is Henry Clay, whose papers are scattered in several small collections in Washington, Tennessee and North Carolina. The avidity with which universities and the great research libraries (such as the Huntington in San-Marino, California, and the Newberry in Chicago) have competed in the open market for manuscript materials, which may attract scholars or build massive collections on particular periods or topics, has led to further dispersion. The splendid *National Union Catalogue of Manuscripts in the United States* is fortunately at hand to aid scholars, but even with this indispensable aid, many hours can be spent in locating the papers of individual public men.

The conscious purpose with which many public men have preserved their papers has disadvantages as well as obvious advantages. Many collections have obviously been carefully weeded and that which seemed insignificant has been discarded. In some cases this may have been done by the man himself; in others, by an executor or biographer. Consequently one frequently finds that the unconsidered trifles, which can throw light upon a man's daily life, have disappeared. Letters on private matters are comparatively rare, while reams of correspondence on local politics and patronage questions have been carefully preserved. In many cases, of course, this selection may reflect the normal habits of a man of business who filed away everything to which he might subsequently make official reference, while throwing away family letters or letters from friends which seemed to have only passing significance. More serious were the moral standards of nineteenth-century editors or biographers who believed it their duty to suppress or destroy evidence of questionable, wasteful or even frivolous activities. Life was real, life was earnest, and the historical record must show it to have been such.

As a result, the papers of American public men present the picture of a sober, serious, and industrious official world. There is little to be learned of their lesisure, or even of the social life of the politicial world in which so much business is actually transacted. The responsible and high-principled life of the public man, as revealed through his papers, is separated by an unbridgeable gulf from the world of political scandal and gossip revealed by occasional journalists, by the rare acidity of a diarist such as Gideon

Welles, or in the fictitional world by Henry Adam's *Democracy* or Mark Twain's *Gilded Age*. Somewhere between the serious image presented by the collected papers and the world of petty intrigue and social triviality lies the real truth of a human personality; but this truth may lie for ever hidden and one can only speculate about the private foundations upon which the public edifice was built.

This is not to say that the papers of public men are devoid of those evidences of fallibility and emotion to which all men are subject; but the evidence must be found largely within the framework of correspondence which was deemed worthy of preservation. Anxiety, obsession and cruelty can be found—as can assurance, realism and generosity—but they must often be read between the lines of correspondence on minor political questions. One fortunate exception sometimes survives: public men away from home would naturally write to their wives and admiring wives would preserve the letters; but here again the letters had often to survive a process of selection or editing determined by principles that modern historians might find unacceptable.

The papers of public men are found in three different types of collection. The first consists of the man's own collection of papers; the letters he received, the printed materials he may have preserved, the drafts he wrote or the copies he preserved. Usually the collection has been arranged and pruned as described above, but with this qualification one has the world as the man saw it crossing his desk. The second type of collection is more artificial in concept and aims at a more comprehensive picture; the core of such a collection may consist of the first type, but it will be supplemented by letters received from the subject, by all kinds of printed materials including speeches, pamphlets, written reports and possibly letters about the man or his affairs which he himself never saw. The third type of collection consists of material selected for publication, and many such collections will have appeared in print or have been incorporated into a biography of the 'life and letters' type so common in the nineteenth century. In course of time all three types of collection may become subsumed in the magnificent collected editions of papers which are witnesses both to the financial endowment and to the meticulous thoroughness of American scholarship. Before the end of the present century it will be possible to fill whole stacks of large libraries with the multi-volume editions of the papers of Jefferson, Hamilton, Madison, Clay, Calhoun, Jefferson Davis, Grant and the whole Adams family. Washington, Jackson, Lincoln, Buchanan, Daniel Webster and Rutherford B. Hayes are already there; but the rising tide of discovery and critical scholarship will probably demand either that the work is done over again or that supplementary volumes are issued. Every reference is annotated; every person or event is identified; and often a single footnote will summarise weeks of patient research. The knowledge that these vast scholarly projects are on hand has a curious effect upon American historical enquiry. Who will embark upon a major interpretative work under the shadow of meticulous and comprehensive scholarship to come? Who will doubt the eventual benefits to scholarship of these great projects, but who will deny that they absorb an enormous amount of industry and energy which might otherwise be directed to more general studies? What seems to suffer is not the work of broad interpretation—for there will always be restless and penetrating minds ready to undertake that task—but the writing of general history at a level higher than that of the text book and lower than that of the specialised study. Even at the local level, or amongst public men of the second rank, the same forces operate, and one can predict with some certainty that wherever a public man has left a considerable body of materials, and wherever a publisher, university or foundation is prepared to take the financial risk, there will be found a body of scholarly men ready to devote their days to the pursuit of the elusive letter or to the identification of the most obscure individual mentioned in correspondence.

Faced with this proliferation of published work, and in the certain knowledge that the presses will continue to turn out volume after volume of the papers of public men, one is naturally led to ask whether the individual scholar has need or incentive to go to the papers themselves. The teams of scholars and research assistants will do the job more thoroughly and more comprehensively than any individual; and when their editions see the light of day they will almost certainly correct, if they do not render obsolete, all earlier work. To this objection there are several possible answers. If there is any truth in the aphorism that every generation must write its own history, it follows that every generation *ought* to write its own history. The multi-volume editions of collected papers extend along the library shelves into a future beyond the working lives of even the youngest historian now embarking upon a professional career. The world of scholarship may be able to afford to wait for definitive editions, but the world which historians have to serve will become indoctrinated with bad history if the professional historians are not prepared to provide them with the best history which they can construct. This is an argument for not delaying work which one feels ought to be done, and for not delaying answers to questions which have to be met, because of hypothetical calculations about the possible effects upon one's own reconstruction of the past of work which may not appear until one is too old to care. The second line of reasoning is more tentative and elusive. However complete the printed collections of material, there is no real substitute for seeing the papers as they were once written, handled and read by the men of the past. It would be useless to elaborate upon this. The ordinary members of the public who see a surviving copy of Magna Carta, or the death warrant of Charles I, or the Declaration of Independence have an experience—and know that they have an experience—which is quite different from reading the text in a printed book. The professional historian may look at manuscript evidence in a more sophisticated way, but he will share with the uninstructed the same sense of immediacy and contact with the past that no printed word can bring. The final reason for going to the papers of public men without waiting for the definitive edition is that when all the discoverable papers have been collected, and when every reference has been verified, there will still remain a large area in which the historian must use his acquired skill to bridge the gap between what is recorded and what happened. This brings one to consider more specifically the information to be derived from this source of historical knowledge.

The novice historian goes to a collection of papers expecting to discover much about the man whose name it bears. A few nineteenth-century public men kept letter books in which a copy of letters out was retained, but this custom does not seem to have been widespread amongst politicians though common amongst businessmen for whom an exact record might be necessary. A public man in high office might have a copy clerk who would transcribe a letter before it was despatched, and sometimes the writer would make a rough draft from which the clerk would make a fair copy for despatch. Very often, however, no record remains of an outward letter amongst the private papers of a public man. If he wrote as an official, a copy will probably have been preserved in the archives of the department in which he served, but no copies were made of the great bulk of correspondence between political leaders or between the leaders and their supporters. The day of the typist and of carbon copies made and retained as a matter of routine had yet to dawn. Occasionally one has the good fortune to encounter a politician who liked to think on paper. Martin Van Buren, when pondering his attitude to the annexation of Texas, and later his reaction to the Free Soil nomination in 1848, left sheet after sheet of drafts corrected, re-drafted, and corrected again, and only his sprawling, ill-formed handwriting hinders the historian who wishes to penetrate his inner thoughts during these crises; but even here there is a limitation, for what Van Buren was trying to frame were public documents which would leave open as many doors as possible and give no hostages to fortune. By contrast, the Rochester collection of Seward's papers contains very few letters or memoranda by Seward himself, and those which are found are frequently photostat copies from other collections. So, too, the Library of Congress collection of the redoubtable Thaddeus Stevens contains hardly any letters by Stevens himself; the same is true of other politicians of the Civil War era such as Wade, Butler, Sumner and Elihu B. Washburn. The diligent biographer who really wants to find out what his subject wrote will have to identify his correspondents, locate their papers (if they survive), and then search in hope. A less pertinacious researcher will merely have to infer the contents of a letter from the reply received, and to realise that the existence of a draft (or even of an apparent fair copy) is not proof that the letter was sent in that form, or ever sent at all.

A troublesome handicap in using the papers of public men is the gap which often appears in the correspondence or periods during which the number of letters seems to be abnormally thin. There are many obvious reasons for this. The bulk of a Congressman's correspondence was with people in his Congressional district, and this became unnecessary when he returned home after a session. One soon learns to spot regular fluctuations in the volume of correspondence, but the real difficulty arises when unexplained and irregular gaps occur, or when large intervals occur without apparent reason.

The papers of a public man may, therefore, be singularly disappointing as a source of information about the man himself; but this said, one must then add that they can be an invaluable source of information about the political and social environment in which he lived. One comes to see him not so much as an individual, with views of his own, but as part of a web of relationships. Upon the one man converge all kinds of requests, offers, information and complaints; yet it would be easy to discover other individuals, within the same network, who give precisely the same impression of being at the vortex.

Why do people write letters to public men? Without attempting a dogmatic classification, one can suggest the following categories:

1. Other political leaders writing in an official capacity, or privately, with a political objective, or privately for social reasons.
2. Political supporters from state or district; of whom some may be regular correspondents engaged in local organisation, and others may be well-wishers giving occasional advice or information.
3. Applicants for state or Federal posts who hope for aid in obtaining them.
4. Other persons soliciting help for a wide variety of causes, interests, or personal aspirations.

5. Private persons who wish to express serious arguments on public matters.
6. Critics—who may sometimes be abusive.
7. Cranks.

Correspondents in the second category, if not the most numerous, were frequently the most important. A public man who wished to remain in office or to seek re-election or to promote ambitions for higher things, had to keep himself closely informed of opinion and events in his constituency. By law a Senator or Representative must be a resident of the state in which he is elected, and by convention a Representative must be a resident of his district; it follows that there is no possibility (as in Great Britain) that a man who fails to be elected may be found a safe seat elsewhere. If he fails in his state or his district, he has failed as a politician; the best that he can expect (if he has served his party or the administration well) is an official appointment that will provide some prestige and a salary, but remove him from the political arena. With far fewer official posts than at the present time,[1] the nineteenth-century politician depended even more than his twentieth-century successor upon the good-will of the voters. For most of them, too, it was equally important to ensure that within the party the wing or faction with which they were identified remained in the ascendancy. It was therefore natural that the correspondence of men in Congress was filled with letters about local party matters. In many cases he would rely mainly upon one close supporter, whose task was to keep the fences repaired at home, but this would be supplemented by letters from many others writing more or less regularly. Paradoxically, therefore, the papers of a man in national politics may reveal far more information on the local scene than on major issues. Out of session the position could be reversed, with comparatively little coming in on local politics—most of the informa-

---

[1] There was no modern profusion of boards, commissions and agencies to provide a haven for disappointed politicians; for men who had obtained some eminence there were only ministries abroad, collectorships at the large ports, territorial governorships, and a small number of senior posts in the executive departments.

tion could be gathered on Main Street—but possibly some letters on national questions from other political leaders; but these tend to be less common and less revealing than one hopes.

It is in the first category that the researcher normally hopes to find the pearls. Here one hopes to find the letters which illuminate national policy, or illustrate to a marked degree the character of the writer. There are, indeed, rich resources to be explored, though the intensity of American scholarship has ensured that most of the best has already appeared in print. The correspondence of Calhoun and his political friends unfolds the whole panorama and unhappy development of southern sectional politics.[1] Before that, much serious argument can be found in the papers of the great figures of the early national period. Yet as time goes on, the argumentative, discursive letter, in which a major political figure argues, under the seal of privacy, important issues, tends to become less frequent. For this, various reasons may be suggested, of which the first is, perhaps, the plain fact that the quality of mind in public life declined. The greater number of newspapers, the ease with which Congressional speeches could be printed and circulated, the explosion in pamphlet literature, all diminished the need for argument in private correspondence. Under special circumstances one may get letters giving first-hand accounts of events. After Martin Van Buren left the White House in March 1841, he intended to return in 1844; consequently, he kept in close touch with his friend Silas Wright, Senator for New York, who wrote frequently about events in Washington. After his election Lincoln was kept closely informed of events by Lyman Trumbull and others, though he gave little in return. Any aspirant for the Presidency had to establish contacts in Washington and in centres of political activity across the country. The papers of Associate Justice John McLean amply document the efforts of a man who constantly tried and constantly failed to get influential politicians to take up his cause, but

---

[1] Cf. *The Correspondence of J. C. Calhoun*, ed. J. F. Jameson. American Historical Association, *Annual Report 1899*, vol. II. And for other influential southern politicians see U. B. Phillips, ed., *Correspondence of Robert Toombs, Alexander H. Stephens and Howell Cobb. Ibid.* 1911, vol. II.

whose papers therefore provide ample evidence on the activities of second-rate politicians in Washington, New York and Ohio.

Applicants for official appointments bulk largely in the correspondence of public men, particularly of Senators who might expect to have the virtual nomination to Federal posts in their states if they were administration supporters. Many others received constant requests even when they were most unlikely to have any influence upon the outcome. The distribution of patronage was closely linked with the retention of political support at home, and a public man might receive a good deal of advice about the effect of particular appointments (or of disappointed aspirations) upon his own standing and that of his party. He was expected to help friends, but no one wanted to be associated with an unpopular appointment, while everyone wanted to share in the credit when a popular local man received his just reward. It would require more research and considerable delicacy of touch to trace the history of patronage in the United States. One's impression is that it developed during Jefferson's Presidency, with a tacit and gentlemanly understanding that the man appointed would be the man approved by the leaders of his party in his state—and that once appointed, men would not be removed unless they became notoriously incompetent or personally objectionable. The system received some rude shocks during the Jacksonian period when room had to be found for a flood of new applicants sponsored by men who had hitherto been outside the inner ring. The need begat the skill, and lifelong politicians such as Martin Van Buren and Thurlow Weed evolved a remarkably efficient system for weighing the claims of individuals and estimating the effects of particular appointments upon a whole range of individuals, factions and interests. The correspondence about patronage tended therefore to grow, as so many individuals had to be approached over such minor appointments as postmasters of country towns or lower appointments in the revenue service. The accession of a new party to power in 1861, followed by the tremendous expansion of patronage opportunities in the government and armed services, swelled the correspondence of even the lesser politicians to unprecedented dimensions, and imposed an almost intolerable burden upon the leaders. After the war the party managers—an informal group of powerful Senators, the Speaker, and a few old hands in the House—tried with varying success to gather up all the reins of the patronage system, which meant establishing the right to review all appointments before they went to the executive. On the other hand, two Presidents, John Tyler and Andrew Johnson, tried to use Federal patronage against Congressional leadership, with notable lack of success.[1] The reason for their failures can be readily understood when one studies the correspondence about Federal appointments and realises the extent to which a decision on an appointment came at the end of long and delicate negotiations, balancing individual interests against party, local opinion, and the need to make an appointment which would not throw discredit upon the administration. The attempt to cut through these procedures was bound to ruin the influence of the appointee before he even assumed his duties.

It is therefore worthwhile at times to linger over the apparently tedious details of a patronage appointment, and to ask oneself how important it seemed to those affected and why it did so. A natural impatience with small issues which obscure the big problems may foster misunderstanding of the political system as a whole; or this impatience may combine with the muckraking tradition in American historiography to render grave injustice to individuals who were doing their best with the situation as they found it.

Requests for a public man to use his influence are not confined to patronage matters. 'Internal improvements' in the pre-Civil War era—railroad politics from 1840 onwards, public lands, tariff schedules—could all provide fruitful and (for participants)

---

[1] For an analysis of Johnson's failure, and for some general observations upon the limitations of Presidential patronage as a political weapon, see Eric L. McKittrick, *Andrew Johnson and Reconstruction* (Chicago, 1960), 377–94. Especially (p. 379) the comment that: 'The cardinal principle was that bestowal of office was a reward for services, past and future, rendered to the party.' The President who regarded party loyalty as a disqualification and who expected future loyalty to himself was not playing according to the recognised rules. It was a different and quite acceptable process for a President to favour his own faction against others *within* the party.

important sources of correspondence. The anti-slavery agitation and fugitive slaves might figure largely in the correspondence of public men. Public lands and government contracts occur with rather less frequency in the correspondence of rank-and-file Congressmen, as these questions were more likely to be presented directly to the departments concerned or to influential Senators. A very frequent item in political correspondence dealt with local newspapers. Editors or would-be editors pointed out the value of their assistance to the party cause, and requested aid either in the form of public advertising or a private subsidy through a subscription list.

From all this it is possible to reconstruct the interests and pre-occupations of a public man, even though his own opinions may remain shadowy. He played several roles which interacted with each other, but which could be analysed separately. He had departmental or legislative responsibilities, and he was a member of a national party. He was a member of a local party organisation, and within the local party he was a leading member of a group of friends or associates which could be dignified or insulted by the name of 'faction'. He might have private business interests; an overwhelming number of nineteenth-century politicians had private law practices, and even while Congress was in session, the most eminent of them might become engaged in cases before the Supreme Court. Private or constituency interests might bring him into close contact with one of the executive departments; and if he enjoyed membership of an important Congressional committee, he would be open both to executive 'influence' and to solicitation from numerous groups and individuals. A prominent politician might be consulted by the President, and even humbler legislators—who happened to occupy key positions on important issues—might find interest in their views and political prospects expressed at the White House. Unfortunately for the historian, many of these intimate and personal contacts left no record on paper.

It is rarely that one finds even a general statement, from the inside, of the kind of relationship which had to develop between executive and legislative leaders. A good deal of information can be gleaned from the diaries of John Quincy Adams and James K. Polk, but both were too self-centred and too self-righteous to provide a candid picture. A rare analysis, from an earlier period, was made by Thomas Jefferson when writing to Barnabas Bidwell, whom he hoped would become the administration leader in the House:

> I do not mean that any gentleman relinquishing his own judgment, should implicitly support all the measures of the administration; but that where he does not dissaprove of them he should not suffer them to go off in sleep, but bring them to the attention of the house and give them a fair chance . . . when a gentleman through zeal for the public service, undertakes to do the public business, we know we shall hear the cant of backstairs counsellors . . . But if members are to know nothing but what is important enough to be put into a public message, and indifferent enough to be made known to all the world, if the Executive is to keep all other information to himself, and the house to plunge on in the dark, it becomes a government of chance and not of design.[1]

This letter expresses very clearly the dilemma posed by the separation of power. Possessed of information which could not always be made public, and with a clear idea of what measures ought to be adopted, the President might see an imperative duty to inform and persuade members of Congress; but hostile members could always raise a cry against 'backstairs counsellors'. For the historian this has the unfortunate consequence that important evidence of 'decision making' is often lacking; personal, private and unrecorded interviews can be inferred but not documented.

Finally, a public man took his place in the social life of Washington and of his own state. Evidence of the former is likely to be more abundant, for Congressmen separated from their wives found this the most congenial topic for letters home. Comments are, however, likely to be most full when he first arrived, with impressions fresh but superficial; as the novelty wore off he became more sensitive to the inner currents of Washington society, and was likely to say less. And, of course, once a man was

[1] Noble E. Cunningham, *The Jefferson Republicans in Power* (Chapel Hill, 1963), 90.

fully established and hoped for a long public career, he was likely to make arrangements to bring his family to Washington during sessions.

This draws attention to another gap in the evidence about public life. In the United States, during the nineteenth century, there are very few examples of the 'court memoir' familiar to European historians. There are obvious reasons for this. Washington was not a cultural capital, and men came there only to transact political business or, as newspaper reporters, to write about political questions. There were few literary 'men about town' with the interest, opportunity and leisure to record first-hand impressions of life in the national capital. After the Civil War the habit grew for public men themselves to write and publish reminiscences; thus Blaine, John Sherman, George Boutwell, George F. Hoar and other lesser figures wrote autobiographies which provide important political evidence; but with the possible exception of Hoar they lacked the literary skill to bring their political world to life. Before the Civil War the only major figure to write a political autobiography was Thomas Hart Benton, and his *Thirty Years View* was largely a pastiche of speeches, interspersed with undocumented narrative. One result is that even close study leaves one with a very shadowy idea of what the leaders of the nation were like. It is possible that more might be done to rescue, from newspaper files, more personal impressions of public men and of their world. Until this is done one has to rely too heavily upon the reports of foreign visitors whose comments were occasionally revealing but more often superficial. Most foreign visitors, who looked like gentlemen and were able to obtain the necessary introductions, had the opportunity in Washington of attending a White House reception, visiting Congress if in session, and perhaps having personal meetings with one or more political leaders.

The historian of national politics is more fortunate in available diaries. John Quincy Adams and James K. Polk have already been mentioned. In an earlier period William Maclay of Pennsylvania provides a unique picture of the first Congress at work. Edward Bates and Salmon P. Chase left diaries of value to historians of the

Civil War period, and Rutherford B. Hayes kept an important diary during some parts of his public life. The most important diary, written from the inside, was that of Gideon Welles; it also illustrated clearly the difficulties in using a diary as a political source. It may be that the habitual diarist is psychologically a man with an urge to explain and justify himself, or to demonstrate his own probity and foresight. Gideon Welles was an exceptionally self-centred person, and he seldom made any effort to understand those with whom he disagreed; yet at the same time he was highly intelligent, diligent and efficient. One may sometimes wonder how he found time to record events so fully while head of the naval administration of a nation at war; but nevertheless the diary is full, explicit, and informative. It convinces by its very detail; it is also bitterly prejudiced against individuals and often deficient in political judgment. Seward and Stanton have suffered injustice at his hands, which is difficult to correct, and during Reconstruction he not only misrepresented the Republican case against Andrew Johnson but also seriously miscalculated the political situation, continuing to forecast victory for 'conservatism' when the tide was running strongly in the opposite direction. The diary is invaluable as a source; but one must always remember that one is seeing events through the eyes of one man who—just because he is a diarist—is not as other men are.

There are two important diaries kept by men on the periphery of public life: Philip Hone and George Templeton Strong. The former was a New York merchant, mayor of the city, and a friend (though not an intimate friend) of Whig notabilities in the Clay and Webster camps. To judge from his diary Hone was not a very exciting person, but he knew everything that was going on in upper-class New York circles, had an interest in literature and theatre, and gives one a rare insight into the mind of that easily misunderstood creature, the conservative Northern Whig. The diary of George Templeton Strong is more lively and often more revealing. The value of Strong's diary is found partly in his indiscriminate recording of the important and the trivial; so that one gets an impression of life as it was being lived, and not as someone, with an eye on posterity, thought it ought to be.

Strong's political ideas were not deeply reasoned and his judgments were often emotional; but for this very reason his diary enables one to chart with accuracy the response of well-educated northern men to the Civil War. He became Treasurer of the United States Sanitary Commission, and the diary provides much important evidence about the relationship between the official world of politics and this first voluntary organisation resolved to perform a great public service.

Next to literary men, public men have been most liberal with their pens. Devotion to public life necessarily means that there is left a trail of letters, speeches, partisan writings; this activity also increases the likelihood that the man will be noticed by contemporaries in various ways; information about a public man will therefore turn up in all kinds of places—in the papers of other public men, in newspapers, in diaries and reminiscences. For the most part he appears as a *public* man, and it has been argued in the preceding pages that it may be difficult in nineteenth-century America to glimpse the personality behind the public face. Nevertheless we do know a great deal about him, and with rare exceptions there is no one else of whom we know so much. The question which then arises is whether the public man is, in any sense, a typical man, and whether the character of the rank-and-file can be diagnosed from a study of their leaders. The question is more interesting and more difficult to answer in America than in Europe, where leaders were, by class and upbringing, isolated from the mass of their fellow countrymen. The public man in America emerged from the mass, but the very fact of success separated him from his origins.

In contrast to public men, servants of the public have left few memorials. No history of nineteenth-century Britain would be complete without mention of the professional civil service, and men in its upper echelons were important if unobtrusive members of the political establishment. In the United States the history of the civil service is known principally through the writings of critics and reformers who were unlikely to extol merits or overlook deficiencies. Yet, as already shown, the increase in public employees was a great and significant aspect of nineteenth-century American history. Whatever illusions men might nourish, or however bitterly they might attack government expenditure, the army of civil servants grew and the country depended more and more upon their services.

The conventional history of the civil service maintains that until the Jacksonian period its quality and morale was high, that 'rotation in office' began a decline brought about by political patronage, insecure tenure, and a failure to attract the best-qualified men; and that this process culminated in the widespread corruption of the 'gilded age' from which the reformers sought to rescue the nation. Inspired by British example, the reformers hoped for an upper class of professional administrators, recruited from the universities, appointed and promoted on merit, and immune from political influences. The lower ranks would be appointed on similar principles and might expect to rise as high in the service as their talents would take them. The Civil Service Act of 1883 was the first great success, and pointed the way to a new era, although many obstacles and reverses lay ahead. There is no reason to discredit this account, but it tells one remarkably little about civil servants themselves.

Civil servants are normally unable to conduct their own defence, and evidence about the use of patronage tends to confirm the unfavourable story.[1] Civil servants who work efficiently are the faceless men of history, and only the failures, the incompetent, or the scoundrels are likely to figure in Executive correspondence or become the subject of legislative debate. The papers of public men provide evidence of the scramble for office, but are unlikely to record good behaviour after appointment. The normal functions of the civil service, and the record of the great number who were censured for neither indolence, incompetence nor malfeasance, must be extracted from forgotten Congressional documents, executive communications, and unpublished departmental archives. It is often as important to read between the lines as to compile

[1] The long series of attacks begin with Thomas Hart Benton's *Report on Executive Patronage* in 1826 (19th Cong., 1st Session, Senate Document 88). Cf. Leonard D. White, *The Jeffersonians* (New York, 1951), 390–93.

positive evidence. Generally speaking the standard of conduct in the Federal departments was high, and professional ethics were more consistent than critics implied. The main difficulty in assessing the evidence is that at every stage some persons had interested as well as disinterested motives for discrediting the civil service. The 'disappointed office-seeker' is a stock character, and there is always an 'out group' with good reasons for attacking the 'ins'. Before 1830 civil servants were attacked because they were unresponsive to popular demands, formed an 'aristocratic' élite, practised nepotism, favoured their own friends, and continued in office long after old age had rendered them incapable. These were the charges vigorously advanced in Benton's *Report on Executive Patronage* of 1826, and echoed by dozens of Jacksonians. By contrast, according to the modern authority on administrative history,

> Stability of officeholding made its own contribution. Men working together year after year molded each others' values, habits, and dispositions. Newcomers, appearing in an office at infrequent intervals, and one by one, were readily assimilated to the unwritten but effective code of ethics that a few short years had fixed. Competition for vacancies in clerkships, always keen, reminded incumbents of the goods they possessed in their own holding and confirmed them in their intention to pursue a course of action above reproach.[1]

The semi-permanent officials of the upper rank at Washington came from the same background as their political masters, and lived on easy social terms with them, and this solidarity of the official establishment was a major reason for the fury of the 'outs'.

Equally the displacement of leading members of this élite by Jackson explains the ardour of critics who attacked the eroding effects of democracy upon the public service. Some notorious scandals provided ammunition. Yet the volume of criticism must be set against other imponderable factors: no government could tolerate sustained inefficiency or wrongdoing on the part of its servants and if honesty was not its own reward it offered most men

[1] White, *op. cit.*, 413.

a better prospect than misbehaviour in office, while the rules of any administrative service are framed to divide the blame for error and thus to encourage vigilance. The ethics of the public service were under pressure but 'the outcome was not total defeat for the ideals of the Federalists and the Jeffersonians'.[1]

Controversy over the civil service produced a number of by-products which can be traced through Congressional debates and committee reports. The charge that unqualified men were appointed was followed by complaints that good candidates were turned down for want of 'useless' knowledge. Attacks upon the retention of superannuated clerks were balanced by allegations of wrongful dismissal. Complaints of perquisites taken by officials were accompanied by a steadfast refusal to pay adequate salaries. Urgent demands for greater efficiency contrasted with denunciations of departmental heads who had refused employment to respectable veterans of the Revolution or of 1812. Thus, while the civil servants themselves remained silent, one can investigate a great many curious notions about the way in which government should be run.[2]

After the Civil War the arguments continued on much the same lines, though the critics had acquired greater sophistication through study of British experience and because everyone had learnt from the imperatives of war. In the last decade of the period covered by this book discussion attained maturity with the publications of the Civil Service Reform Association, the debates preceding the passage of the 1883 Act, a large number of government reports, memoirs, and many magazine articles.[3] It is worth recalling that this outburst of criticism was the outcome of very rapid expansion of the Federal service and of resentment at the way in which an 'in-group' of Republican politicians, mainly from the Mid-West, had checkmated the influence of eastern

[1] Leonard D. White, *The Jacksonians* (New York, 1956), 436.

[2] The best of all the Congressional investigations was that conducted by Thomas W. Gilmer in 1844 (27th Cong., 2nd Session, House Report 741).

[3] See especially Ari Hoogenboom, *Outlawing the Spoils: A History of the Civil Service Reform Movement 1865–1883* (Urbana, 1961), *passim* and bibliography, 270–73.

intelligentsia. It is also useful to be reminded that the worst examples of official dishonesty were concentrated into a comparatively short period, and that behind the scenes the novel tasks of modern administration were being tackled.

> For a full century the characteristic figure in the rank and file was the person who sat at a desk and used a pen: the auditing clerks and the department copy clerks. Immense masses of handwritten accounts, letterbooks, and manuscripts accumulated in every agency, the product of painstaking, laborious and usually excellent penmanship.[1]

Day was dawning for technicians, scientific advisers, academic experts seconded to the public service, and offices equipped with typewriters and telephones. But the historian of the nineteenth century, though staggered by the mountains of material, has yet reason to remember with gratitude the faceless regiment of departmental clerks.

Another class of public servant has received scant attention from historians. For most of the years between 1790 and 1860 the United States relied upon a tiny professional army, supplemented by state militias.[2] In time of war the regular Army was supplemented by the militia and by volunteers, but the War of 1812 and the Mexican War were fought with forces which were small even by the standards of the early nineteenth century. The professional Army was frequently engaged in fighting Indians and keeping the peace on distant frontiers; but most of these operations lie outside the scope of this volume. Military cadetships at

---

[1] Leonard D. White, *The Republican Era: 1869–1901* (New York, 1958), 390.

[2] An Act of 1802 fixed the professional Army at two regiments of infantry and one of artillery—a total of about 3,350 men. On the eve of the Mexican it was only 27,373. Because there was no retirement age, and promotion was solely by seniority, elderly officers—remarkably numerous in proportion to total numbers—led the Army. Great Britain was somewhat better served under the system by which commissions could be bought and sold. An authoritative modern study is Russell E. Weighley, *History of the United States Army* (New York, 1967).

West Point were eagerly sought, and nominations were a useful item in political patronage. Many southern gentlemen did a spell of military service, but often military ambitions could be satisfied by attachment to the state militia. Foreign visitors were surprised to find so many civilians addressed as 'Colonel' or even as 'General' but soon realised that this might be won by short service in an Indian war or nominal duties with amateur forces. The civilian 'colonel' carried his title as evidence of status and esteem, but it was an American tradition to be suspicious of professional soldiers.[1] There was no officer caste forming a part of the ruling class as in Europe. A military record was a good qualification for public life, but the best recommendation was to be called from the plough to war, to demonstrate leadership and military skill, and to return to civilian employment.

What applied to officers applied equally to enlisted men. Though the Constitution protected the right of citizens to bear arms, and they were expected to rally to the flag in emergencies, professional soldiers were little in evidence. Whereas in Europe public ceremonies were usually, in part, military occasions—with bands, guards of honour, precision drill and splendid uniforms—the Americans got by with little more than the minimum required for police duties. When the real fighting had to be done it was assumed that volunteers would show their spirit.

These attitudes mean that there are few sources for military life. The official record can be studied in the archives of the War Department, and there is certainly material there which has never been fully exploited by historians. Materials relating to appointments, promotions, military administration and supply would, perhaps, make dull reading, and yield much detail of little general significance. Nevertheless organisation for defence is a primary function of any government, and the early efforts of the United

[1] While a volunteer or a militia officer might earn exalted rank cheaply, the professional officer (dependent upon the seniority rule and hindered by a top-weight of superannuated generals) might wait many years for promotion. Middle-aged lieutenants and captains were not uncommon; the average age of senior officers tended to be high in a country where that of politicians and successful businessmen tended to be low.

States deserve more attention than they have received.[1] In the light of subsequent events the puny efforts of the early Republic may seem ludicrous, but the principles which prevented the pursuit of military glory may bear examination.

It is surprising how little one actually knows of the ordinary soldier during the Mexican War. Newspaper accounts are unreliable, and provide little realistic comment. For most Americans the hardships of the soldiers in the heat and dust of Mexico were obscured by eulogistic accounts of heroism, dash and leadership. Pictorial records were mostly set pieces designed to show (perhaps from imagination rather than observation) the picturesque aspects of war: sun, brightly coloured uniforms, and impressive terrain helped the illusion. There may survive private letters which tell a different story, but few have appeared in print.

With the Civil War the atmosphere changed dramatically. Everyone was involved in the war, and large numbers of young men served in the armies. Sheer numbers made it statistically probable that, in a literate people, some soldiers would write informative letters, keep diaries, write descriptions of individual engagements, and record reminiscences before the memory faded. Indeed, measured by the published and unpublished output, the Civil War was the most literate war ever fought. The foremost authority on life in the Union and Confederate armies found letters of Confederate private soldiers 'in amazingly large quantities' while 'extant letters of Union soldiers greatly outnumber those on the Confederate side'.[2] He found comparatively few diaries by Confederate soldiers and in general they were less revealing than letters; but 'several hundred' unpublished Union diaries were discovered in addition to the considerable number already in print. The official sources of both sides also contain such material for studying the lives of the soldiers as regimental

[1] The best account of the early history of the War Department is given in the relevant chapters of Leonard D. White, *op. cit.* He relied mainly upon printed executive documents, Congressional Debates and Reports, and the *Army and Navy Chronicle* (from 1834).

[2] Bell Irvin Wiley, *The Life of Johnny Reb: the Common Soldier of the Confederacy* (Indianapolis, 1943), 419, and *The Life of Billy Yank: the Common Soldier of the Union* (Indianapolis, 1952), 438.

records, courts-martial, and reports on health. For the Union a semi-official source is the published and unpublished reports and papers of the United States Sanitary Commission.

If the Civil War produced an incomparable mass of written evidence, it was also the first to be photographed extensively. The work of Matthew B. Brady is well known but he did not stand alone. In addition, the war stimulated artists, and great volumes of sketches and prints survive. The illustrated magazines, especially *Harper's*, made enormous demands on the skill and ingenuity of artists and lithographers, and probably invention had sometimes to outrun material. Lithographed illustrations in magazines often took the harsh edges off life in the armies, and pictures of military and naval events would be somewhat stylised. Heroism and drama were what the magazine readers wished to see; but the war was too close to too many lives for the record to depart far from the truth. Photographs were more revealing; the cameras of the day were incapable of taking action scenes, and for this very reason the photographers concentrated upon camps, transportation, portraits, group pictures and the sad aftermath of battles. Thus the daily life of the soldiers and railroad trains are preserved and the information provided inexhaustible.

Both in the literary and the pictorial record the Civil War was unlike any previous war. The experience also cast a brilliant light upon aspects of society which normally passed without record. The letters and diaries of soldiers have been used mainly by military historians, but they also reveal many of the thoughts, attitudes and assumptions of hundreds who would, in normal times, have passed into obscurity without leaving more evidence of their existence than an entry in a census schedule or on a tax roll. The multiple records should therefore provide a unique cross-section of a nineteenth-century society; but to analyse them with this purpose in mind would require not only skill but sensitivity and delicacy of touch.

After the Civil War professional soldiers retire into their customary obscurity so far as general historiography is concerned.[1] There is, however, a swelling volume of information

[1] One monograph on the late-nineteenth-century army has recently appeared:

about the aspirations and activities of veterans. The Grand Army of the Republic formed in 1866 became one of the largest and best-organised pressure groups in American history; and its activities are exceedingly well documented.[1] Abundant literature was issued by the Grand Army, records of state and national 'encampments' are available, and pensions occupied much debating time in Congress. The demands of the veterans were frequent topics in political correspondence, and occupy large files in the archives of the Treasury and War Departments. For some reason all this activity has attracted the animosity of historians, but it deserves to be recorded that, for the first time in history, a national government was compelled to compensate adequately the men who had fought its battles. Exaggerated claims were inescapable, but the outcome was a notable advance in the slow process by which governments have been brought to recognise their social responsibilities.

Jack D. Foner, *The United States Soldier between Two Wars: Army Life and Reform, 1865–1898* (New York, 1970).

[1] There is a good-humoured account in Wallace E. Davies. *Patriotism on Parade* (Cambridge, Mass., 1955), Chaps. VII–IX.

CHAPTER 7

States, Cities and Courts

The records of the Federal government cover only a small part of the governmental activities of American society. In the nineteenth century most matters which affected the daily lives of the people were the responsibility of the states, and many of these functions were in turn delegated to counties and cities. By 1890 the thirteenth, fourteenth and fifteenth amendments, and the enlarged interpretation of the commerce clause, had set the pattern for greater Federal intervention, but American society was still a loose-limbed structure in which local autonomy was a real and persistent fact of life. Looked at from above, and through the perspective of the National Archives, the United States might appear to be an integrated nation in which authority flowed smoothly through well-recognised channels. Looked at from below, there was no uniform pattern; the country was a honeycomb of lesser executive, legislative and judicial bodies—each with responsibility for a particular aspect of life—and dealing either with many concerns in a limited area or with single concerns in a wider area. Responsibilities could be delegated completely, or remain divided; some of the authorities were appointed, but an increasing number were elected, though the electorate might differ from office to office and area to area.[1]

The states were sovereign bodies safeguarded by the Constitution. Their powers could not be varied by Congress, and their boundaries could not be altered except by their own consent. By

---

[1] Charles S. Sydnor observes that 'extremely little work has been done on the history of local government in the South'. *The Development of Southern Sectionalism 1819–1848* (Baton Rouge, 1948), 372. The same could be said of other parts of the country. Little of the published work on local government in New England extends into the nineteenth century.

contrast, the powers and boundaries of the counties and cities depended upon state legislative enactments. Though the older counties had established traditional boundaries, they could be divided or amalgamated; new counties could be formed out of large old ones, or from extensive and recently settled areas. The first task for a person wishing to investigate local history is often, therefore, to establish the geographical divisions of counties within states. For cities the important date to establish is the year of incorporation. Once granted, incorporation was very seldom withdrawn, so that quite small places—which had either declined or failed to fulfil an early promise of growth—might be cities with mayors, councilmen, or other appropriate authorities. Conversely, some quite large places could remain for a period under county government.

The sources for much social history lie buried in the archives of states, counties, and cities. The regulation of economic life was a state responsibility: weights, measures were agreed on a national basis, but the maintenance of standards was a function of the States; so were roads, canals, railroads, markets, tolls, direct taxes and local rates; titles to property and laws for conveyancing; water, sanitation, and public nuisances; health and education; public order, crime, and law enforcement. A most important function of a state was the right to endow, by incorporation, a number of people with a legal personality able to sue and be sued, and to exercise designated powers. Corporations might be municipal, commercial, or charitable; and once created they became record-keeping bodies with responsibilities as well as privileges.

By far the largest part of the judicial system of the country came under the states, and the number of cases heard in Federal courts was very small indeed when compared with the vast range of private litigation and criminal prosecutions commenced and terminated in the state judicial system. The records of the state courts, therefore, provide ample material for the life of society as a whole. Much of this evidence has been lost; still more lies unexplored in the archives of state, county and municipal courts. In most instances the decisions of the state supreme courts were printed—because these were of immediate significance for practising lawyers—but the decisions of inferior courts were likely to be noted publicly only when they established a new point of law or extended an old principle to new circumstances. As the printed records were invariably compiled for the use of lawyers, their material is selective, and the historian who is more interested in social or economic history than in legal doctrine may be compelled to search amongst the dusty and forgotten records of the inferior courts.

It has often been remarked that, for anyone familar with medieval English history, the American system presents a fascinating study in the survival of institutions. Grand juries are still vigorous and important bodies; courts of oyer and terminer sit; the sheriff is the key man in the enforcement of law, and the *posse comitatus* can still be called out at his bidding. County courts retain some administrative functions, and the courthouse (especially in the southern states) is normally the executive and political headquarters of the county. In New England towns selectmen function in much the same way as the ruling group chosen by the freemen in a medieval English borough. On the other hand, the District-Attorney was an important new official who emerged as the principal agent for the prosecution of crime.

The journals of state legislatures are readily available, but the debates are seldom preserved in print though legislative proceedings may be noticed in the local press. A great deal of light can be thrown, not only upon political and administrative structure but also on theories of government, in the records of State Constitutional Conventions. Normally these were regarded as sufficiently important for the debates, proceedings, votes and proposals to be printed in full. As most states revised their Constitutions twice or more during the nineteenth century, the conventions provide a source of great importance for understanding the political and administrative anatomy of the country. The biographical record of state legislatures and conventions is recoverable, though there are bound to be omissions; and from this it should be possible to build up a picture of sectional, economic and class interests within the state.

The records of the state executive departments should be extensive but are often sadly depleted by loss or neglect. The messages of governors were widely reproduced in the press and will normally be entered in the legislative journal. The orders and regulations, issued by the executive departments, will also be readily available; but the correspondence is often incomplete. Nineteenth-century state officials often preserved the minimum of correspondence, and the secretariat was small, untrained and impermanent. There was often an imprecise line drawn between private and public correspondence with the usual result that much which would now be regarded as 'official' was removed by the individual responsible. The deficiencies of the records were compounded in many states, until comparatively recent times, by carelessness in keeping the archives. In many little attempt was made to preserve the records from decay, even when they were not destroyed; in few was any attempt made to classify or catalogue the archives. Early in this century the American Historical Association expressed its concern at the situation, and resolved to bring pressure to bear upon the state authorities to set up programmes for the collection, care, and classification of state records. State historical societies also interested themselves in this matter, and in some instances voluntarily undertook a part of the labour involved. As a result most states have taken steps to improve their archives; but the neglect of former years, the expense, and the considerable work now required means that much remains undone.

It is probable that more historians will be drawn in the future to the state archives. More and more it becomes apparent that the impressions derived from the national records alone are incomplete and often misleading. Political historians have been amongst the first to realise that in a federal society it is necessary to study the articulated limbs as well as the national body. The history of an American political party is the history of a large number of autonomous state parties, and the state party may well prove to be a bundle of semi-independent county organisations.

Economic historians have realised the importance of studying economic developments in detail, but a wide gap still separates the large surveys of economic history, working mainly from national records and statistics, and the detailed studies of districts or industries. Work on the economic activities of the states has been done with notable success for a few states over limited periods of time, but much remains to be done for the country and the century as a whole.[1] It is a work of some importance, because the economic and social history of the United States, especially in the later years of the nineteenth century, has been based too much upon the broad generalisation of men who were personally hostile to many of the developments of the age and who were ill-informed about the real nature of the economic process.

Social history (however defined) has the greatest need to use state and local records. Indeed it is only by the use of these records that one can hope to establish the precise categories on which social analysis should depend. Or, to put the point in another way, it is only by the accumulation of exact information from local records that historians can resist the temptation to use sociological concepts as a substitute for knowledge.

A by-product of the Works Progress Administration of the New Deal era was a giant project on historical records which included inventories of local records. The task was never completed but a large number of volumes (photographically reproduced from typescript) were produced.[2] These inventories are unlikely to be available except in large libraries and it may therefore be useful to examine the records available in three samples.

[1] An excellent example of what can be done is Milton S. Heath, *Constructive Liberalism: the Role of the State in Economic Development in Georgia to 1860* (Cambridge, Mass., 1954). Extensive use of state records enabled Mr Heath to present a picture very different from the conventional view of government non-intervention. It does for Georgia what the well-known study by Oscar and Mary Handlin did for Massachusetts in *Commonwealth* (New York, 1947).

[2] Cf. S. B. Child and D. P. Holmes, *Bibliography of Research Projects Reports: Check List of Historical Records Survey Publications* (Washington, 1943). Some of the inventories were published too late for inclusion amongst the printed works listed.

An exceptionally full record survives for Lehigh County, Pennsylvania.[1] This was formed in 1812 with three county commissioners, a sheriff, a coroner, and three auditors as the official staff. The commissioners and auditors were elected for three-year terms; the sheriff and the coroner were selected by the governor from names proposed by the freemen of the county. The governor appointed an officer responsible for weights and measures. The commissioners appointed a clerk and a treasurer. The sheriff and the commissioners drew the names of jurors. Lehigh County formed a part of the Third Judicial District for which the governor appointed three judges, a prothonotary, a clerk of the courts and a registrar of wills and deeds. The judges appointed six road viewers when necessary. In 1838 the number of elective officers was increased; the county treasurer became elective in 1841, the county court judges in 1850, three directors of poor relief in 1844, a superintendent of schools in 1854, and a board of prison inspectors in 1867. By the State Constitution of 1874 the district-attorney was made an elected officer. During the same period the commissioners, whose original responsibilities had been purely fiscal, extended their responsibilities to elections, poor relief, county property, and the appointment of a growing number of officials.

Thus Lehigh County exhibited a typical story of nineteenth-century administrative evolution. The growing complexity of society necessitated an extension of administrative powers and the creation of new *ad hoc* authorities; but at the same time more and more officials were directly elected. In some areas development caused a complicated overlap between state and county authorities; for instance, poor relief was for long a direct responsibility of the state government, though executive powers in each township or borough were delegated to two elected overseers, and administration cut across county boundaries until 1884 when it was reformed on a county basis. In education free public schools were established by the State Statute of 1834, which also provided for the election of local boards of school directors in each district;

[1] *Inventory of the County Archives of Pennsylvania: Lehigh County* (Allentown, 1946).

but until 1849 districts were not compelled to set up boards or establish schools. A county educational authority was set up in 1854 with a county superintendent, elected by the local school boards, but he was responsible directly to the state and not to the county commissioners. Roads and bridges were primarily the responsibility of townships, with elected officials empowered to levy a road tax under the general direction of the county surveyor. Again the surveyor was separately responsible to the state, not to the commissioners, though they might have some influence on county projects through the allocation of tax revenue.

The Judiciary consisted of a presiding judge and two associate judges for each circuit; these became elective in 1850. Local justice was administered by justices of the peace and aldermen elected for six years. The Court of Common Pleas dealt with all civil matters; the Court of Quarter Sessions with lesser crimes and misdemeanours, roads, bridges and other minor questions; the Court of Oyer and Terminer with more serious crimes. The State Supreme Court was the court of appeal. In Pennsylvania there was no separate Court of Chancery. The grand jury was primarily an accusing body which heard only the evidence for the prosecution, but it also approved public works and inspected various county institutions such as prisons and lunatic asylums.

Lehigh County is a model for keeping records. As early as 1790 the state of Pennsylvania ordered county commissioners to erect a building for holding courts and keeping legal records, and in 1827 the judges of the Court of Common Pleas were made responsible for the records, and required to inspect them annually. The Prothonotary of the Court of Common Pleas was the official in charge of all court records, and his records include oaths, bonds, trial and argument lists, pleadings, preparatory papers, notes on testimony, depositions, briefs, and judicial opinions on points of law. In addition there are records of every judgment of the county courts, and of judgments of other courts affecting property in the county, divorces, bankruptcy, records of jury service, registers of the professions, and records of lunatics and habitual drunkards. The Prothonotary also kept the records of the Circuit Courts prior to their abolition in 1834. Finally he also kept a record of the charitable corporations incorporated by the county under authority delegated to it by the state.

The range of source material in county archives can be judged by the administrative records of Lehigh County. These include deeds and wills; the proceedings of the Board of County Commissioners; papers of the sheriff and coroner; papers of the county treasurer, controller, surveyor, engineer, superintendent of schools, and prison inspectors; the records of the county board of elections and of the grand jury. The Recorder of Deeds kept the original copies of every conveyance, mortgage, agreements relating to public lands or real property, charters of incorporation and trusts. The Clerk of the Courts of Quarter Sessions and Oyer and Terminer preserved records of criminal prosecutions, and of certain administrative responsibilities (exercised by these courts) for roads, bridges, and municipal accounts. From 1869 to 1911 the clerk also kept evidence of the medical qualifications of doctors and licences for transient medical practitioners.

This account of the records of Lehigh County has been given in some detail to illustrate the wide field covered in well-preserved county archives. Another sample, taken at random, is that of Jessamine County, Kentucky.[1] Whereas in Pennsylvania it was possible to speak of the county as an administrative unit, though some offices had direct responsibility to the state, in Kentucky it would be misleading to think of the county as, in any way, a unit of government. Administratively it was a headless body, a mere geographical term defining the jurisdiction and responsibility of various officials performing functions delegated to them by the state. It was a district for the administration of justice, law enforcement, elections, tax assessment and collection. Under autonomous officials it was a unit for education, poor relief, and roads. There was a county court with a clerk who kept a record of titles to property. The direct accountability of the various officials to the state authorities meant that many of the records, which in Pennsylvania accumulated in the County Court House in Kentucky found their way to the state capital. By contrast, in a Massachusetts county, there was a central

[1] *Inventory of the County Archives of Kentucky*, No. 57 (Louisville, 1940).

administration, consisting of three commissioners and two associate commissioners, which touched directly or indirectly every aspect of government in the county. The county archives therefore cover a wide range of topics and many questions would be settled—and thus leave their only record—at the county level (probably in the records of the commissioners).

City government was likewise complicated by varying patterns of administration, and, in the older towns, by many archaic survivals. Thus the city of New Haven, Connecticut, was incorporated in 1798 but its organisation was much older.[1] At the time of incorporation the officers elected annually were the selectmen, the town clerk, the lister (replaced by the assessor of taxes in 1819), the collectors of rates, the constables, the grand jurors, the tythingmen (whose duty was to prevent violation of laws concerning the sabbath), and the town treasurer. In addition there were a number of minor officials such as surveyors of highways, sealers of weights and measures, gaugers, inspectors, and viewers. During the nineteenth century the number of major officials was increased by an agent and treasurer of the school fund (1838), a registrator of births, deaths and marriages (1852), elected school boards (1856), and a registrar of voters (1868). This is the bare record of a complex and ancient system of municipal administration which evolved gradually to meet changing conditions during the nineteenth century. The selectmen were always effective administrative heads of city government, but much of their business was conducted orally and their decisions made on the spot; consequently their written records are meagre. The town clerk kept the official records.

Similar complexities make the study of the larger cities extremely difficult. Few preserved such interesting and archaic offices as the New England towns, but their affairs were complicated by endless wrangles with the State governments over responsibilities and jurisdiction. As major prizes in the struggle for political power they provided the stage for intense rivalry between local parties and between factions within the parties.

[1] *Inventory of the Town and City Archives of Connecticut*, No. 5, *New Haven County*.

Any increase of power by the city government was therefore likely to be resisted externally by the state legislature (normally dominated by rural representatives) and internally by rival municipal factions who might claim to represent the interests of the ratepayers and reform. Extended responsibilities for the city meant larger patronage for the ruling party. These institutional and inbuilt checks upon enlarged government were more effective than any theory of politics in explaining why American cities continued to be ruled by authorities with powers which were inadequate to meet the problems of urban growth.

Over a forty-year period from 1790 there was very little alteration in the functions of the Common Council of the city of New York.[1] Wharves, markets, street paving and maintenance —with occasional references to water supply and cleaning— continued to provide the normal business for the city government. The control exercised was very loose and consisted mainly in the approval of contracts negotiated according to precedent. The city was responsible for its own police, but in practice the police authorities seem to have been largely autonomous. The fire service was privately operated. The administration of a great port was complicated both by the overlapping responsibilities of the state and also by the presence of Federal authority. The Customs House under its collector was a stronghold of party patronage and also exercised considerable influence upon the way in which commercial business was transacted. The Naval Officer of the port was a Federal official. Ships were under Federal law until they docked, and even then they might be reached by the long arm of the commerce clause. The legal status of seamen on shore leave, or waiting for employment, was often obscure. Federal, state, and municipal authorities shared the responsibility for incoming immigrants, with the result that nothing very effective was done to protect travellers against abuses on sea or land.

In the second half of the nineteenth century the government of cities was complicated still further by the rise of political bosses dependent upon the vote of low-paid workers and recent im-

[1] Information derived from *Minutes of the Common Council of the City of New York, 1784–1831*, 21 vols (New York, 1917–30).

migrants. Notorious abuse of the power so gained added further weight to the case against entrusting city authorities with greater power. Much of the literature on city government in the later nineteenth century emanates from 'reform' groups whose main concern was to discredit corruption and to save property owners from the depredations of unscrupulous politicians.

The present chapter is concerned with government rather than with urban life (which will be dealt with elsewhere). City archives are well-stocked with materials, but for the most part the history of municipal government has been written from the newspapers and from personal records. The official sources themselves may be suspect, especially in the later part of the century, when the facts committed to paper were often intended to conceal rather than to enlighten. Even so, the government of a great city deserves to arouse more interest than heretofore; who was responsible for what, who paid for what, and how were the functions carried out? Further questions may arise from considering the omissions from the official record; how far were public services provided by private associations and how far was charity a substitute for municipal action?

The great mass of material lying buried in state, county and city archives raises some important issues for historical strategy. It is clear that local historians must use these materials if their work is to progress beyond reminiscence and rumour; the question is whether they can be ignored by historians who are trying to take a broad view of national history. On the one hand it can be argued that the vital decisions, affecting the destiny of the nation were taken in the Capitol, the White House, and the Supreme Court, and that the national historian must necessarily focus upon these national institutions. The internal history of Lehigh County, Pennsylvania, or of New Haven, Connecticut, may be of absorbing interest for those with local affiliations, but they cannot have much bearing upon the main course of American history. On the other hand, the national institutions are no more than the peaks in a landscape which is full of activity. The character of a democratic society can hardly be understood unless one gets down to study how the processes worked amongst the people most closely affected by government.

The sources for state, county and city history can provide a texture to life which cannot be discovered in any other way. Indeed this tangled web of administrative and elective processes may well prove to be the distinguishing characteristic of American society, and the experience which marks it off from that of Europe. In this view the essential meaning of 'the Great Experiment' may be grasped through the obscure records housed in county courthouses rather than through the rhetoric with which Americans have tried to explain their way of life. The difficulty for the historian lies in framing the generalisations which will indicate and emphasise this local experience without tedious explanations of detail.

CHAPTER 8

Political Activity and Participation

The basis of all American government is popular choice, and the constant endeavour of politicians is to influence or control it. Grandiose designs or selfish conspiracies will come to naught if elections cannot be won. The fact is obvious but bears repetition. There is therefore a constant incentive for political activity, and the frequency of elections means that the next test at the polls can never be far from the mind of a public man.

It is a truism (since Alexis de Tocqueville said it) that America is unique in not having had to undergo a democratic revolution. In practical terms this meant that when the Constitution was made, it was only necessary to adapt machinery for representative government which was already in full working order. The House of Representatives was closely modelled upon the directly elected houses of state assemblies, and it was expressly provided that the voting qualifications should be the same. The composition of the Senate was new; but the idea of an Upper House came from British practice and State experiment; moreover, the Senators were chosen by state legislatures by any procedure the individual states might adopt. Apart from the novelty of Federalism, much, therefore, was taken for granted, and existing practices in popular government were utilised. This was a part of the basic data with which the Americans began their national existence, and from the earliest days the undergrowth of politics has been the experience of frequent elections. Elsewhere governments preceded popular participation; in the United States popular participation preceded government. Practices which, in other countries were thought to undermine property, good order, religion and the principles of government, were accepted in America as the normal way of getting things done.

157

At the end of the eighteenth century all states imposed some restrictions upon the right to vote, and if the representative principle was the basis of political society, the states retained the power to say who should be represented. Not until 1869 did the fifteenth amendment impose restrictions upon this right, and even then states were free to fix the qualifications for suffrage, provided that they did not refer to race, creed or previous condition of servitude. Throughout the whole period covered by this volume, the exclusion of women from the suffrage was challenged only by rare individuals. Before the Civil War very few states, even in the North, allowed free Negroes the right to vote. Before the adoption of the Constitution the possession of freehold land had been abandoned as the exclusive qualification for voting, but most states retained in some form the idea that in order to vote a man must demonstrate a permanent and settled position in society. Often the stake had to be higher to qualify for the right to vote for state senates than for the lower houses. Residential qualifications were everywhere required, and in most states the payment of taxes, the possession of some property, or service in the state militia were required of voters. The details can be readily ascertained from state constitutions of the day.[1]

The formal qualifications of voters may, however, be a poor guide to who actually voted. Large numbers with the right to vote did not do so, and the reasons for this abstention often require careful assessment. Lack of interest, the fact that the result was a foregone conclusion, or distance from the polling places were frequent reasons. A low turn-out may, therefore, mean that the nominations for office were tightly controlled, that no effort was made to present political issues to the people, or that only perfunctory efforts were made to persuade voters in remote districts to exercise their rights. Conversely a high turn-out, in the early days of the Republic, indicates that it was worth someone's while to make quite exceptional efforts to overcome these obstacles. Intimidation to prevent voting became common

[1] Not only did more men become qualified to vote but also, and probably with greater significance, more state and local officers became elective. For examples see Chapter 7 above.

in the southern states in the later nineteenth century; elsewhere there is little evidence of its use, and as the competition for elective offices increased, the law was more likely to be stretched to inflate the vote than to depress.

Even when restrictions upon the suffrage seemed severe, they were often ignored or evaded. It was the responsibility of the officials in charge of polling places, in the first instance, to accept or reject votes, and a local man might well hesitate to turn away any man of good standing in the community. Long before adult male suffrage became the rule, the law was often administered only to exclude vagrants, casual labourers, recent immigrants, and criminals. This laxity might be stretched still further when would-be voters were known to favour the returning officer's party. This practice reached notorious proportions in some cities, where there were always numbers of men with doubtful qualifications who might be enlisted to vote on the right side. In New York in the heyday of Boss Tweed compliant judges would issue naturalisation certificates to almost any recent immigrant who was prepared to vote the Democratic ticket; indeed, complaints of this practice were being made as early as 1844. Other devices to inflate the vote were by getting men to vote twice or more under different names, getting votes cast in the names of men who were dead or removed, or introducing voters from other districts. This is not, however, the place to examine the extent or nature of electoral frauds; the point established is that the legal qualification for suffrage is a poor guide to actual voting.

Voting frauds were often notorious, but led infrequently to petition or litigation. Probably every Congress had before it some petitions against the result of elections, but few led to extended Congressional proceedings; the expense of establishing a case would be considerable and before it was complete it would be time to prepare for the next election. There is, therefore, no long record of argument in the House of Representatives over contested elections to serve as a source for electoral practices, but a good many cases were argued in state courts.[1] There were

[1] Frederick C. Brightly, *A Collection of Leading Cases in the Law of Elections* (Philadelphia, 1871); this is a work of reference intended for lawyers which

disputes over Senatorships; these usually turned upon an interpretation of the state law for the choice of Senators by the legislatures, but several cases occasioned debates in the Senate.[1]

In general it is therefore dangerous to draw too fine a conclusion from voting figures. Elaborate calculations of 'swings' may easily be influenced by human factors which have disappeared from view in the bare record of numbers. Even larger generalisations may require careful scrutiny. For many years historians assumed that a great upsurge of voters brought Andrew Jackson to the White House, and that this was in some way connected with the enlargement of the electorate by the abandonment of suffrage qualifications. It required only a look at the figures to demonstrate that voting in state elections (where the same suffrage qualifications applied) had often run as high or higher than the Presidential vote in 1828, and that the most spectacular increase in voter-participation came between 1836 and 1840. It is likely that future historians will be on their guard against errors of this kind, but they were common before the present age of quantification. At the other end of the scale, however, figures can be made to carry more weight than they will bear, and their correct use depends upon a wide understanding of the political environment.

With these qualifications it must, however, be emphasised that in the United States there is more information about elections, running over a longer period, than in any other country. J. R. Pole remarks that 'Governments have long been in the habit of leaving ample and reasonably continuous records of the more legitimate side of their activities', and consequently voting records are remarkably complete.[2] Where the official record is blank, it is almost always possible to fill the gap from press

---

notes leading cases and decisions in state courts. It contains much information about the interpretation of electoral laws.

[1] *Compilation of Senate Election Cases 1789–1913* (Senate Document No. 1036, 62nd Congress, 3rd Session), Washington, 1913. This work prints extracts from debates in the Senate on contested elections and contains much useful information.

[2] *Political Representation in England and the Origins of the American Republic* (London and New York, 1966), 565.

reports or from other political year-books or almanacs. It is probable that since 1824 the records of every national or state election are recoverable, and even before that date there is abundant evidence on most of them.[1] It has been possible to compile election figures for several states from the middle of the eighteenth century, and every Presidential election has been recorded, county by county, from 1824 to 1896. Only South Carolina, where the Presidential electors were appointed by the legislature until 1868, eludes the count. With due caution (as indicated above) it is possible to work out quite sophisticated calculations, while even the simple process of drawing electoral maps based upon these county statistics will reveal some surprises for men bred upon traditional statements about the regional and occupational character of the parties. Some difficulties may be encountered in ascertaining county boundaries, and it is wise to consult contemporary maps, watch for the creation of new counties and note the division of old ones.

The next step in the reconstruction of electoral history should be to record the results of Congressional elections. Some difficulties may be encountered in ascertaining the boundaries of Congressional districts as these could be changed after each decennial apportionment of Congressional seats, or at other times after disputes within the state over the under-representation of recently settled areas. In the east it was normally the coastal areas which were over-represented; old cities which had not grown rapidly also tended to be over-represented, while new or rapidly growing cities were under-represented. West of the Appalachians the over-representation of rural areas was the rule, especially those along rivers which contained the earliest settlements. So far Congressional elections have received close attention only in special studies of a few regions, but if the task could be done nationally, several new vistas in political history would be opened. On several important occasions a notable 'swing',

---

[1] Samuel P. Hays estimates that 98 per cent of all the county returns for Presidential, Congressional and Gubernatorial elections during the nineteenth century are recoverable. 'The Use of Archives for Historical Statistical Enquiry,' *Prologue*, I, No. 2.

which set the pattern of party strength for some years to come, took place in mid-term elections, and there were others, less prolonged in their effects, which had a notable impact upon history; 1810, 1826, 1842, 1850, 1858, and 1874 provide examples of long-term effects and 1798, 1838, and 1866 of short-run. Each of these mid-term elections saw decisive shifts in opinion or the introduction of new forces into public life.

Use of election returns in conjunction with the census may open the way to further deductions about the popular basis of political power.[1] In addition to population statistics, information about occupations, land-holding, property and manufactures can be related to voting patterns. The census shows the foreign born, but does not break up the people into ethnic groups. Religion is recorded and may be relevant. Sources in the local archives such as tax returns and assessments can reveal much about the prosperity of the district and its distribution of wealth. Thus the bare figures of the ballots cast begin to assume character and meaning. Local newspapers can provide further information to supplement the statistics. The main difficulty in this kind of research is that it is inordinately lengthy, and the rewards may be doubtful. While economic historians have learnt the value of micro-studies, political historians may well question whether the reward is worth the effort. The anatomy of a single congressional district may lead to the classic dilemma of the specialist who comes to know more and more about less and less. Perhaps the example of Sir Lewis Namier in the study of British eighteenth-century politics may inspire American historians to delve more deeply into constituency patterns, but the task will be harder. Namier dealt with a society which was not in a rapid state of change (for the bulk of his studies were concerned with rural

[1] Some recent examples of the use of voting statistics to correct ideas advanced by contemporaries and subsequently accepted are George Daniels, 'Immigrant Vote in the 1860 Election: the case of Iowa', *Mid-America*, 44 (1962), 146–62, and David J. Keppner, 'Lincoln and the Immigrant Vote; a case of religious polarization', *ibid.*, 48 (1966), 176–95. Daniels shows that Iowa Germans were predominantly Democratic in spite of the claims of German Republican editors, while Keppner shows that Philadelphia Germans divided on religious lines.

constituencies and small country towns), and the voters were few and often identifiable. Most of his material was drawn from the correspondence of patrons, members and agents, and did not require him to evaluate the moving currents in a wide suffrage society.

Analysis of the 'structure of politics' on the classic Namier model is therefore based largely upon the correspondence of public men, and in Chapter 6 reference was made to the wealth of material on party organisation and constituency affairs which can be drawn from that source. However the letters of Congressmen and their political friends often leave precisely the gaps which can only be filled by the kind of micro-political study suggested above. Public men knew the character of their districts, and required to be informed only of unexpected changes or to be corrected when they made palpable errors. Information may be gleaned, here and there, about the activities or opinions of individuals and groups, but it is never the systematic analysis that modern students of politics demand.

A source of a different kind is campaign propaganda, the parties' own press, and other forms of political literature.[1] There is obvious distortion, but properly used these sources can yield valuable information which cannot be found elsewhere. Analysis of voting figures tends to be a cold, unemotional task, and while consistent patterns, changes and swings may be charted, the emotional drive remains elusive. The partisan literature can at least provide the picture which the faithful presented of themselves, the image of their opponents, and the arguments which they stressed in order to catch the uncommitted. We may remain puzzled by the crudity of the arguments and the credulity of those who were influenced by them, but one must at all times remember that the 'average' voter is not drawn to the polls to serve a special interest or to promote a single policy, but because he is persuaded that the general attitude of one party or candidate is to be preferred to the others. It is an emotional response, but is, nevertheless, rooted in tradition. It was the business of the party

[1] Cf. Lee Benson, *The Concept of Jacksonian Democracy: New York as a Test Case* (Princeton, 1963) makes constructive use of this material.

politician to keep this tradition alive, and to persuade reluctant voters that it had immediate relevance to their needs. Once some sort of contrast had been established between the parties, the sporting instinct and the will to win could be brought into play. Partisan literature can, therefore, be highly misleading if it is used as a substitute for hard research into voting behaviour; but it is often the only means available for understanding why people voted at all.

In the first quarter century of the new nation voting figures were often poorly preserved, and often exist only in scattered newspaper reports. It follows that for this period greater reliance must be placed upon the papers of public men and upon the partisan press. Fortunately the small scale of the political society, and the quality of many of the public men, make this more rewarding than might be true of a later period. The leading authority on the Jeffersonian party writes,

> The slow means of transportation and communication of the Jeffersonian era dictated that political leaders and party workers fashion many of their plans and conduct much of the party's business through correspondence. Thus the letters of active participants in the political scene afford a particularly rich source of early party history.[1]

Moreover, in this early period the party politics of the federal society were still in their formative and experimental stage, so that much had to be spelt out which could later be left unsaid. Even so, it remains true that we know much more about the leaders as individuals than about the voters. The 'Great Experiment' depended upon voter participation; but it is often uncertain how they participated, to what extent, and why. This kind of ignorance is not the measure of the incompetence of historians, but merely that the nature of the sources makes an informed deduction more profitable than fragmentary data. Unavoidably political study in these early years tends to be somewhat top-heavy, though from time to time close study of local materials can reveal something of the undergrowth of politics.

[1] Noble E. Cunningham, *The Jeffersonian Republicans in Power* (Chapel Hill, 1963), 306.

The very success of early party leaders in stimulating local political organisation meant that, as the years went by, the role of national leaders as party managers became less important. Their services became to provide a national image which could be used by local leaders rather than to take command of operations themselves. This tendency became marked after the break-up of the caucus system. So long as the choice of Presidential candidates was made by the Congressional party, the national alliance could operate with some degree of central control, even though exercised informally. The rise of the convention system for Presidential nominations meant the coming of the now familiar divorce between the Presidential party and the Congressional party. No one could predict who would be the party's Presidential candidate in four years' time, nor the direction which he would give to national politics. A Presidential candidate, and still more a President in office, would want to see his own men in positions of influence; but a failure to win re-nomination or defeat in the election meant that they would be forced to abdicate in favour of new men. There was not only a separation between the Presidential party and the Congressional party, but also between Presidential leadership and national party organisation; the latter tended to drop back into purely administrative tasks during campaigns and to become invisible between them. Indeed, between 1840 and 1852, when political participation was at its highest level and two national parties fought on terms of near equality, national party organisation had almost ceased to exist; it was called into being to preside over Presidential campaigns and then mainly as a centre for propaganda, liaison and information.

This development affected the nature of the sources. The period is of great intrinsic interest because, for the first time, one sees a two-party system operating in a mass democracy over a long period of time. Indeed, it is perhaps only during this period that one first finds the assumption that the two-party system is the normal and not the abnormal way of conducting politics. Yet it is extremely difficult to document the character of the parties as national organisations. What Presidents and Presidential candidates tried to do can be fully studied from the newspapers, the party platforms, personal correspondence and the speeches of their supporters in Congress. But the unifying concepts and the organic unity of the party is far more elusive because there is no body of source material which throws light upon the national aspects of party as a continuing organisation.

It is, however, possible to obtain a great deal of information about the functioning of vigorous local organisation. There are limitations upon what the sources can reveal, for politics at the state level, and still more at the city level, were often face-to-face affairs in which decisions were made and directives issued without the necessity for committing a word to paper. Indeed, as the management of local politics often involved transactions and promises which could easily be misunderstood (even when not discreditable), the less evidence remained the more satisfied were the local leaders. For a quarter of a century Martin Van Buren was regarded as a supreme master of political management in his own state of New York, and he has passed into textbook history as the exemplar of success in professional politics; yet if one tries to study the art of political management through Van Buren's voluminous surviving papers, one will find clues rather than solutions, and the complex interaction of influence, pressure and persuasion which produced success eludes one. The renown of Thurlow Weed as a master tactician may be equally difficult to document; he has been called 'the wizard of the lobby' but, like other practitioners of mysterious arts, little evidence remained of his magic once it had performed its task. Thus the study of state party organisation, which presents the apparently simple prospect of abundant material concentrated in a few places and dealing with a close-knit social organism, comes to demand the most difficult of the historian's arts: the reconstruction of a situation in which the most important decisions can only be inferred from indirect evidence. There is the added danger that those who claimed to have access to inside information— especially those whose livelihood depended upon producing good stories for the press—were often guessing from scraps of evidence or even fabricating the evidence for themselves.

The later history of party organisation has, as yet, been inadequately studied. It may be suggested that the rise of the Republican party and its consolidation during and after the war provides a field of special interest in this connection. Like other American parties the Republicans began as a local organisation, but one has to go back to the first decade after 1790 to find local organisation inspired by the same fervour. The Republican party of 1854 had more in common with its Jeffersonian predecessor than a name; in both instances one found local groups inspired by a conviction that really vital issues, fundamental for the whole character of the nation, were at stake. Later the identification of the Republicans with the cause of the Union and the reconstruction of the South kept up the impulse to organise not merely for power but for a cause. Politics would no longer be conducted purely on a professional basis in terms of power and patronage; it was necessary to appeal to all kinds of other factors—to religion, political ideas, and patriotic sentiment—and to enlist the aid of all kinds of amateurs whose influence might be of use. In other words, it is necessary to move on from political mechanics to political ideology. The sources are challenging and abundant; and though their exploration has only just begun the first results indicate that a new dimension has been introduced into American historiography.[1]

The later history of the Republican party illustrates a further development.[2] Still inspired by the original emotional and ideological impulse, the Republican party became primarily an organisation for ensuring stability in government. The 'spoilsmen' have been treated with scant respect by historians, but it is sometimes worth while to see them as they saw themselves: not as men helping themselves and their friends out of the public purse, but as political experts devoting their talents to the difficult task of weaving together the intricate structure of support necessary for efficient government. One aspect of this task can be amply documented and this is patronage, for the use of patronage is

[1] Eric Foner, *Free Soil, Free Labor, Free Men: The Ideology of the Republican Party before the Civil War* (New York, 1970) is a stimulating example.

[2] Robert D. Marcus, *Grand Old Party: Political Structure in the Gilded Age* (New York, 1971) provides the argument for this paragraph.

almost certain to leave positive evidence on the record. There had to be correspondence with men in the district where the post was to be filled, with the government department concerned, and with others who might influence the outcome. Controversial appointments might explode in Senatorial debates over nominations, though these would normally take place in executive session, when the Senate sat in private. Notorious cases would be certain to make their impact on the press. Indeed, so ample is the documentation that it has tended to exclude everything else.

Far more tentative and hypothetical are the relationships between politics and business. Again the best-known, and therefore least creditable, examples are well-documented, while normal relationships remain obscure. It was the task of Congress and the executive branch to find out about business, just as it was the interest of business to influence government. The natural channel for the flow of information was through the lobby, through representations to the executive departments, and by evidence presented to Congressional committees. The process could be abused, but even justifiable actions could easily be misinterpreted. At this level, too, it is difficult to distinguish between the fair operations of government and dubious party management.

There is therefore a contrast to be drawn between the study of voter participation and of party organisation. The former was largely taken for granted by earlier historians, but today the stimulus provided by the emphasis of modern political science has led to an increasing interest in this field. Once the need to investigate is apparent, the materials are found to be abundant. Voting statistics can be bolstered at many points by evidence from the newspapers. On the other hand, party organisation has always attracted a good deal of attention from historians, but on examination many statements prove to be based upon no evidence, upon evidence out of context, or upon attempts to read back contemporary party differences into the past. Moreover, much of the evidence for the inner working of the party system does not exist, because it consisted of verbal commitments, promises or threats. No heads were counted to decide the way in which things should be done, and no written agreements were made.

Where correspondence tends to be abundant—as between Congressmen and their active political supporters, much is unwritten because it is well-known to both correspondents. One has, therefore, an interesting example of a case in which it is possible to count every tree but often difficult to map the wood.

Between the voters and the state and national parties were conventions and caucuses. District and state party conventions are usually noted in the local press, but the details may be vague. Occasionally, and in periods of tension, the proceedings of such conventions were widely reported and might be reprinted in pamphlet form. For instance, the cross-currents of New York Democratic politics in 1848 can be disentangled with some success from printed records of the conventions which led to the split between radical and conservative wings and to the sudden emergence of the Free Soil party. Other conventions, in which the party managers succeeded in pushing things along predictable channels, left less imprint upon contemporary sources. It is probable that in some cases a manuscript record remains of the proceedings in the state archives, the state historical society, or amongst private papers. Lacking this kind of information, a good deal of obscurity surrounds the making of nominations and (from 1832) the choice of delegates for the national conventions.

There is no shortage of material on national nominating conventions. The newspapers reported them liberally, and the proceedings—often including abridged versions of the speeches— were often published. The conventions would be preceded by printed propaganda on behalf of leading candidates; the discussions on policy would be formalised in the party platform. By custom, the leading contenders for the Presidential nomination were not present at the Convention, and their leading supporters would naturally wish to keep them informed; there is therefore a good chance that these letters survive in the papers of the candidate, and, if so, they will go beyond any printed record in intimacy and frankness. Other participants in the convention may well have written letters about the incidents, speeches and votes, and these are likely to go into much greater detail than normal political correspondence.

Another political process which is amply documented is the constitutional conventions of the various states. Indeed, the records of these conventions, supplemented by newspaper reports, provide invaluable insights into the working of the political system and into political ideas and attitudes. Often the interest and importance of the occasion warranted more than a formal record, and the proceedings and speeches were subsequently published in book form. There is, perhaps, no more significant or revealing a body of source material on political culture in America or in any other country. Of course, one cannot expect everything, and there are inadequately reported constitutional conventions. The conventions held in the southern states in 1865, under Johnson's plan of reconstruction, were reported in a very meagre fashion, and studies of the southern states at this crucial period have suffered from this lacuna in the evidence. The conventions in 1867 and 1868, held in pursuance of the Reconstruction Acts, received fuller treatment.

Constitutional conventions are, perhaps, the best source for examining American political ideology. The questions which must be asked are more complex and fundamental than might be expected. One of the basic propositions of American political life—taken over from the British seventeenth century—was 'no taxation without representation'. What was understood by 'representation'? Did it mean representation of a geographical area (a state or a county), or the representation of individuals? Was there some magic about the territorial unit or was it merely a matter of convenience? Did 'representation' mean that an elected member had a power of attorney for his constituents on all questions, on some questions, or only on those questions which he had enumerated at the time of his election? Did the right to be represented imply the right to instruct representatives, and was a representative morally obliged to resign if he displeased his constituents? The specific questions on the authority conveyed by election were raised infrequently with regard to members of the House or of state lower houses; the tenure was normally so short that it was more practicable to wait for the next election to decide the issue. These questions were however raised not infrequently with United States senators and state senators. The liability of a senator to act upon instructions from his state was frequently discussed and never settled. The problem of nomination for office received early and urgent attention with caucus and convention, party regulars and party rebels, professionals and amateurs all brought into the dispute.

A theoretical argument which runs through constitutional conventions is whether the different elected authorities should represent different constituencies. The original concept was that the principle of checks and balances would not work unless the executive, the upper and the lower houses derived their authority from different sources. The solution in the constitution for the Presidency was to construct a system of indirect election, and this quickly became a system of direct election. The original idea of the United States Senate (which already prevailed in most state senates) was that the Senators should represent property and continuity, while the directly elected lower house represented numbers and changing opinion. In the Federal convention the great compromise made the Senators chosen by state legislatures, thus making them representatives of the majority party and qualified by political success rather than by possessions. In the separate states the qualification for the right to vote for Senators was a perennial talking point, and gradually the logic of democratic representation wore down the property qualifications, until Senators and Representatives (and, in most cases, Governors) were chosen by voters with uniform qualifications, and only the size of their constituency and the length of their tenure distinguished members of the 'upper' and 'lower' houses. The debates on this issue in several state constitutional conventions provide a fruitful source for the study of ideas about representation.

The institutions, processes, and concepts of the world's oldest democracy provide a field for study which transcends their purely American significance. As commentators from Crèvecoeur and Tocqueville to Bryce and Brogan have insisted, they are of wider importance. We should speak not of American democracy but of the American version of democracy. The vast range of sources enables us to document in detail a movement of great importance in human history; the sources are there, but definitive methods for their use have yet to be determined.

PART III

The Life of the People

Introduction

Political and economic history offer central themes for investigation; the important sources cluster around major institutions or activities, and though investigation flows into many channels one can fix boundaries for the territory to be surveyed. Conversely, where a gap exists in the record it is usually possible to identify it. Social history operates in a different historical medium; it deals with influences which are all around us and it is difficult if not unrealistic to abstract one category of experience from the whole. Nor will it ever be possible to define the scope of the study or to know what has been omitted.

Not every social historian would admit the truth of these generalisations. Some would argue that social institutions are as capable of definition as governmental or economic. One can certainly define some social units such as towns and farms; one can also describe certain social groups by occupation, race or status. What can be defined can also be studied; and if units and groups can be identified the relationships between them should be analysed. One need not be content with incomplete descriptions, but can build research around phenomena which are as recognisable as governments, administrative systems, courts of law, industries, banks, or trading relationships. The difficulty, in the present state of knowledge, is that while it is possible to say with certainty what a government is, and to describe accurately an economic activity, there is more complexity and less agreement in defining a social system. In this field one man's description is likely to be another man's heresy.

The social historian deals with sources in the same way as any other historian, but for him the problem of selection is peculiarly difficult. He is bedevilled by problems of relevance and significance. A single issue of a single newspaper is crammed with detail of every kind, and the social historian has to construct a coherent picture from this and similar sources. A political historian knows what he is looking for, and a cursory inspection will determine whether materials relevant to his study exist. Moreover, he has a ready-made scale of significance, for his selected theme will itself set the order of importance. The social historian has no such guides—for everything which happened is relevant to his study—unless the order of priority is fixed in accordance with a predetermined theory which may not be generally acceptable.

Social history suffers from three occupational diseases: personification, substitution and abstraction. Personification makes large entities act as single persons: cities, races, classes *do* things collectively, and soon they are spoken of as though they were single persons. If one means that the government of a city took a certain decision, one refers to verifiable fact, and in this sense 'a city' can take actions; but when one leaves the safe ground of recorded decisions by duly constituted authorities, and begins to speak of the city as a collective person in other contexts, there is danger ahead. So, too, it is necessary to distinguish between what 'a race' thinks and does, and what some members of the race say they do or should do. Substitution is the simple process of making something that one knows serve in place of other things that one does not know. For instance, one may not know how all members of a class thought, but have a good deal of evidence about the thought of some it is tempting to generalise about the many from evidence of the few. Abstraction is the danger of cutting oneself off from the real world, and dealing with supposed influences upon action; a symptom of this disease is frequent use of the words 'image' and 'ethos'. Conventional historians have, however, showed equal fondness for 'forces' and 'factors' which are often abstractions used to avoid the need for investigation.

In the following pages the more obvious sources for social history will be mentioned, but the major problem will be left unresolved. Is the task of social history primarily descriptive or analytical? Is it intended to provide a background of knowledge against which the history of institutions can be studied, or to provide 'models' to explain the activity of men in society? This is a dilemma which pervades a great deal of social history, and the road taken by individual historians largely determines their approach to the sources. For one school everything is relevant which contributes towards knowledge of how men lived in the past, so that the trivial and apparently inconsequential must be included. The other school attempts to identify certain groups, causes of conflict, or patterns of behaviour; and then to look at the sources in this light. The latter should not be too readily blamed for 'making the facts fit a theory', because they follow in the path of conventional political history which has normally looked for the sources to document a policy, a controversy, or the structure of government.

There is an overlap between social history and intellectual history; indeed the separation between the two may sometimes be artificial, for the study of how men lived necessarily includes consideration of how their minds were influenced. In the following pages, for instance, the press is given prominence in 'the life of the people', whereas it might have been treated in Part IV as 'the mind of the people'. Its inclusion in this Part can be defended on grounds of convenience, for newspapers form so essential a source for social history that it would be difficult to discuss the sources for particular aspects of society without first considering the press. The general rule followed has been to reserve for the last Part consideration of theories and arguments which can be associated with particular individuals or groups, or with broad themes which can be separated from the general course of popular thought and studied separately; but the distinction is not rigid and there is a constant interaction between the two fields.

CHAPTER 9

The Press, Periodicals and Pamphlets

The United States has never had a national press. There has been a metropolitan press, and in the later part of the nineteenth century the metropolitan dailies circulated in a large surrounding area. Before the Civil War some weeklies achieved a wide circulation; but no newspaper achieved anything like a nation-wide circulation, and at the end of the period purely local news-papers continued to flourish under the shade of the metropolitan press. From the start, however, American newspapers as a whole, catering for a literate population, commanded a larger potential market than their European contemporaries, and the precocious development of advertising kept the cost of successful newspapers low. In 1833 a reasonable estimate gave 1,200 newspapers, which was almost three times more than in Great Britain or France at that period.[1] By 1860 there were 3,000 and the comparison with European countries was still more favourable; in 1870 there were 574 dailies, 4,295 weeklies, and 222 published either twice or three times a week.[2]

These figures bring out the importance of the weekly in nineteenth-century journalism. A daily probably sold only in its city and the immediate neighbourhood, but a weekly with postal subscribers might reach far afield and become the principal means by which people in the more remote areas were kept informed of events. A landmark in the history of the weeklies and of periodi-

---

[1] Frank Luther Mott, *American Journalism: a History of Newspapers in the United States* (New York, 1941; revised eds. 1947, 1950), 216. Except where otherwise stated the information in the following paragraphs is derived from this invaluable work. There are studies of the southern press by Thomas D. Clark: *The Southern Country Editor* (Indianapolis, 1948), *The Rural Press and the New South* (Baton Rouge, 1948).

[2] *Abstract of the Census* (1870).

cals was the Postal Act of 1852 which reduced rates and allowed them to be pre-paid by the publishers and not on receipt by the subscribers. While the dailies had a total circulation of about two and a half million, the weeklies reached about ten million. The historian of opinion should therefore pay particular attention to the weeklies, which reached a very large number of people and reflected the editors' judgment of what their readers would wish to select from the plethora of passing events.

Figures tell only a portion of the hectic history of American journalism, for the failure rate amongst newspapers was high and the mounting totals indicate a continuing excess of new ventures, optimistically launched, over large numbers dying ignominious deaths. There were good reasons—besides a naïve expectation of bounding sales—which encouraged men to start newspapers. Not only did local fame and fortune await the successful editor but also influence and political prestige. Indeed, next to lawyers (though a long way behind), editors were the most likely men in the nation to achieve public distinction. If comparatively few reached governorships or became Senators, they were certain to stand high in local party councils. Politics also persuaded many public men to purchase, subsidise, or start newspapers as their personal organs. Presidents regarded the choice of an administration newspaper in Washington as a question of national importance; while a few leading editors played dual roles as political oracles and party leaders. Thurlow Weed, Thomas Ritchie, Horace Greeley, and Henry J. Raymond all became recognised as powers in the land through their editorial influence. It is therefore of considerable importance to ask, of any particular newspaper, what political influence sustained it, and whose political ambitions it was intended to serve.

A share in the public advertising was an important piece of patronage for a struggling newspaper. Official announcements, advertisements for contract tenders, and information about appointments were constantly being issued by federal, state and city governments; for the newspaper they were not only a source of revenue but also a guarantee of purchase by people with an interest in these things. A page of public advertising will indicate

to the historian that the newspaper enjoyed some official patronage. In the early days this might make all the difference between
success and failure, because few newspapers could cover costs out
of circulation.

In the 1830s a new phenomenon appeared upon the scene. This
was the cheap daily which deliberately ignored patronage, and
set out to capture circulation with methods deplored by the old
school of editors who had imagined themselves already half-way
to statemanship. The first penny daily was the New York *Sun*
in 1833, followed by the New York *Morning Herald* in 1835; the
latter, under the brilliant but unscrupulous editorship of James
Gordon Bennett, was one of the success stories of the age; in
spite of doubling its price in 1837 the *Herald* reached a circulation
of 50,000 by 1850. In the twentieth century such a figure would
be regarded as a dismal failure for a big city newspaper, but in
the mid-nineteenth century it was a beacon of success.

Unfortunately the lighter touch of the new journalism diminishes their value as historical sources (except, perhaps, for the
historian of crime, humour, or popular taste). Editors reduced
the ponderous reporting and comment upon national and
international events, gave more space to local events, and to
stories which were interesting in themselves not merely because
they involved well-known people. Though the popular newspaper of 1850 looks restrained by the standards of the modern
press, it seemed sensational and shocking to conservative contemporaries and to upper-class visitors. The strongest impression
of a modern reader is not one of immorality but triviality;
and he may have to remind himself sharply that this is as close
as he is likely to get to the lives of ordinary and unrecorded
Americans.

A new epoch began in 1841 with the foundation of Horace
Greeley's New York *Tribune*, which he would edit with outstanding success for over thirty years. The *Tribune* combined the
dash and vigour of the popular dailies with serious purpose. It was
intended to interest and occasionally to shock, but the quality
of the writing was always high; for a whole generation it educated its readers in a wide range of reforming and humanitarian

causes and taught them to associate with these aspirations first the Whig and then the Republican party. By 1860 it had a daily circulation of 45,000, but its weekly edition was even more influential because of its wide distribution. Many years later John Ford Rhodes, who could remember the period and had immersed himself in its literature, wrote:

> I can emphatically say that if you want to penetrate into the thoughts, feelings and grounds of decision of the 1,866,000 who voted for Lincoln in 1860, you should study the New York *Weekly Tribune*... it was the greatest single journalistic influence in 1854 with a circulation of 112,000.[1]

For the historian the *Tribune* is not only an index of Republican feeling but also an insight into what progressive Republicans thought their party ought to be. In the South the *Charleston Mercury* and the *Charleston Courier* are equally invaluable for anyone who wishes to understand the rhetoric and well-springs of secession.

The New York *Times*, beginning in September 1851, aimed to serve a different purpose. In conscious imitation of its London namesake it aimed to provide the news and all the news, and to capture educated readers by sober comment and stylistic distinction. Its editor, Henry J. Raymond, became a power in the Republican party (he was chairman of the national committee in 1865), but spoke to and for a different brand of Republicanism than Greeley. The latter educated the rank-and-file with serious purpose; Raymond sought to influence the educated and well-to-do. The success of the paper in achieving its objective makes it a valuable source for historians; its reporting, both of domestic and foreign events, was fuller than that of any other newspaper, and though it spoke for the more conservative type of Republican, bias was less obtrusive than in most contemporaries.

[1] Quoted Lucy M. Salmon, *The Newspaper and the Historian* (New York, 1923), 471, from *Atlantic Monthly*, May 1909, 655. The *Tribune* has also been described as 'the first and only great vehicle this country has known for the ideas and experiments of constructive democracy'. J. R. Commons *et al.*, eds., *History of Industrial Society in America*, vii, 23.

In a way the older *National Intelligencer*, published in Washington, had tried to fill the role claimed by the *Times*. It was the principal Whig paper in the country and attempted to give full reporting; it survived for many years but hardly thrived. The local circulation was too small, particularly when Congress was not in session, to sustain an expensive newspaper; its editorial style was dull, and it tended to ignore events which were politically inconvenient. For instance, if one is studying the crisis of 1850 one can read the files of the *Intelligencer* without realising that a great controversy was brewing until in February there is a single disparaging reference to northern and southern extremism. However, the *Intelligencer* does enable one to penetrate into the Whig mind and especially the opinions of those Whigs who followed Henry Clay to the last.

Three newspapers in the state of New York rose to political influence in the years before the Civil War. The New York *Evening Post* was edited by William Cullen Bryant; it was at first a 'regular' Democratic paper, but after 1844 it moved more and more towards the radical anti-slavery position. The literary distinction of its editor and its radical leanings made the *Evening Post* the favourite newspaper of the New York intellectuals, most of whom ultimately became Republicans. The Albany *Evening Journal* was edited by Thurlow Weed, friend and political manager for William Henry Seward. Weed was one of the most adroit politicians of the day and a key man in the alliance which brought together the reforming Whigs of the North and the westerners who rallied to the banner of William Henry Harrison in 1840. Weed was distrusted by the silk-stocking Whigs of New York city and Boston, and he had as much responsibility as any man in defeating Clay's bid for nomination in 1840. He was accused, probably unjustly, of giving less than whole-hearted support to Clay in 1844 and thus contributing to the loss of New York and the Presidency. The *Evening Journal* was not a great newspaper and had little distinction or originality; but it was keenly watched as an indicator of the secret councils in the northern Whig and later Republican party. The New York *World*, edited with success by Manton Marble, was the organ of the conservative

New York Democrats; during the Civil War it was very luke-
warm in its support for the Union cause and vigorously supported the Peace Democracy in 1864. During the Reconstruction
period it was said to be the one northern newspaper with a large
circulation amongst southern readers. The assurance with which
it attacked the Radicals may have done a good deal to encourage
southern intransigeance. For a time the *World* accepted municipal
advertising from the city of New York, and supported the discreditable William M. Tweed; but in 1870 it broke abruptly
with 'the ring' and gave strong support to Samuel Tilden in his
successful attack upon boss rule.

After the Civil War one moves into a world of journalism
which grows more familiar to modern eyes. Improved methods
facilitated the printing of larger editions more quickly; the increasing size of cities provided a stronger circulation base; and
commercial advertisers bought more and more space. Under
this stimulus daily newspapers became larger; while the rapid
dissemination of telegraphic news by the Associated Press and the
spread of syndicated articles reduced the importance of the
weekly. Advertisers found it worth their while to place advertisements further from home, and even small local newspapers
might expect a share in the advertising for widely distributed
products. A new generation of editors was ready to take advan-
tage of the new conditions, and among them the best known was
Joseph Pulitzer who transformed the *World*.

To an increasing extent the great city newspapers maintained
staffs of specialist journalists, and kept permanent representatives
in Washington, in other parts of the country, and in foreign
capitals. The historian will find the late nineteenth-century
newspapers far more professional, and much better informed,
than their predecessors; but he will also miss the sense of dealing
with living people and handling human problems that one
gets from the thin, poorly printed, and often badly organised
newspapers of the earlier years.

The value of newspapers as historical evidence is obvious, but
their use is also full of dangers. The first danger lies in the assumption that, because something is in print, it is either typical

or influential. Most frequently an editor is writing what he thinks his readers want to read, but he may be misjudging them or he may be deliberately expressing a minority view. Editorial comment upon election results can be particularly unreliable; in particular an editor would consciously or unconsciously be influenced by a desire to justify his pre-election forecast or to attribute its inaccuracy to a single, identifiable and unpredictable cause. Nor is circulation a reliable guide to influence. The *Charleston Mercury* and Thurlow Weed's *Albany Evening Journal*, from 1840 to 1860, had far greater influence than their circulation might suggest, while Bennett's New York *Herald*, with a comparatively large and rising circulation, had little political significance. To understand either a single editorial or editorial policy over a period, or the selection of and prominence given to news, one may have to understand a great deal about the political and social environment.[1] In other words, the time for the analysis of newspaper material is at an advanced stage of an investigation and not, as so often happens, in its preliminary phase.

In the first half of the nineteenth century a great deal of the material in newspapers consisted of extracts from other newspapers, journals, or published speeches. Editors in different parts of the country exchanged copies, from which the recipient could publish extracts at his discretion. A number of columns were often occupied by these extracts from other newspapers, and the editorial might well fasten upon one of them for comment. One is therefore obtaining a double vision of the way in which opinion was moving in the country; first of what was being said or noticed in other parts of the country, and second, of what the local editor thought worthy of repetition or comment. Of course, many of these extracts deal with spectacular crimes, natural disasters, or unusual occurrences; but they also formed the most used channel through which information and political impressions flowed. By the middle of the century some eastern newspapers were using ingenious means to get early spot announcements

[1] 'The task of the historian is often not to ascertain what the press says, but to go behind the face of the returns and to determine why it says what it says, and what is the effect of what it has said.' Lucy M. Salmon, *op. cit.*, 36.

of European news, but the full story had to wait until the newspapers from Europe had been received, digested, and material extracted for publication. Sometimes, however, extracts from foreign newspapers were reprinted in full. This foreign news normally has little value for the historian unless he is trying to reconstruct the 'image' in the American mind of the outside world.

It is well known that southerners first experienced the shock of northern abolitionism through extracts from Garrison's *Liberator*, reprinted in the columns of their own local newspapers. The motives of southern editors in giving this kind of prominence to Garrison, while ignoring more common and typical expressions of friendship to the South, need not be discussed here; but the question illustrates the way in which an intelligent use of newspapers as a historical source will take one far beyond the mere recording of what appears in print. Theodore Weld adopted the same technique when he used southern newspapers as the major source for his influential *American Slavery As It Is* (1839). In turn, Charles Dickens used a great deal of Weld's material (without acknowledgement) in his *American Notes*. Incidentally, Weld's use of southern newspaper material also demonstrates the great value of advertising material for social historians; much of his indictment of southern slavery consisted of advertisements for runaway slaves with descriptions of their scars and other distinguishing marks.

Extracts on political questions reprinted from other newspapers were normally selected to provide supporting evidence for policies favoured by the editors or their political patrons. This might be either evidence of support in other parts of the country or of incidents demonstrating the need for action. From 1865 to 1870 Republican newspapers, and especially the *Tribune*, printed copious extracts from southern papers illustrating atrocities against freedmen and white unionists; at the same period the *World* was documenting, with equal thoroughness, the case against the Freedmen's Bureau and Radical Reconstruction. Neither was in the least degree objective, but set side by side they help to explain why different northerners came to have two entirely separate and incompatible views of the southern problem.

Advertisements in newspapers provide an invaluable source of information about economic life and social customs. They were the major channel through which not only governments and business men could reach the public, but also served anyone with services to offer, meetings to announce, or ideas to propagate. Coaches, canals, ships and railroads, imported goods, books and wine, lectures, concerts, theatrical performances and religious services pass like a pageant before one's eyes. The vivid impression of bustling activity of reformers in the mid-century was described in the following words:

> The columns of advertisements in a newspaper might announce for Monday night a meeting of the anti-slavery society; Tuesday night, the temperance society; Wednesday night, the Graham bread society; Thursday night, a phrenological lecture; Friday night, an address against capital punishment; Saturday night, the 'Association for Universal Reform'. Then there were all the missionary societies, the society for the diffusion of bloomers, the séances of spiritualists, the 'associationists', the land reformers – a medley of movements that found the week too short.[1]

A major difficulty for the historian is to assess the accuracy of press reports. The first amendment, and similar provisions in most state constitutions, protected newspapers against direct government interference, but the importance of public advertising has already been indicated. In the later years of the period one has to reckon with the undocumented influence of advertisers or of private interests with local political influence. In general one can surmise that private influence of this type was more likely to be general and cumulative than manifest on single occasions; an editor would have to calculate the effect—upon advertising revenue, official favour, and circulation—of reporting certain kinds of material with a special prominence and emphasis. At the other end of the scale, the law of libel limited what the press could report about individuals; but only a bold, obstinate or aggressive individual was likely to take legal action, and in

[1] J. R. Commons *et al.*, eds., *History of Industrial Society in America*, vii, 13.

practice newspapers could go a long way without fear of reprisals. In general it is unsafe to accept as evidence an unconfirmed press report, and even its repetition in another newspaper, or its supposed confirmation by later evidence in the same newspaper, is not conclusive. Too much popular history has placed too much credence upon newspaper reports without considering the full implications of the freedom of the press or assessing the motives at work in reporting particular incidents.

An interesting American innovation was the press interview with notable persons; the first appeared during the Civil War, but was rare until after 1868.[1] The historian will be too much aware of human fallibility to accept uncritically the evidence of a personal interview; at least, if he encounters any statement which appears surprising, he will wish to look either for corroborative evidence or for a subsequent denial. This is, of course, still more true of remarks attributed to individuals but not directly reported. Particularly in the later years of this period political partisanship was intense—and lacking major issues, often relied upon personal attacks—and certain kinds of individual were extremely unpopular with many classes of reader. Railroad magnates, predatory financiers, and political bosses were fair game and unlikely to receive disinterested treatment except in those newspapers which they owned or influenced. The later nineteenth century saw a number of unattractive people in positions of power, but the element of caricature which has pervaded study of the 'gilded age' owes a good deal to uncritical acceptance of hostile newspaper reports.

Another danger lies in the excessive influence, upon historical interpretation, of those newspapers which are most available, most articulate and (as described above) most frequently quoted in other sheets. It seems that accounts of economic conditions, from 1816 to 1818, may have been distorted by paying too much attention to north-eastern newspapers with their emphasis upon the difficulties of shipping and manufactures, and too little to those from the prosperous cotton belt. At a later period the economic retardation of the South has been exaggerated by

[1] Lucy M. Salmon, *op. cit.*, 233.

attention paid to South Carolina newspapers and neglect of those from Georgia, Alabama and Mississippi. The southern Whig press has hardly been noticed except by local historians. It is only recently that historians have begun to use the lesser newspapers of the mid-west as evidence for Republican politics and racial attitudes, and the changes in opinion which led to acceptance of the fifteenth amendment have yet to be studied in the Republican press.

Thus newspapers, in all their diversity, provide the most intimate and vital source for the life and opinions of the people; but no source requires greater circumspection in its use or makes more demands upon the accumulated skills of a trained historian. In the hands of the novice or the enthusiastic amateur they can be used to provide documentary evidence for what is, in fact, local, idiosyncratic, or merely untrue.

Throughout the nineteenth century many Americans depended more upon magazines than upon newspapers for their knowledge of the world. The number of magazines grew rapidly, but the failures were even more numerous than amongst newspapers. In 1795 five magazines were recorded, by 1800 there were twelve and by 1810 forty. But only three of those started in the eighteenth century lived for more than two years, and not until 1811 was a magazine able to celebrate its tenth birthday.[1] Nevertheless the men who launched magazines were inspired by the same spirit of hopeful enterprise as the editors of newspapers. By 1825 there were nearly a hundred extant, and in the first quarter of the

---

[1] Frank Luther Mott, *A History of American Magazines* (New York, 1957), 3 vols, i, 120. This, like the same author's study of newspapers cited above, is an invaluable work. It is, perhaps, unavoidable that Mott's own preferences should influence the emphasis which he gives to various types of magazines. Wallace E. Davies, who has made a close study of the patriotic press in the late nineteenth century, observes that 'Mott devotes two sentences to veterans' magazines, mentioning only three of them, sandwiched next to the barbers and the launderers in the chapter on "Journals for Printing and Other Crafts" '. *Patriotism on Parade* (Cambridge, Mass., 1955), 104. Mott can also be criticised for insufficient emphasis upon the religious magazines; but on magazines dealing with politics and the main stream of literature he is excellent.

nineteenth century probably five to six hundred had lived (and mostly died). In 1824 the *Cincinnati Literary Gazette* proclaimed

> This is the Age of Magazines –
> Even skeptics must confess it:
> Where is the town of much renown
> That has not one to bless it?[1]

The next quarter century saw a further flood of magazines with perhaps 600 in circulation in 1850, but the rate of failure remained very high with the average life estimated at not more than two years. The number fell between 1850 and 1860, but the expectation of life increased to about four years.

Most of these magazines were either literary or religious, with the latter showing much greater capacity for survival. The majority of literary magazines hardly got beyond a local coterie in their quest for circulation, and 'even the names of a large proportion of these ephemerae are sunk in oblivion'.[2] Even successful magazines had very small circulations; the *Port Folio* (a lively political magazine, strongly Federalist in its politics) had only two thousand readers in 1801; and the *North American Review* — destined to become a major cultural influence—had only between five and six thousand in 1820. Religious magazines were better placed to break through local barriers and to circulate more widely amongst members of the denominations they represented, but even so, circulation was likely to be confined to ministers and a handful of pious laymen. In a literate society, however, the circulation, though limited, might cover a wide social spectrum. In 1857 the *National Era*, organ of the politically active abolitionists, lamented the onset of depression for 'many of our subscribers are among the intelligent mechanics and industrial classes of the North, and we hear by every mail that some of them, thrown out of employment, cannot find the money to renew their subscriptions'.[3]

A major publishing event was the appearance, in 1811, of *Niles' Weekly Register*. This could be classified as either a magazine

---

[1] Mott, *op. cit.*, i, 126. Quoting from *Cincinnati Literary Gazette*, 28 Feb 1824.
[2] *Ibid.*, i, 342.   [3] *Ibid.*, ii, 5.

or a weekly newspaper; though its format made it resemble the latter. It continued publication until 1849, and provides a major source of information for historians. Hezekiah Niles was a Baltimore man, strongly National Republican and later Whig in politics, but he aimed to provide a comparatively impartial summary of the week's political events. Niles printed lengthy extracts from official documents and political speeches; he supplied information about finance, trade, prices, and economic affairs in general; he often reprinted passages from newspapers in different parts of the country, but the extracts were usually longer than those in the newspapers; finally, he allowed a good deal of space for correspondence on political and economic questions. As a source for the history of the first half of the nineteenth century *Niles'* is therefore invaluable; it is true that almost all the information can be obtained elsewhere, but what one has is an unfolding picture of the world of politics and economics as it was seen by educated Americans of the period.

Major magazines devoted to politics which printed original contributions were the *American Whig Review*, appearing under slightly varying titles from 1840 to 1852, and the *United States Magazine and Democratic Review* from 1837. The former has been somewhat neglected by historians, though it contained articles of considerable importance; the latter has been a quarry for quotable phrases and arguments illustrating Democratic thought in the age of Jackson and after. Another magazine which has been much used by historians was *De Bow's Review*, first published in New Orleans in 1845. J. B. D. De Bow was a man of experience and distinction. He was superintendent of the census for a short period, and the primary purpose of his *Review* was to gather information about the South and to disseminate views and arguments about the southern society and economy. The use of *De Bow's Review* as an historical source illustrates, however, the danger of reliance upon a single powerful journal. De Bow believed that the South was exploited by the North, and more than anyone else he was responsible for giving currency to the interpretation of southern society as a 'colony' paying tribute. Like Niles, he relied mainly upon reprinting articles, speeches, and statistical information; but to a much greater extent than Niles he chose his material to make a case and preach a doctrine. He aimed to reach the larger planters, merchants, and would-be manufacturers of the South; but the majority of the southern upper class which followed Henry Clay in the 1840s was unrepresented. One can therefore study in De Bow the genesis, rise and development of southern separatism, but one is not getting a true cross-section of southern opinion. Nor was De Bow in any way representative of the 'plain people' amongst whom he was unlikely to find many readers.

A different kind of venture was represented by the *North American Review*, founded in 1819 with Edward Everett as its first editor. Though published in Boston the *North American Review* aimed at a national circulation, and the example of the *Edinburgh Review* was consciously imitated. The main interest in the *North American* is, however, its function as a lively transmitter of European ideas; much of its space being given to articles on European (and particularly British) literature, society and politics. The *North American* achieved its greatest success under the editorship of Alexander Everett (brother of Edward) between 1830 and 1836. After that it continued for many years but became more and more the staid journal of the Boston upper class.[1]

The *Southern Quarterly*, edited in Charleston, South Carolina, was a deliberate attempt to assert the claim for southern cultural independence. Its articles—mainly (following the *Edinburgh Review*) in the form of lengthy reviews of books—were polemical and very well written. Like *De Bow's*, the *Southern Quarterly* represented only a portion of southern opinion; it appealed especially to old nullifiers and young secessionists, but employed its rhetoric in winning converts to the cause. It is a valuable source for southern thought of this *genre*.

Eighteen-fifty was a landmark in the history of American magazines, for it saw the appearance of Harper's *New Monthly Magazine*. It aimed at a much wider circulation, and to cover, more or less at random, all cultural questions which might interest educated readers. It included pictures and specialised in

[1] Most information in this and the following paragraphs is derived from Mott's *History of American Magazines* (see p. 188 n. 1).

serialised fiction (mainly from British novelists), biography, and travel accounts; but in later years it also included some articles which made a serious contribution to political debate. *Putnam's Monthly Magazine*, founded in 1853, aimed to provide the rising American intelligentsia with a forum for writing and criticism, but it failed to survive; for a little less than five years, however, it is an important source for intellectual history.

The anti-slavery movement imitated the denominational religious press by using magazines as a principal means of keeping members in touch with one another, drawing attention to meetings and publications, and disseminating views about slavery. In format William Lloyd Garrison's *Liberator* was a newspaper rather than a magazine, but the contents put it rather in the latter category. Though the circulation of the *Liberator* was never large, copies were widely distributed (some even reaching British friends of American abolitionism), and probably passed from hand to hand in many local anti-slavery societies. As a source of information about slavery, national politics, and even non-Garrisonian anti-slavery men, it is tendentious and unreliable; but anyone who wishes to understand the ideological main-spring of American abolitionism cannot ignore the *Liberator*. It was also much better written than less extreme anti-slavery journals such as *The National Anti-Slavery Standard* and the *New Era* which first appeared as the organ of the Liberty Party and later of Free-Soilers who supported abolitionism. The *New Era*, however, achieved some kind of immortality by publishing, as a serial, *Uncle Tom's Cabin*. Black abolitionism was represented by *Frederick Douglass' Paper* and the *Afro-American Magazine*.

A new epoch in the history of magazines began in 1857 with the appearance of *Harper's Weekly*. Like its monthly progenitor, it published some serialised fiction and other literary features, but it was designed largely to cover politics. It also carried pictures, and these became an increasingly important part of the magazine, as an invaluable record of life during the period. *Harper's Weekly* was Democratic in politics, and vigorously critical of anti-slavery agitation; in 1860 it solved the dilemmas of that year by largely ignoring politics and concentrating upon the visit of the

Prince of Wales. Eulogistic notices appeared of the seceding southern Congressmen, but when war came *Harper's* gave reluctant support to the Union. A great change came in 1862 with the appointment of George William Curtis as editor and Thomas Nast as principal artist; both were vigorous Republicans and for over twenty years *Harper's Weekly* was to be a unique and powerful influence within the Republican party. Nast was a strong Radical, Curtis was more moderate; but both belonged to the reforming wing of their party. Mr Frank Luther Mott must have read more dull, decayed or pathetic magazines than any living person, and one can therefore give special weight to his verdict that 'the old files of *Harper's Weekly* are a delight to the casual reader and a rich treasury for the historical investigator'. During the war artists were sent to the front, and serving officers were encouraged to send in material (which got *Harper's* into some mild trouble with the military authorities). After the war it became celebrated for its successful attack upon the Tweed ring in New York. In 1884, however, it lost many Republican readers by opposing Blaine and supporting Cleveland.

Throughout *Harper's* long Republican period the caricatures of Thomas Nast had an immediate impact and have since been reproduced more frequently than those of any other American caricaturist and illustrate countless histories. Nast's caricatures were vigorous, skilful, and often merciless. He left that genial rogue William Marcy Tweed without a shred of reputation or dignity; he invented the Elephant and Donkey symbols for the two major parties; and he pilloried every prominent man on the other side of politics. With him, however, caricature was something more than pictorial polemics and became a conscious instrument for moral regeneration.

A landmark of another kind was the launching in 1865 of the *Nation*, designed as a 'journal of opinion' to stand comparison with the *Spectator* of London. The idea was originated by F. L. Olmstead, journalist, distinguished author of *The Cotton Kingdom*, and secretary of the United States Sanitary Commission, in which capacity he met and worked with most leading men of the New York and Philadelphia upper middle class. It was this 'informed public' that the *Nation* was intended to enlighten. But when the *Nation* was eventually published, Olmstead had moved to the west, and the editor was E. L. Godkin, an expatriate Englishman, who became an oracle in the land for many years to come. Godkin enlisted many prominent contributors, most of whom have been identified, but the articles were anonymous and frequently suffered severe editorial pruning and rewriting, so that it is the periodical which has a distinctive style rather than the individual writers. The first orientation of the *Nation* was definitely Radical; as time went on it became more and more interested in civil service reformation, low tariffs, and proportional representation. By the 1880s it was 'mugwump' and a long way from regular Republicanism. James R. Lowell believed that the *Nation* did 'more good and influenced public opinion more than any other agency, or all others combined, in the country'; but the distinction of the *Nation* lay in its deliberate appeal to the highly educated and its refusal to make concessions to popularity. Its faithful and influential subscribers never exceeded 12,000 and were often much fewer than this. Thus, for the historian, the problem of evaluating the *Nation* is entirely different from that of other nineteenth-century American magazines; it represents the convictions of an élite, as interpreted by one vigorous and masterful mind.

Four other magazines of special importance may be briefly noticed. The *Atlantic Monthly*, founded in 1857, was to be a more lively and modernised organ of New England intelligentsia than the *North American Review*. It had three distinguished editors (J. R. Lowell to 1867, James T. Field, 1867–71, and William Dean Howells, 1871–81); it carried some important articles on Reconstruction, but its major interest is for the historian of American literature. *Vanity Fair*, which began in 1859, was the first attempt to provide a comic, illustrated paper which was not vulgar; in many ways it was an early progenitor of the modern satirical press, but in the North at war it attacked the wrong people—abolitionists and Negroes—and collapsed in 1863. Another venture on the same lines was *Puck*, which began in 1877 and reached a circulation of nearly 90,000 by 1890; closely following the English *Punch*, its main aim was to provide high-class humour, but it became a political influence through its caricatures (mainly by Joseph Keppler). A very different member of this mixed bag was *The Scientific American* which began as a weekly in 1845. In 1846 it came under the control of Orson Munn and Alfred Beach, who successfully ran a double career as editors and patent agents. Every patent handled by the firm was noticed, and there were major articles on many of them. Many other articles on scientific and technological matters were included, and the magazine is thus a prime source for these aspects of American history. In 1876, to mark the centennial, the *Scientific American Weekly Supplement* was launched, which was devoted more to theoretical questions. Munn and Beach were early enthusiasts for aviation and underground railways; these and their other interests mark them out as prophets of twentieth-century civilisation.

A specialist press grew alongside newspapers and journals appealing to a wider audience; provided that it was fairly modest in its aims, the specialist journal could keep a ready-made core of readers. The most important examples were in law and medicine, both serving professions in which up-to-date information and argument was of the first importance. The medical magazines are not likely to provide much for the general historian, though much for historians of medicine and science. The legal journals, though of primary interest to historians of the law and constitution, also contain important articles dealing with fundamental American concepts of justice, freedom, and equality. Considering the fact that the courts were often the battleground for political ideas and interests, and that most public men were also lawyers, general historians have paid surprisingly little attention to the legal press. Journals published by economic interest groups have long been used by historians specialising in the fields served by this press.

One magazine of specialised interest deserves separate notice. *Hunt's Merchant Magazine* was published monthly from 1839 until 1870; from 1865 onwards it also published the weekly *Commercial and Financial Chronicle* which survived. In its heyday

Hunt's was the principal magazine for intelligent businessmen (perhaps a precursor of *Fortune*), and its files contain a mass of lucidly presented material on economic subjects. The general historian might, perhaps, devote more attention to this unique compendium of nineteenth-century business which sought not only to inform but also to impress upon its readers the importance of maintaining high moral standards in commercial life. For information on the journals of particular industries and of organised labour the reader may be referred to specialised bibliographies of their respective subjects.

During the nineteenth century there were therefore emerging four main types of periodical: the literary or political review, all started, no doubt, with ambitious plans, but achieving in only a few instances longevity and enlarged circulation; the religious and polemical magazine designed to serve a cause rather than to make money; the popular magazine aiming to provide material of varied character for an educated public which was growing in size but expected to have its interest aroused by attractive presentation; and professional journals covering a wide range of interests, but mainly designed to promote the fortunes of a particular occupation or social group. Each of these types has importance as a source of history, and it requires only the discrimination of historians to decide what their use should be. Collectively they provide a growing body of information about the life and thought of the people.

One obstacle, gradually overcome, was the cost of printing and distributing publications. The Postal Act of 1794 permitted the carriage of magazines by mail, but required the consent of local postmasters; this was not usually difficult to obtain, though in the 1830s it provided the precedent by which southern postmasters could confiscate abolitionist literature. The postal charges were however high, increased with distance, were borne by the subscriber, and thus added substantially to the cost of a magazine. Reference has been made above to the Post Office Act of 1852 which remedied this. This real break-through came with the extension of the railroads, which greatly lowered distribution costs, whether by mail or as freight. During the Civil War the cost of paper rose sharply, and in the South both paper and ink almost disappeared. At the same period, however, production costs were being progressively reduced, and even *Harper's* illustrations were handled comparatively cheaply.[1] After the Civil War, therefore, the economics of the press moved on to a modern basis, and as circulation increased, advertising revenue grew. Greater economic security could, however, introduce carelessness over the standards of editorship; the periodical of the late nineteenth century was cheaper and technically vastly improved, but the struggling magazines of the pre-Civil War period were often of greater literary distinction and, for the historian, of greater interest in the arguments employed.

The nineteenth century was a great age for pamphlet literature. In any large library these ephemeral productions—with which innumerable forgotten men hoped to make significant contributions to knowledge or debate—fill much shelf space. They range from slight productions of three or four pages to small treatises of a hundred or more. The range covered is enormous, from political polemics to religious meditation and scientific papers. Pamphlets played an essential part in any political campaign, and every tide of political controversy left loads of hastily-produced and ill-printed pages stranded on the foreshore. A few have survived as major contributions to debate; the great majority will never be read again save by the diligent searcher after historical knowledge.

A description of nineteenth-century pamphlet literature would itself fill many pages, and it is possible to indicate only the main course of development and the principal categories in this class of literature. Pamphlet literature played an important part in the revolutionary period, and the political controversy of 1790 to 1800 produced a growing volume; but at this early period the

[1] Intense political activity combined with these changes to promote many new publishing ventures. In 1850 there were 1,630 political newspapers and periodicals; in 1860 there were 3,242. J. C. G. Kennedy, *Preliminary Report of the 8th Census* (Washington, 1862).

cost of paper and printing was still high, and poor communications limited distribution. The most prolific age for pamphleteering was from about 1840 to the Civil War. After the Civil War the magazines provided an alternative outlet for serious discussion, and the importance of the pamphlet diminished, although the number published actually increased. The trend was towards using the pamphlet for specialised or freakish writing which would not appeal to normal newspaper or magazine readers.

For the historian the number of pamphlets published, and the range of topics covered, is often more important than their text. Reprints of political speeches account for a high proportion of pamphlets during the peak period, and if these were first delivered in Congress, they are probably more easily found in the *Congressional Globe*. The pamphlet version is, however, normally the speaker's final revision, and may therefore be stylistically superior; but as speakers also revised their own speeches for the *Appendix* to the *Globe*, there is not likely to be a great deal of difference between the two versions. Indeed, many pamphlets of this class are reprints from the *Appendix* to the *Globe*, circulated from Washington under the Congressmen's franking privilege. It may, however, often happen that the speech appearing in pamphlet form is one first made to the Congressman's own constituents, and in this case the pamphlet may be the only record, save what might be found by patient research into local files.

Pamphlets were also issued to record the proceedings of societies and other unofficial bodies, and by private individuals as serious contributions to debate over public questions. The slavery controversy brought forth an enormous flood of pamphlet literature, and this illustrates the special role of the pamphlet. Abolitionists were unlikely to have their pieces accepted in 'respectable' journals, while few northern journals would accept more than the barest minimum of occasional items covering slavery; if the abolitionists were to reach the public at all, and if pro-slavery arguments were to be heard in the North, the pamphlet was the only means of doing so. The student of the slavery controversy must therefore immerse himself in the pamphlet literature produced on both sides of the argument.

For somewhat similar reasons the spokesmen of organised labour, who had little hope of gaining the public ear in any other way, resorted to pamphlets to argue their case. The special value of pamphlets, as a historical source, lies, therefore, in those areas where the parties to a controversy were denied access to the normal channels of communication. One should not, even in such instances, expect too much. A pamphlet was in the form of a public appeal; it was rhetorical rather than exact; it may convey conviction and commitment, but the facts adduced in support are often suspect. Pamphlets may convey a lively sense of ideological struggle, and are therefore not to be neglected; but unproven assertions may be more frequent than verifiable facts.

In assessing the importance of the press, periodicals, and pamphlets it is important to remember that one is dealing with a literate people. Even in the South the number of completely illiterate adult whites was not so great as is sometimes supposed. The printed word reached more people than in any other country, with the possible exception of Scotland, and the male readers were also voters who could decide great issues and make or break the careers of politicians. In Europe the majority of newspapers were written for a minority of the people, while periodicals and pamphlets were intended, almost exclusively, for a very small and highly educated public. Foreign visitors contrasted the tone of the American press unfavourably with their own; they failed to recognise that literacy and wide suffrage required the American press to play a different role. A modern reader, accustomed to modern journalism, may well be more impressed by the restraint and responsibility of editors, journalists and publicists in this first democratic society. The New York *Herald*, and other minor city newspapers, might exploit crime and report in lurid terms, but the great majority of newspapers intended to be serious and were taken seriously.

British visitors found the newspapers crude in expression and often naïve in inspiration; but what they really missed was the background of allusion and shared knowledge which bound together men who had passed through the same educational mill.

There was a great deal that a British newspaper or magazine did not need to say because writers and readers dealt in the same common currency of ideas and experience; the American press had to say more, but in doing so could easily fall into rhetoric, exaggeration, or over-simplification.

The historian must always bear this simple fact in mind. The 'public opinion' which he tries to diagnose from the pages of newspapers is not the opinion of an educated élite; but it is the opinion of men who had to decide important issues. Magazines had a more limited objective, and their tone often consciously imitated that of their distinguished British contemporaries, but success and influence depended upon winning a wider audience. Not only was the American upper class intelligentsia much smaller than that of Britain, but it was also scattered more widely; it was difficult for any magazine to flourish without a strong local base, and outside Massachusetts this meant drawing in readers who were fully literate but not highly educated. This applies with even more force to pamphlets which were, so often, written to influence public questions. A pamphlet which could be appreciated in a London club might be wholly ineffective in America.

CHAPTER 10

Planters, Farmers, and Agricultural Labour

It was noticed in an earlier chapter that official statistics on agricultural production were scantier, before 1860, than one might expect in a predominantly rural country. Except for cotton, there was little political incentive for discovering the facts; Congress was not called upon for legislation affecting agriculture, and the decennial censuses provided all the information that was necessary about the number and type of farms. There is, however, a good deal of unpublished information in the Federal Archives and in the archives of the separate states. Most of the information in the Federal Archives refers to disposal of land from the public domain, and therefore provides more evidence for the early stages of settlement and development than for stable agriculture in the older regions. Manuscript census returns provide more information about land-holding than the published tables. State archives can furnish tax returns, title deeds, and records of litigation. Both the Federal and local archives may provide maps which mark the land holdings.

The activity of the Federal government was considerable. The leading authority on agricultural history, writing of the period between 1815 and 1860, has observed,

> The business of surveying, sectioning, advertising, selling and collecting the proceeds constituted the largest single area of economic activity in the country and a major obligation of the Federal government. It is difficult for people of later generations to realise the extent to which the government was engaged in the land business in the nineteenth century ... No problem so continuously absorbed the attention of Congress ... as that of the management, sale, and donation of this great empire.[1]

[1] Paul W. Gates, *The Farmer's Age* (New York, 1960), 51.

There were twenty-one land offices in 1818, thirty-six in 1822, and seventy-eight in 1860. Each office kept a register of tracts, surveys with descriptions of land, and a record of all sales and payments. The registrarship and receivership at each land office were valuable pieces of patronage, as the commission on sales was $2\frac{1}{2}$ per cent, of which 1 per cent went to the registrar and $1\frac{1}{2}$ per cent to the receiver. The latter was, however, responsible for the safe-keeping of considerable quantities of cash, which he might be compelled to hold until it was convenient to visit a bank authorised to receive deposits.[1] The land offices sent duplicate copies of their principal transactions to Washington, and ultimately all the land office records were transferred to the Federal Archives. The records not only covered surveys and sales, but also investigation of squatters' claims and negotiations with large purchasers. A new era opened in 1862 with the Homestead Act which required the investigation of the use and cultivation of land after five years' occupancy. It is safe to say that no other nation has so full, varied or voluminous a record of agricultural settlement and early growth.

An example of what can be accomplished is the study of a single township in Wisconsin from materials in the National Archives.[2] A detailed map, prepared by David Dale Owen for the General Land Office of South West Wisconsin, was the starting-point. This included detailed annotated plans of townships with the names of owners of houses, the length of time of residence, and the nature of the holdings; also the names of owners or operators of mills, mines and furnaces. This was compared with the manuscript census schedules, and miscellaneous records of the General Land Office (e.g., records of purchase). In this particular area the main attraction was the existence of lead mines; a law of 1807 laid down that land where lead was located should not be sold, but leased to operators, and in 1821 the responsibility for the supply of lead was transferred to the Treasury and the Ordnance Department. This carried the

[1] Gates, *op. cit.*, 54.
[2] Jane F. Smith, 'The Use of Federal Records in Writing Local History', *Prologue* (The Journal of the National Archives), i, No. 1 (1969), 29.

search for information to the records of these departments, and in 1824 a Superintendent of Lead Mines was appointed. The Superintendent corresponded with the Secretary for War, the Adjutant-General, and the Commissioner of the General Land Office. In 1827 Colonel Henry Dodge, later to be Governor of Wisconsin Territory and a United States Senator, arrived, and the papers of an important public man are therefore included in the range of enquiry. Indian troubles bring in the archives of the Bureau of Indian Affairs. In 1834 a large number of immigrants, especially from Cornwall, arrived, and disputes over the occupancy of land led to a report by the General Land Office. Finally, the records of the Post Office yielded information about postmasters and mail routes.

This case history has been cited because it happens to have been investigated, and because it provides a good example of the way in which national archives, drawn from several departments, can be used to build up the history of a single area. Doubtless the picture would be given more life and character from local sources, but 'at all periods in our history Federal records have provided the broader framework to give local records greater meaning'.[1] The Wisconsin example is not typical because important minerals meant that the Federal Government was involved in the development of the district for a longer period than normal. There was also an unusually complete map prepared at what proved to be a crucial period in the history of the township. Nevertheless, the Federal Archives are likely to provide essential information about many purely rural areas, and in some sparsely populated regions (without courts, newspapers, or local business) they may well prove to be the only available sources.

It is often more difficult to obtain detailed information once the early days have passed. The sources (e.g., newspapers) may be more abundant, but the evidence will be unsystematic and often reflect the views and special interests of editors. As usual, with this kind of source, evidence of what was exceptional will be easier to find than evidence of what was normal and unremarkable. Local agricultural societies, where they existed, are

1 *Ibid.*, 51.

important sources of information; their published proceedings were often concerned with propaganda rather than description but their unpublished papers, where these have been preserved, cover a wide range of topics. The agricultural societies tended to represent the views of the larger and more enterprising farmers, and the smaller and unprogressive farmers may be mentioned only as examples of poor agricultural practice. In court records, also, the larger landowners are likely to figure more frequently than the small.

The nature of the sources is therefore likely to distort the picture of farming life, with disproportionate emphasis upon large and active farmers while silence reigns over the lives of their more numerous neighbours. It is also likely that far more evidence survives from hard times than from good. For instance, the panic of 1819 set off a round of angry debates in state legislatures in which the miseries of the farmers were adduced as grounds for stay laws, paper currency, or more generous banking credit. In 1837 and the following years there was a further round of debate, though at this period the misfortunes of manufacturers and indebted states were more frequently discussed. Even when the difficulties of farming were widely discussed the emphasis is likely to be slanted towards the larger owners, for while the distress of small cultivators was a stock item of agricultural oratory, the spokesmen were likely to be substantial farmers or lawyers allied with them.

A very large number of travel accounts—the majority by British visitors—commented upon various aspects of American agriculture. Most of the British travellers, drawn from the upper classes, had been brought up in rural districts, and had been accustomed from youth to casting a critical eye over soil, crops, cultivation and livestock. Accustomed to the intensive agriculture of the British Isles, which had benefited so greatly from eighteenth- and early nineteenth-century improvement, their comments upon wasteful cultivation, untidy fields, and poor livestock were often scathing.[1] In the southern states British travellers were often more concerned to study the effects of slavery than the problems

[1] Gates, *op. cit.*, 3, 23, 428–30.

of farming, and few of them travelled beyond the main plantation areas. American travellers from the North-East were scarcely
less critical of western and southern farming. One is therefore
more likely to receive a sharper impression of the weak points of
American agriculture rather than of its strength.[1]

Of all American agriculturalists the large planters of the South
have left the greatest volume of source materials. Hundreds of
plantation accounts have survived; many planters kept diaries—
sometimes primarily as business journals but often including
many personal details—and letters about plantation management
are abundant. Planters wrote to their overseers and received
letters from them; crops, slaves and politics were staple fare for
letters between planters or members of their families. Planters'
wives added to the volume of literary evidence about plantation
life. Agricultural societies, the writings of agricultural improvers,
newspapers, and debates in the state legislatures add their evidence.
There are numerous court records, especially concerning the
ownership of slaves and claims for freedom. Upper-class travellers
were more likely to visit the great houses, and to record their
impressions. Indeed, a large class of travel literature, pur-
porting to explain the south to the outside world, was based
upon the experience of a comparatively small number of large
plantations (mainly in Virginia, South Carolina, Georgia and
Louisiana).

For many of the great plantations it is therefore possible to
reconstruct daily life in great detail over a number of years and
the cumulative evidence provides exceptionally full information
about a defunct social system. Amongst rural societies perhaps
only Great Britain and France can yield evidence of comparable
extent. It is therefore a comment on the fallibility and relativism
of historical judgment that the two authorities who have studied
this evidence most closely—Ulrich B. Phillips and Kenneth
Stampp—formed very different impressions. It is true that the
major difference between them was in their qualitative judgment upon slavery (which will be dealt with elsewhere),

[1] These points are made frequently in Thomas D. Clark, ed. *Travels in the
Old South: a Bibliography* (Norman, 1956–9).

205

but this affected their views on almost all aspects of plantation life.

The study of the southern plantation offers, then, a unique challenge in the understanding and use of sources. So much is known; but different value judgments mean that the same evidence can appear in very different guises. If, however, one abandons extreme views, reconciliation may be easier to achieve than might be anticipated; every social system will produce some saints and many sinners, good personal relations will often mitigate vicious laws, and few men confess—even to themselves—to being brutes. There will remain a basic disagreement as to whether slavery did more to encourage wickedness than kindly masters did to mitigate its abuses, and this will inevitably influence the use of evidence. A master may admit to severity but not to cruelty; and leave unanswered the question whether sadism was a conscious or unconscious response to the system. Paternalism can be represented as hypocrisy, but it can also result from a genuine impulse to set oneself right with the world and with eternity. In administering discipline a planter might be moved by vindictiveness, but he might equally perform with distaste a duty which he felt that he owed to society.

Econometricians have claimed to deliver historians from the tyranny of subjective judgments; if one cannot judge a man's morals, at least one can estimate his profits. Unfortunately, the claim to objectivity can hardly be sustained. The evidence on costs and prices is abundant, but few southern planters had any idea of modern accountancy. They kept accounts to keep track of their money, not to draw up sophisticated balance sheets or satisfy inquisitive shareholders.[1] There are, therefore, few and crude attempts to cost overheads, allow for depreciation, or to consider investment as a long-term proposition. Most planters—at least in the older parts of the south—were mainly concerned with keeping up the style of life to which they were accustomed, not to place their money where it could earn the highest return. Arguments over the profitability of slavery are therefore likely to

[1] Cf. Richard P. Brief, 'The Origin and Evolution of Nineteenth Century Asset Accounting', *Business History Review*, xl (1966), 1 ff.

stumble over the inadequacy of the evidence and the refusal of planters to act as economic men.[1]

A great deal will, of course, depend upon whether one is studying an individual or an area, or trying to generalise about the whole social system. In the large number of cases a single plantation or a select district can be examined in great detail; but individuals differed, and there were marked contrasts between different regions. The broad differences between planters on old land of the upper South and new land of the south-western cotton belt have always been recognised, but the problem of differentiation can be pushed much further and the common factor of slave labour has led historians much too far along the road to uniformity. If it had not been for slavery, the many contrasts between planters engaged in raising different crops, under different climatic conditions, serving different markets, and operating on different scales would have been more widely recognised and emphasised. Of course, close students of the old South are aware of these things, but general historians have too often allowed their vision to be distorted by preoccupation with one particular type of evidence—that relating to slave labour. In this, of course, they have done no more than reflect the obsession of contemporaries; but the profession of history should demand a little more.

If the planters of the South are the best documented group in the nation's history, the small farmers of the South are almost the worst. The discovery of much about their lives from patient work upon the census schedules has already been mentioned; court records have also yielded some evidence, but the sources remain meagre. Many of the 'plain people' were illiterate, and few of those who were literate were ready with the pen. They kept few

[1] The implied doubt should not detract from the value of the work which has introduced *some* standards of objective judgement into a field long dominated by prejudice. The pioneer work was Alfred H. Conrad and John R. Meyer, 'The Economics of Slavery in the Ante-Bellum South', *Journal of Political Economy*, lxvi (1958), 95–130. The most recent survey of the controversy, with a full bibliography and further calculations, is Robert W. Fogel and Stanley L. Engerman, 'The Economics of Slavery' in *Reinterpretations of American Economic History* (New York, 1971). At the time of writing a major work by the same authors has been announced for early publication.

accounts, and cash for goods sold in the local market was likely to be spent almost as soon as received. Many of their transactions were by bartering goods and services. Occasionally their political needs were aired in state legislatures, but only in a limited and sporadic way. Few travellers came their way.

Contemporaries were as ignorant as posterity about the 'plain people'. Indeed, some sectional misunderstanding can be explained in this way; there was, for instance, the now well-known fact that northern Republicans, led by Lincoln, persistently over-estimated the latent Unionism in the South, and expected the 'true men of the South' (cast in the Jeffersonian yeoman mould) to take command once the dangers of upper class secessionism stood revealed. It should, however, be noticed that where modern scholarly work has begun on this neglected class, it has necessarily operated upon different principles than research on the greater planters. The sources for plantation life consist very largely of personal documents and accounts, and they have been studied to establish, test or challenge generalisations about the system as a whole. The sources for the life of the plain farmers are mainly impersonal, and their use requires concentration upon compara-tively small areas. An analysis of census schedules for a county— let alone for a state—is time-consuming, and can absorb much academic labour. Computers may be brought in to help, but the task will remain formidable.

Another aspect of southern agriculture for which the sources are weak is the important question of the South's commercial and financial structure. In spite of the well-known dependence of southern planters upon the North, very little direct correspond-ence seems to have survived. Indeed, a recent study has shown how much of the work was actually done by factors, so that the full picture must portray the relationship between planter and factor and between factor and northern merchants.[1] Generations of historians have accepted (with minor qualifications) the picture of sectional relations presented by advocates such as J. B. D. De Bow, and other ardent propagandists for southern independence.

[1] Harold D. Woodman, *King Cotton and His Retainers* (Lexington, Ky, 1968) studies the place of the factor in the southern economy.

This thesis was reinforced by economic interpreters who seized upon the 'exploitation' of the South by 'the North' as an explanation of the Civil War. It can, however, be said with some confidence that there would have been no secession if the economic leaders in both sections had had their way. The northern and southern economies did not compete but complemented each other, and for large planters and wealthy northern merchants the relationship had been profitable. This is the obverse of the coin of secessionist rhetoric; but what is required is systematic study of the sources which will enable one to establish a full picture of the diverse and complex economic relationship before the Civil War.[1]

In the same way one knows extraordinarily little about the real economic relationship between the developing society of the East and western agriculture. The finance of agricultural expansion has been studied in the round rather than in detail, and (as in the North and South relationship) contemporary political rhetoric has dominated historical writing for far too long. Speeches against the Bank of the United States are important episodes in political history, but they can be extremely misleading as sources of information about economic relationships. The marketing and distribution of agricultural produce; the supply of manufactured goods, and all the links in the chain between farmer, local merchant, eastern merchant, international trader, and foreign buyer have yet to be studied in detail. Associated with this field are the perennial topics of internal improvement, railroad promotion, and the rivalry between cities for the trade of the great agricultural regions. The western farmer was not an isolated individual; he was part of a great network which tied remote homesteads to an international capitalist system which was growing and changing with unprecedented rapidity. The sources of information about this system will require far more investigation before one can substantiate the text-book generalisations about the relationship between East and West, between businessmen and farmers, between 'capitalists' and 'agrarians'.

[1] A pioneer work is George D. Green, *Finance and Economic Development in the Old South: Louisiana Banking, 1804–1861* (Stanford, 1972).

After the Civil War there is a marked shift of emphasis in the sources available for agricultural history. There is a proliferation of information about western farming—especially on the Great Plains—and, though it is necessary to dig through the layers of political grievance before coming to the bedrock of economic life, it is possible to build up a remarkably complete picture of western farming and its problems. By contrast information about commercial farming in the South dwindles perceptibly. It is still well-documented for those who wish to seek, but the kind of evidence which served so well to build up a picture of the great pre-war plantations almost disappears.

The census schedules, becoming more voluminous each year, undoubtedly have much information to yield about the farming population of the seventies and eighties. So must the records of business: land companies, railroads, elevator companies, packers and processors of different commodities were all of vital importance, and in many case their records remain untouched or but partially exposed. In this period, too, the Federal Department of Agriculture was collecting more and more data.[1] Indeed, it is the guiding concepts rather than the information which has hindered the study of the late-nineteenth-century farmer. Historians have been preoccupied with the relative decline of farming rather than with farming as an essential and growing part of the national economy. This emphasis has not been universal. It is, for instance, possible to study the mechanisation of agriculture in detail, and to explore its effects upon farm life. There are also excellent studies of particular developments—such as meat-packing and refrigeration—and their social impact. The best studies have, however, dealt with the Great Plains, which lie outside the scope of this book. As one might expect, it is the novel and experimental which leaves more traces in the written evidence than the normal or unadventurous.

While much evidence survives on western farming, the sources

---

[1] The first monthly report of the Commissioner of Agriculture was issued in 1863. This was the first attempt to provide regular and accurate information about production; it also included meteorological tables supplied by the Smithsonian Institute.

for southern agriculture became far more meagre than in pre-war days. The 'peculiar institution' no longer drew the fire of critics or response from its defenders. The great houses were no longer on the traveller's visiting list, while the 'plain people' left little more evidence than in the past. The records of the Freedmen's Bureau contain a good deal of information about the state of southern agriculture immediately after the war, but the focus was on the labour problem and on the prospects of restoring cotton production. Much evidence about the transference from slave to free labour is highly suspect. The full story of the later emergence of share-cropping as a principal element in southern agriculture has, so far, been poorly documented.[1] No one has thought it worthwhile to give to commercial agriculture of the new South the same meticulous attention as was lavished on plantations using slave labour.

At the other end of the country, the farmers of New England and the Atlantic states almost disappear from view, so far as the records are concerned. The majority of their farms continued as small businesses, specialising more and more in supplying food for the great urban markets. The foremost survey of late-nineteenth-century agriculture deals with New England in three pages, mainly confined to the state of Connecticut and largely dependent upon personal recollections and oral traditions.[2] However, state governments in the North East, Mid-Atlantic, and Mid-West maintained and expanded their agricultural services during this period, and the majority of state legislators came from rural districts. It is therefore probable that much evidence on farming in these areas could be unearthed from the records of state legislatures and governments.

In all periods of agricultural history the labouring people—whether slave, hired or self-employed—tend to be poorly served

[1] C. Vann Woodward, *Origins of the New South 1877–1913* (Baton Rouge, 1951), 178–86, 206. This makes use of Reports published in connection with the 10th (1880) and 13th (1910) Censuses. There is further information about the sources used in Woodward's Bibliography, *ibid.*, 508.

[2] Fred A. Shannon, *The Farmer's Last Frontier* (New York, 1945).

by the sources. The life and labour of the slaves is, indeed, very fully documented, but it must be remembered that almost all this evidence is derived from masters, overseers, and upper-class travellers. Even a man such as F. L. Olmstead, who was concerned both to describe fully and to discredit southern society, could make little contact with the slaves. For the most part those to whom he spoke were suspicious, inarticulate, and probably appeared more ignorant than they were. The great mass of slaves remain an enigma; on many plantations we can discover their names, their approximate ages, their daily tasks, and their occasional punishments; we know what efforts were made to preach Christianity to them, to provide food, medicine, and clothing; we know about the slave codes, passes, patrols, and the recovery of fugitives. But the subjects of all this information remain silent, or speak to us only through the mouths of white men. Even in the numerous cases concerning the ownership of slaves, compensation for injury done to them, or claims for freedom, Negro testimony survives mainly as paraphrased by court reporters. Slaves were, of course, legally incapable of giving evidence in criminal cases.

An even greater obscurity shrouds another class of agricultural labourer. In spite of the tradition of the family farm, with sons and daughters performing most of the work, a great deal of labour must have been performed by hired men and female servants. Some settled for long periods, others were casual and migrant labourers. Occasionally hired men might themselves own small portions of land, while servants might be the daughters of less prosperous farmers. This kind of labour force leaves least trace upon the records; they were not, like slaves, an object of curiosity or a capital investment; they did not, like industrial labour, organise or strike. The invaluable census schedules may come to our aid once more in building up a statistical picture of hired help, but little other aid is likely to be forthcoming from the sources for the study of this considerable number of people. If more were known, or likely to be known, a new dimension would be added to our ideas on American social mobility.

The shortage of written evidence for some aspects of agricultural life is offset by an abundance of physical evidence.[1] In every part of the country there are men and women dedicated to the preservation of the rural past; implements are collected, furniture restored, and rooms reconstructed. Most of this evidence accumulates in museums, or occasionally in farms or villages preserved as visible reminders of an earlier age. In the earlier part of the period attention tends to concentrate upon a few 'show pieces', mainly connected with great names. Mount Vernon, Monticello, Gunston Hall and other great houses are maintained as memorials to their owners and to the great period in Virginian history. In other parts of the South the houses of many planters survive, either under the care of local historical societies or carefully restored by modern owners, or sometimes in a state of picturesque dilapidation, Very few small farmhouses of this period survive. The back-country of New England can still show farmhouses which have been in continuous occupation since the eighteenth or even the seventeenth century. In the Mid-West many nineteenth-century farms can be found, though few in anything approaching their original state. In some areas, particularly in the more remote parts of the South and northern New England it is still possible (with the help of a little imagination) to carry oneself back visually to an earlier era.

Photography has played an important part in recording the agricultural past. Travelling photographers were eager to meet the farmer's need for pictures of the homestead, the family, horses, prized livestock and agricultural machinery. Many such photographs have vanished with other ephemeral records of the past, but enough remain to provide a pictorial record of rural life in most parts of the country. The back-country of the South is least well-served; areas which were being actively settled in the late nineteenth century show the most complete record. Not only

[1] Paul Gates (*op. cit.*, 425) writes, 'The further we are from the pre-tractor age in agriculture the more valuable become the great agricultural and industrial museums which have sprung up in recent years.' He singles out for special praise the Henry Ford Museum and Model Village at Dearborn, Mich., the Museum of Science and Industry at Chicago, and the Museums and restored villages at Cooperstown, N.Y., Stourbridge, Mass., and New Salem, Illinois.

did a natural pride in achievement cause the farmer to preserve photographs, but it was often desirable to send pictures to the folks in the East or in Europe.

A prime source of information is the agricultural press. There is little of value for the early years of the period, but from about 1820 there is a swelling flood. Some periodicals were confined to single regions, others to a single branch of agriculture, and a minority attempted more general coverage. Some rose and fell with bewildering rapidity, while some of the moderately successful were absorbed by larger journals. The general discussion on the press in Chapter 9 indicated some of the dangers inherent in too great a reliance upon this source, and it is only necessary to amplify these earlier comments. Subscribers were likely to be the more prosperous farmers, and the contents therefore mirrored their interests. Editors had their own enthusiasms and many relied upon financial aid from individuals or companies with something to sell; so editorials or articles might well be advertisements masquerading as fair comment. With these qualifications, however, the agricultural press is an invaluable source for farming lives and methods. The advertisements are often most revealing. In the later years of the period Montgomery Ward and some smaller mail-order houses were operating with the special purpose of serving the rural market; their advertisements and catalogues provided a splendid record of what they thought the farm dweller wanted.

The literature of the Grangers, the farmers' alliances, and the political action groups of the last years of the period was in a class by itself; if only because its appeal was directed to the poor and unsuccessful (though often more readily acceptable to the more prosperous suffering from hard times). It may often be difficult to distinguish between fact, ignorance, and polemical exaggeration; but no source brings one closer to the realities of farming life, to its difficulties and disappointments as well as to its opportunities or the rewards of rural innocence. Just because the farmer was idealised in American mythology, the more conventional literary sources often sacrificed realism to romanticism.

This brief survey of the sources of information on the life of agriculturalists may close with some general observations. Throughout the period covered by this volume farmers and planters formed a majority of the people; in the early years it was an overwhelming majority. To a large extent the long-term political development of the nation depended upon the decisions of rural voters and, despite the growing influence of commerce, finance and industry, agriculture remained the economic back-bone of the country. It provided the exports without which the society could not have bought manufactured goods or met the interest charges on borrowed capital. An unseen but vital factor in American history is that American agriculture has always been able to feed the American people. Agriculture also played a dominant part in the evolution of American political and social ideas, and even at the close of the period and after, the images drawn from the 'agrarian myth' were emotive and powerful. It is therefore with some surprise that one realises how uneven are the sources of information and how easily the information is distorted.

Information about an upper class proliferates in a hierarchical society, and the planter gentry of the old South become familiar even to a casual student of American history; yet scholars have been forced to labour long to discover a rural middle class in the South. Throughout the country thousands of farmers provided for local markets and so facilitated the rise of towns, but these essential activities can only be revealed by diligent research on local sources, and even then the way of life of the people who engaged in them may remain obscure. When the fortunes of farmers became involved in politics—as in the West after the Civil War—evidence accumulates, but most of it is tainted with polemics. Physical and pictorial evidence often provides a better opportunity than written evidence for understanding rural experience; here at least there is a strong element of random choice in the selection and consequently more chance of achieving a balanced view of the whole.

It should be understood that this relationship of the historian to his sources is not exceptional, but merely a particularly good example of a general condition. The greater part of mankind leaves but a trace upon the records, and even the well-documented history of the American people leaves most people with no more than a name which can be recovered from the dusty archives of the census. Of all the events that ever happened, only an infinitesimal fraction are recorded. Confronted with the enormous mass of evidence left by an advanced and literate society, historians may well despair of ever exploring more than a small corner. Yet if they knew all that the sources could tell them, they would still know very little. The degree of certainty which one can acquire must vary with the topic. Diplomatic history may still leave us guessing about the motives and calculations of statesmen; but at least there is a good chance of recovering all the information on which they based their guesses. At the other end of the scale, social history deals with material which is often voluminous but necessarily incomplete. The survival of information depends so much upon social structure, upon the chance that a way of life happened to arouse special interest, or upon the degree to which a social condition became a political issue; and each of these reasons for the survival of information breeds its own bias and distortion. The history of those millions of Americans who lived on farms provides a striking illustration of these difficulties and offers a continuing challenge to those who wish to reconstruct the American past.

CHAPTER 11

People in Towns

During the period covered by this volume the total population of the United States was multiplied by approximately sixteen, but the number living in towns increased much faster. In 1790 there were only twenty-four urban places; half of these were populated by under 5,000 and only two were over 25,000.[1] In 1890 there were 1,348 towns and twenty-eight of them were over 100,000. The natural increase of population in towns was far below that in rural areas, so the great rise of urban population is principally the result of migration from Europe and from the American countryside. It has been estimated that for the period from 1860 to 1900 twenty farmers moved to the city for every town dweller who moved to a farm.[2] It has become a commonplace in American historiography that this great movement of peoples, and all the problems of urban growth, have received little attention compared with the lavish chronicles of western settlement. In recent years the rise of a school of urban historians has done much to redress the balance; yet even so, the average American still fails to reckon the rise of the city as a dominant fact in nineteenth-century history.

Morton and Lucia White remark that: 'We have no tradition

---

[1] A. M. S. Schlesinger, taking a city as an urban place with more than 8,000 inhabitants, estimated that between 1800 and 1860 the city population increased twenty-four times. In 1810 one out of every twenty Americans lived in cities; by 1860 nearly one in six, by 1880 nearly one in four, and by 1900 one in three. Between 1790 and 1890 the city population multiplied by 139, and, with a few exceptions, the larger the city the faster had been the rate of growth (*Paths to the Present*, New York, 1949, 210–33).

[2] F. A. Shannon, *The Farmer's Last Frontier* (New York, 1945), 55, 356–9, and 'A Footnote to the Labor Safety-Value Theory', *Agricultural History*, xix (1945), 31–7.

of romantic attachment to the city in our highbrow literature, nothing that remotely resembles the Greek philosopher's attachment to the *polis* or the French writer's affection for Paris.' Indeed, the hostility of writers has usually been more marked than their sympathy and 'throughout the nineteenth century our society was becoming more urbanised, but the literary tendency to denigrate the American city hardly declined in proportion. If anything it increased in intensity.'[1] One consequence is the poverty of descriptive literature on cities during the nineteenth century. This is a serious lack, for it is often more important to catch the 'spirit' of urban life than to measure its statistical proportions or analyse its municipal government. One Dickens can go a long way, but there was no American Dickens before 1890 and amongst the poets only Whitman's imagination was stirred by city life.

The history of most advanced civilisations has been primarily the history of their principal cities. American historians have been quite exceptional in treating the history of their civilisation as a rural story in which the towns have functioned on the periphery rather than at the centre. It is as though the history of ancient Greece had concentrated upon the culture of the countryside with occasional references to Athens, or as if we knew much of the Campagna and little of Rome. There are historic reasons for this agrarian distortion, but its persistence in a nation dominated by urban culture is remarkable. It may be explained in part by the fact that American civilisation has not centred upon a single city but upon several, and by the fact that no city nourishes strong traditional associations with national institutions and ideas. Washington is the city of government and national shrines but also an entirely artificial creation. Thus it has seemed unnatural to build the national story around urban growth, and even when its importance is recognised, it is difficult to present urban growth as a single and central theme.

The frontier presented F. J. Turner with a great theme in which the episodes of growth could be readily translated into stages of development. This in turn could be related to the surviving evidence of early settlement. No such systematic analy-

[1] 'The Intellectual versus the City', *Daedalus* (Winter, 1961), 166.

sis is presented for urban historians; growth is haphazard, untidy, and influenced by many fortuitous circumstances. The history of a town is the history of its founders and early residents, of its economic activities, of migrants, markets and railroads; of city and state governments; of leading citizens and slum-dwellers; of churches, schools, and local benefactors. Cities were incorporated by their states, and 'home rule' became a perennial controversy between the larger cities and their state governments dominated by rural legislators. In the later years of the period the rule of bosses and the movements for civic reform tend to dominate the scene and crucial facts in urban development are often obscured. All this means that urban historians must make their choice between concentrating upon chosen themes or attempting a synthesis from widely diverse materials.

The problem of the sources for early urban history has been admirably described by Richard C. Wade, and one can hardly do better than repeat some sentences from the essay on sources which conclude *The Urban Frontier*:

> The sources for this book are scattered throughout the Ohio Valley. More than two years were spent in city halls, court houses, libraries, and historical societies working through municipal records, newspaper files and manuscript collections. The original bibliography of this volume ran to more than fifty pages, and then it included only the more useful items.[1]

Wade found in most towns the manuscript books of their city councils, also committee reports, grand jury presentments and tax lists. Records of real estate transactions and town plans often survive. Of especial use are town directories which may well include a great deal of information about the town and its leading businesses and institutions as well as lists of addresses. Newspapers are an obvious and invaluable source; the kind of caution to be observed in their use has already been noted, but their record of local happenings is likely to be far more reliable than their national news or political information. Often the comparatively small cities of the early nineteenth century supported a surprising number of newspapers and some even had their own periodicals.

[1] *The Urban Frontier* (Cambridge, Mass., 1959; Chicago, 1964), 343.

Manuscript sources are almost inexhaustible. City life has so many dimensions that almost every contemporary document has some relevance. A single letter between friends often contains valuable comments on social conditions; a company's account book sometimes reveals economic pressures not discernible in larger statistics; the diary of an ordinary citizen can illuminate otherwise hidden aspects of a community's growth. Finally, travellers' accounts are often useful, particularly in the early stages of a town's history when the visitor could easily grasp the whole visual impact of a town and meet personally a high proportion of the citizens. As a city grew, the traveller often found himself confined to a single district and a narrow circle of like-minded friends.

Other possible sources for urban history are the records of the churches and of national societies (such as the anti-slavery societies), census material in the National Archives, and the papers of United States senators and representatives. Finally, early local historians often preserved oral data and printed sources which have since disappeared.

Wade's book does not take the study of his chosen cities much beyond 1830. One can imagine how similar evidence proliferates as the cities grew in size and their social organisation became more complex.[1] The history of a city is different in kind as well as in scale from that of a country. 'National history' is the history of the people who have governed the country, of major crises and conflicts, or of select themes such as economic growth or political evolution. Histories which claim to be those of 'a people' normally fall wide of the mark, and end by recording the history of those people whom the historian considers important. This is as true of histories which set out to give prominence to the poor and weak, as to those who unashamedly write of the rich and the strong. This selectiveness is no great handicap in national history, because the number of surveys and interpretations provide the

[1] In *Italians in Chicago, 1880–1930* (New York, 1970) Humbert S. Nelli used plat maps, ward maps, voter registration lists, and election returns from the City Hall; conveyances preserved by the Register of Deeds, papers of the Civil Service Commission, reports of the Superintendent of Police, records of parishes, city directories and numerous maps and photographs amongst his principal sources.

range which no one book is likely to encompass. The historian of
a city is, however, trying to present a living social organism in all
its aspects and is not likely to encounter many professional rivals
in the field. He must be comprehensive without losing his sense
of proportion. It is not enough to concentrate merely upon
politics, upon economics, upon leading citizens, or upon the
labouring poor. It is the essence of urban history that it studies the
development and relationship, within a comparatively small area,
of a whole variety of classes, occupations, and interests. To abstract
any one of these is to study the history of a particular group in a
chosen environment, and to abandon the idea of the city as a
social phenomenon demanding treatment as a whole. At the
same time some factors have been more significant than others in
explaining growth but these will vary from city to city.

It is therefore no wonder that urban historians tend to be
worried by questions of method, analysis, and evidence. Quantitative data is not too difficult to obtain, but if a city is a corporate
entity qualitative evidence must be added. Men acquire loyalty
to a city; they seek to clothe it with an identity different from all
other cities; and sometimes they recognise bonds of union which
cross the barriers of class and occupation. Civic pride is an old
and ancient virtue, but it is difficult to define.

If one is studying a close-knit social organism, it is impossible
to make statements about one element without making statements about all. Descriptions of (say) immigrants in a city cannot
be made without reference to the attitudes of other city dwellers,
to municipal government, and to all the institutions of urban life.
The same generalisation would apply to studies of particular
aspects of urban life: politics, culture, or economic activity. The
task of separating out the themes, upon which historians are
accustomed, rightly or wrongly, to concentrate, becomes
difficult if not impossible when they are so inextricably inter-
twined as they are in a modern city.

There is a great mass of literary evidence for the history of
cities in the later nineteenth century; but much of this evidence
clearly betrays its class origin without revealing whether the
opinions expressed were typical. There is, for instance, a growing

mass of protest by middle-class reformers against the conditions of city government, but obscurity veils the large mass of middle class people who expressed no opinion on the subject. Even greater difficulty is experienced in deciding what weight should be given to working-class comments when we know that only a very small minority were articulate or even concerned by the issues which their leaders discussed with such vehemence. Some light is shed when immigrants form a large enough group to organise their own churches and societies, and to support their own newspapers. In recent years there has been revealed an increasing body of evidence about black people in the northern cities. Yet the fact that evidence of this kind reflects the opinions of political and ethnic minorities means that it provides inadequate information about the city as a whole. Paradoxically the corporate identity of a city becomes more elusive as more light is cast upon its component parts; the synthesis becomes a vague hypothesis rather than a verifiable statement.

Curiously enough the businessman, who occupied the centre of the stage, often remains a shadowy figure delineated by his critics rather than presenting his own portrait. The typical businessman remains unidentified because everyone took him for granted; yet most Americans of the nineteenth century tacitly agreed that business enterprise was the mainspring of city life. Business records normally deal with the economic man, and, important though they are for economic historians, they tell little of assumptions, aspirations or ideals. A glance through the footnotes to Edward C. Kirkland's sensitive re-creation of the mind of the businessman will show both how widely it is necessary to range and also how few businessmen can be quoted to explain their own way of life.[1] Rockefeller and Carnegie left

[1] *Dream and Thought in the American Business Community 1860–1900* (Ithaca, 1956). Professor Kirkland writes (Preface, vii–viii), 'I have sought to immerse myself in the available statements made by businessmen in books, magazine articles, private correspondence, and testimony before Congressional and other committees, and in statements made by the press and periodicals directed towards the concerns of the business world—for example the *Commercial and Financial Chronicle*.' This seems to be a fair summary of the research programme to be undertaken by anyone who wishes to understand American businessmen

their own records, but they were hardly typical even of the very rich and still less of the ordinary man of business. Something could probably be achieved by the laborious process of piecing together —from local newspapers—reports of speeches and of society meetings, obituary notices, and letters to the press.[1] State historical societies and private attics must contain thousands upon thousands of letters for and about long-forgotten middle-class citizens; but so far little has been done to explore—let alone to understand—the business mind of the nineteenth century.

The nature of the sources for the life and thought of the ordinary businessman, of moderate success and moderate means, helps to explain the difficulty of penetrating his character. The conventions of the time respected the privacy with which a man of means could surround his life, and held fervently that a man's business was his own concern. This was the typical response to criticism, and one seldom gets an elaborate explanation in answer to public attacks. In the larger cities businessmen seldom played an active part in political life, and as citizens left their mark in private associations and occasional public benefactions. When a city became sufficiently conscious of its richer citizens to be interested in their social life, the newspapers might note their comings, goings and 'conspicuous consumption'. The gossip columns of the press may be insignificant in their detail, but revealing in their total effect.

---

during this period rather than to assess them exclusively through the arguments of their critics. The reticence of businessmen is noted by Gerald T. White, 'The Business Historian and his Sources', *American Archivist*, xxx (Jan, 1967), 20.

[1] Sigmund Diamond in *The Reputation of the American Businessman* (Cambridge, Mass., 1955) used obituary notices of six business magnates (Girard, Astor, Vanderbilt, Morgan, Rockefeller, and Ford) to assess the 'basic assumptions and evaluations concerning the social ideals of their writers'. This method might well be employed in other contexts; for instance it might be profitable to study the obituaries of prominent citizens in a single city over a long period. More formal records may be preserved in lawyers' offices and in the law departments of large firms 'Since lawyers think in terms of precedents and thus historically their records are of great value to the researchers. And, fortunately, lawyers are extraordinarily conservative in throwing old records away.'(Gerald T. White, *op. cit.*, 27.)

Materials for urban history of a quite different kind are found in architectural survivals, town plans, lithographs, and early photographs. In a few instances—such as Harper's Ferry and Knotsberry Farm in California—there have been deliberate attempts to preserve or re-create the physical environment of small nineteenth-century towns; but in most living towns the buildings which were once the heart of the city have long since disappeared. In a few back streets or poor districts it is still possible to recapture the physical appearance of nineteenth-century towns. A striking example on a large scale is the city of Baltimore, where street after street of red brick nineteenth-century houses survive, each with its once carefully washed marble doorsteps. Around Capitol Hill in Washington one can still fancy oneself in a nineteenth-century world of frame built houses. Many small New England towns still preserve their original appearance (carefully protected and controlled by vigilant committees), and though they perpetuate the styles of a still earlier colonial world, they were the environment of much nineteenth-century life. Moving westward one can trace the architectural styles of New England along the belt of Yankee migration to the Great Plains. In the same way improvement and the automobile have not yet entirely eradicated the physical features of the small nineteenth-century southern town. Until very recently one could see a score of them on the somewhat isolated 'eastern shore' of Maryland, and further south, in Faulkner country, one can still encounter towns where little seems to have changed since 1850.

How valuable are these architectural survivals for general historians? How does it aid one's understanding to experience the scale and design of an earlier society? This kind of evidence cannot be quantified or defined; it may be impossible to describe. Moreover, 'the sense of place' is the most difficult thing for any historian to communicate to his reader. It may do much for the historical imagination to experience the physical world of the past, but it is not easy to pass on, unless the historian has in him a vein of poetry; this, it must be admitted, few of them have. The medieval historian can hardly fail to communicate the majesty and purpose of a great cathedral, but a modern historian has a more difficult task when confronted with the aura of an ugly row of Victorian houses or even with a neat New England church. He may, however, leave imagination behind, and by a study of techniques and function learn a good deal about the aims and limitations of nineteenth-century urban life.

Town plans have obvious utility for local historians; for others their immediate impact may be to bring home a sense of scale. In a typical small town of 5,000 to 10,000 inhabitants, there were, perhaps, from 1,000 to 2,000 adult males. The town plan may well enable one to identify enough house lots to guess where the majority of them lived, and from this to calculate the probable frequency with which they met and the likelihood of knowing each other by sight. In this way one can grasp what it meant to live in a 'face-to-face' society. Research, however, becomes faith or speculation if one asks whether these small urban societies exhibited the virtues which the older writers attributed exclusively to the city state.

Of more direct utility are the surviving pictorial records of urban life. With lithographs or other hand-made pictures there is an obvious element of selectivity; to make a picture required time and skill, and it was not a task to be lightly undertaken without purpose or prospect of reward. Pictures of the early period, therefore, tend to depict scenes which someone thought worthwhile preserving. Historic events, public buildings, principal streets, coaches, railroads, hotels and business premises. Early photographs tend to be equally selective and stylised, but as the process became more common and techniques improved, a greater degree of spontaneity prevailed. Photography during the Civil War demonstrated its capacity for crystallising the passing scene, and for catching the agony and dirt as well as the placid and respectable. Family portraits, crowded streets, and the seamy side of city life are presented, and it becomes possible to visualise the urban scene as never before. The photograph could also become a useful instrument in the hands of civic reformers.

It is possible that more might be done to analyse scientifically the evidence presented by these pictorial records. Historians have used them as aids rather than as sources; they have looked for the pictures to illustrate their arguments rather than used them as basic materials for the reconstruction of the past. Yet there are many instances in which the picture—whether contrived or natural—can reveal information which has left no imprint upon the written record, and there are other instances in which it can suggest the direction in which a search should be conducted. One can imagine the excitement which would reverberate amongst classical scholars if one could suddenly be presented with a full and intimate pictorial record of ancient Athens; the modern historian with similar material under his hand often neglects it.

When one turns from attempts to study cities as a whole to particular aspects of city life, the task of historical reconstruction can be easier. An ethnic minority, a church, an artistic coterie, or a club will have records which describe, in varying ways, their activities. With some luck in the survival of evidence it will be possible to study particular economic activities. The affairs of large concerns, such as railroads, will have left abundant evidence in state and municipal archives, in business records, in private correspondence, and in public comment. Even more prevalent will be the sources for the history of local politics.

Each aspect of urban life will present its own source problems. An ethnic minority, particularly in the early days, is likely to be composed of people whose language or lack of education makes it difficult for them to communicate with other citizens. More-over, the shifting residential pattern within a large city may make it difficult to keep track of the ethnic components. Writing in 1890 Jacob Riis described the situation in New York city.

A map of the city, colored to designate nationalities, would show more stripes than on the skin of a zebra, and more colors than any rainbow. The city on such a map would fall into two great halves, green for the Irish prevailing in the West Side tenement districts, and blue for the Germans on the East Side. But intermingled with these ground colors would be an odd variety of tints that would give the whole the appearance of an extraordinary crazy-quilt. From down in the Sixth Ward, upon the site of the old Collect Pond that in the days of the fathers drained hills that are no more, the red of the Italian would be seen forcing its way northward along the line of Mulberry Street to the quarter of the French purple or Bleecker Street and South Fifth Avenue, to lose itself and reappear, after a lapse of miles, in the 'Little Italy' of Harlem, east of Second Avenue. Dashes of red, sharply defined, would be seen strung through the annexed District, northward to the city line. On the West Side the red would be seen overrunning the old Africa of Thompson Street, pushing the black of the Negro rapidly uptown, against querulous but unavailing protests, occupying his home, his church, his trade and all, with merciless impartiality.[1]

Amongst the other ethnic groups Riis noticed the Russian and Polish Jews 'hardly less aggressive than the Italians', while dovetailed with the Germans 'the poor but thrifty' Czechs, but 'the two races mingle no more on this side of the Atlantic than on the rugged slopes of the Bohemian mountains; the echoes of the Thirty Years War ring in New York after two centuries and a half.' Arabs, Chinese, Finns, Swiss, and Greeks could all be located on the imaginery map, but it would have to be re-drawn every few years.

There is a church in Mulberry Street that has stood for two gener-ations as a sort of milestone of these migrations. Built originally for the worship of staid New Yorkers of the 'old stock', it was engulfed by the colored tide, when the draft riots drove the Negroes out of reach of Cherry Street and Five Points. Within the past decade the advance wave of the Italian onset reached it, and today the arms of United Italy adorn its front.[2]

The sources for these aspects of urban history must therefore be scattered and obscure. Much can be recovered from newspapers, directories, church records, and city archives, but the task of reconstruction is difficult and uncertain. Every attempt to cut a cross section, and to describe a great city as it was at a single point in time, is necessarily deceptive. Change and movement is the essence of the story, and here the historian must often resort

[1] Jacob Riis, *How the Other Half Lives* (New York, 1890), 18–19 (Reference to Sagamore Press edition, 1957).
[2] *Ibid.*

to impressions rather than to quantitative or verifiable evidence.

The history of city politics provides many opportunities for the exploitation of new evidence and new techniques. The statements of contemporaries were invariably tainted with bias; it was important to claim greater strength than one possessed, and it was an obvious tactic to discount both the size and influence of opposition support. On the Democratic side editors and political spokesmen were anxious to identify their opponents as rich and privileged, friends of monopoly and foes of humble virtue. On the Federalist, Whig, and later Republican side it was important to stress respectability and concern for honest enterprise, while stressing the violence, corruption and immorality of the Democrats and their bosses. The party 'images' are important for an understanding of political attitudes, but there is no short cut to the realities.

Lee Benson's pioneer study *The Concept of Jacksonian Democracy: New York as a Test Case* was not confined to the city, but can well be taken as an example both of what can be done and of the limitations imposed by the sources. He used the official canvass for state offices, which is preserved in manuscript; but this does not give the votes by urban wards. The *New York Annual Register* (1830–45) and the *New York State Register* (1843, 1845–46) cover the vote for President and Governor by ward for 1830, 1834, 1838, 1840, 1842, and 1844. The *Tribune Almanac* (1834–1900; from 1838 to 1854 known as the *Whig Almanac*) gives town and ward returns for 1858, 1860, and 1864 only.[1] For the years after the Civil War fuller information on voting in the larger cities is probably available, but they have not been used in any major studies. Thus the political history of most cities remains to be written in a way which will satisfy the requirements of modern historians. Even an organisation such as Tammany in New York city, which has been the subject of a number of studies, lacks a thorough investigation of its organisation, methods, and voting strength. The main difficulty is that the political 'machines' of

[1] Lee Benson, *The Concept of Jacksonian Democracy: New York as a Test Case* (Princeton, 1961), Chap. XI, *passim*.

the later nineteenth century were so odious to the respectable and well-educated that no one considered it worthwhile to study them dispassionately as political institutions. Historians have yet to shake off the habits of mind of their illustrious predecessors.

It may seem unnecessary to demand the investigation of the obscure and parochial politics of nineteenth-century cities, yet much could hang upon the outcome. In the first place urban voting plays so essential a part in twentieth-century politics that a study of its history might add significantly to our understanding of the present. In the second place light might be thrown upon crucial problems in historical interpretation. Lee Benson's work was largely inspired by a belief that much harm had been done by 'the proposition that socio-economic cleavages are the obvious place to begin a study of American voting behaviour' and advanced 'a counterproposition . . . that at least since the 1820s, when manhood suffrage became widespread, ethnic and religious differences have tended to be *relatively* the most important source of political differences'. The difficulty in establishing this 'counter-proposition' lies in the fact that Protestant immigrants from the British Isles (who provided an important element in Whig support) were the newcomers who slipped quickly into a comparatively good socio-economic position, while Catholics from Ireland and Germany remained insecure for a considerable period after arrival. It is, however, clear that a great deal of work is necessary to emancipate history from the cruder forms of economic determinism, and that an excellent field for research is provided by the cities. Despite the rapid changes in the fortunes, and ethnic composition, of the various districts, enough evidence must survive to provide an informed analysis of the structure of urban politics.

The history of the larger cities has suffered from a weakness of the conceptual framework. Should one attempt the 'biography' of a single city, attempt to generalise about urban experience, or study national events in an urban environment? Or should one attempt to analyse the stages in urban growth (which will occur at different periods in different cities) and so build up an

229

'anatomy' of urban development? Should one try to isolate and describe the entrepreneurs and public men who were responsible for decisions, and to study the timing and consequences of their actions? Or is the history of cities to be found in the masses who crowded into their back streets? As everything in the urban environment is related to everything else, abstraction breeds unreality, but a comprehension of the whole demands so many different materials and so many different techniques that it has so far defeated historians.

These difficulties have been so far insuperable because most professional urban history has begun with the larger cities. Yet small towns might not only prove easier to handle in pioneer studies but also provide important contributions for an understanding of nineteenth-century history. For if economic power was coming to be located in the greater cities, political power was still focused upon the main streets of countless small towns where lawyer politicians felt the pulse of their constituencies.

There are, of course, a great many local histories of the smaller towns; and modern urban giants often show a lively interest in the records of the little communities which provided the nucleus for later growth. But most of these histories are deliberately parochial and are often untouched by the broader aims of social analysis. For many Americans the adjective 'small' has a peculiarly emotive force when applied to 'small' businessmen or 'small' towns; the instinct which produces this respect is a sound one, but it usually seizes upon the picture of 'smallness' fighting a losing battle against overwhelming 'bigness'. For the historian of the nineteenth century the emphasis is often misplaced, for small towns, small businessmen, small lawyers, and politicians who started from small beginnings, were the mainsprings of social and public life. The majority of legislators sat for rural constituencies, yet the majority were also lawyers, which meant that their professional lives must have been spent in small towns which were the headquarters for the business and professional activities of their districts. Small towns which were county seats or communication centres could be particularly important. In economics and in politics the most important decisions were often made in small towns, while the rivalries between them were often the most significant local issues.

How small is 'small'? The census classified anything with over 2,500 inhabitants as an urban place, and this was very small indeed. In such a town the 400 to 500 adult males could all know each other, and even when one steps up from this to a town of 20,000, the scale was still small enough for the leading citizens to know each other intimately and to be known by repute to their humbler fellow townsmen. In most parts of the United States, for most of this period, the small towns were also very homogeneous societies; overwhelmingly Protestant, mostly dominated by men of Anglo-Saxon descent, and sharing the common experience of life in a growing community, the small towns were coherent and cohesive even when politically divided. In considering the role of slavery in sectional differences, it is worth remembering that the presence of Negroes was the one quantifiable difference between a northern and southern small town.

Small towns have not lacked their historians, but most of them have been distinguished by local patriotism rather than by professional skill. What is required are studies inspired by the intrinsic importance of the subject rather than by genealogical zeal. A great many national issues will be better understood when we know more about their local roots and about the local pressures behind the public men. And as knowledge about the small town as a social institution advances, a good deal more will be understood about basic American attitudes and assumptions. So far urban history has tended to mean the history of the larger cities, but there is a clear case for more intensive study of the small towns where, during most of the nineteenth century, a majority of urban Americans lived.

In a challenging article, written in 1968, Sam B. Warner, jr, noticed that: 'From the moment American historians began writing self-conscious urban history they assumed that the city was a particular kind of place, an environment or set of environments, that called for special historical investigation . . . Thus far, however, historians have failed to study the sources of this uniqueness in any systematic way.'[1] It may be a commonplace that urban life moulds lives, thoughts and traditions of people in a special kind of way, but if so, the facts have yet to be explored and presented in a manner which defines and explains what these peculiarities are. We are therefore dealing with an area of historical enquiry in which sources are plentiful, but the questions they should answer have not been framed; much of the raw material has been unmined, some only partially refined, and some employed in manufactures unrelated to each other. The situation has not been helped by the habit of generalisation either from particular examples or from an oft-denied but nevertheless intractable belief that cities are somehow alien to American civilisation.

One generalisation has become so widespread that it calls for special comment. Time and again urbanisation and industrialisation are linked together as twin forces which 'explain' changes in society. This is particularly noticeable in many analyses of sectional conflict before the Civil War which stress the emergence of industry and the growth of cities in the North as explanations of the differentiation between the two parts of the country. Now, clearly, the rise of some cities is closely related to the rise of some industries; conversely, industry is unlikely to develop without access to the commercial services of a city; but urban society and industrial societies are two different things. A city can flourish with little or no industry, while the majority of large-scale industries began in rural situations—close to water power, coal, or mineral resources—and the clusters of dwellings around them were entirely distinct from the old cities with their complicated patterns of class and economic function. In the later part of the period more industries were being drawn to the older cities, but to the periphery, not to the centre. A great deal of craft industry, carried on in small workshops, flourished in the older cities from the earliest times, and overall figures for industrial production may conceal differences between this kind of small-scale pro-

[1] Sam B. Warner, jr, 'If All the World were Philadelphia: a scaffolding for Urban History 1774–1930', *American Historical Review*, lxxiv (Oct, 1968), 26–43.

duction, which was indigenous to the older urban environment, and factories which arrived late in the day.

Urbanisation and industrialisation are phenomena of advanced civilisations, and their development in nineteenth-century America makes them essential objects for analysis and research; but they are distinct, and an unwary use of the sources without an understanding of these distinctions produces more darkness than light. The assumption that the city is 'a particular kind of place' which calls for 'special historical investigation' must lead to the conclusion that there are many different kinds of city and several different kinds of environment. The warning is necessary because the more obvious sources for urban history may often give an impression of uniformity which ought to be challenged. One city newspaper is very like another, and cities tend to produce similar educational institutions, trade associations, voluntary societies, and religious activities. So, too, business records, if one can discover them, may have marked similarities with each other. Even the visual record of lithographs and photographs may give the impression that one city was very like another. It is true that the universals of city life are the very things which historians must attempt to grasp and analyse, but they must not be content with apparent similarities. The depth, variety, and complexity of urban relationships must be studied systematically before one can venture to the higher plane of generalisation.

To meet these difficulties Professor Warner suggests that it is possible to construct tables to illustrate patterns of urban population and occupation over long periods, and that an analysis of this data would reveal patterns of change in the urban environment, establish comparisons between different cities, provide the material for a general theory of urban culture, and, by 'an orderly presentation of a few facts, . . . provide a kind of intellectual scaffolding for urban history'. To illustrate the possibilities of his method, he tabulated data available for Philadelphia in 1774, 1860, and 1930. The first Table gave for each of these years a percentage of the population employed in industry, clerical work, and all other occupations. The surprising fact to emerge was a sharp fall in the proportion of industrial labourers between

1774 and 1860 (from 13·3 per cent to 8·1 per cent), followed by a slight rise (8·1 per cent to 8·7 per cent) in the next seventy years, but a very marked rise over the whole period (0·8 per cent to 13·9 per cent) in clerical workers. A further breakdown of industrial employment showed decreases in each category over the whole period except building and textiles; between 1774 and 1860 the picture was more varied, with some increases and some decreases. Non-manufacturing occupations increased on the whole, from 47·6 per cent to 54·7 per cent, with professional and consumer occupations showing most gains. The whole series suggested that urban manufacturing was at a peak in the late eighteenth century, while non-industrial employments rose conspicuously in the following 150 years. This, in turn, may suggest that one criterion for 'urbanisation' is the proportion of the population engaged in clerical and professional occupations. Another table established population shifts between the 'ring' and the 'core' of the city. In 1860 65·1 per cent of the Negroes lived in the core, but 62·1 per cent of European immigrants lived in the ring. By 1930 80·3 per cent of the Negroes lived in the core and had been joined by 70·5 per cent of the Irish, 72·6 per cent of the Poles, and 70 per cent of the Russians. Further figures showed the rise of large manufacturing establishments, and the consequent emergence of 'work groups'. Even without formal organisation, the 'work groups'—concentrated in single areas and employed in two or three large factories—constituted a new and significant social unit. At the other end of the income scale, there was a growing tendency for business and professional men to join in trade associations and professional societies, while clubs and fraternal associations provided the means by which prominent citizens evolved new patterns of loose but important links.

When we speak of 'the rise of the city' or of 'urbanisation' we are not therefore dealing with a simple phenomenon, but with a social organism with a constantly varying internal structure. A comparison between the structures of various cities at various times may, therefore, become the basis of one set of generalisations about the process. This kind of analysis is, however, only the beginning; it will still be necessary to discover the effects of the changing patterns upon social behaviour and public policy. All this suggests that the study of people in towns has far to go. Indeed, it is the intrinsic difficulty of the task rather than lack of interest which has prevented Arthur Schlesinger's call for an 'urban interpretation' of American history enjoying the same influence as Turner's 'frontier thesis'. It is also true that in no field of historical study is an alliance with sociology more important, but its terms have yet to be negotiated. The sources are abundant; the concepts which govern their investigation await formulation.[1]

[1] Oscar Handlin has a perceptive essay on 'The Modern City as a Field for Historical Study' in *The Historian and the City*, ed., Oscar Handlin and John Burchard (Cambridge, Mass., 1963), which collects papers (with some additional material) delivered at a Harvard conference in 1961. A useful recent collection of essays is Alexander B. Callow, ed., *American Urban History: an interpretative reader with commentaries* (New York, 1969). Neither collection touches upon the history of small towns.

CHAPTER 12

Afro-Americans

The 'simple annals of the poor' invariably present historians with a
challenge. Amongst so many who are inarticulate and illiterate
the man who expresses himself on paper, or for the record in
public, is necessarily atypical; but rarity ensures that his evidence
will be given enhanced value and authority. One is constantly
tempted to substitute the known fragment for the unknown
mass. Additional difficulties arise when the poor are enslaved, of
different race, and denied opportunities of advancement. There is
an unavoidable tendency to attribute depressed conditions to the
deficiency of the victims, and this bias forms an additional hazard
for fair assessment of the sources. There is a mass of evidence
about slaves and a good deal about free Negroes before and after
Emancipation; but the greater part consists of material compiled
by white men who assumed that they knew about Negroes,
without the necessity of allowing them to speak for themselves.
Even in non-slave states before the Civil War the great majority
of Negroes were the worst educated part of the population, the
poorest paid, and the least well served by the press. Conditions improved, both North and South, after Emancipation, and
there is a growing volume of source material contributed by
Negroes themselves; but even this derives mainly from a tiny
minority separated by training from the experience of the
mass.

In the South, before the Civil War, no subjects were more
frequently discussed than slaves and slavery. Internal pressure
and external criticism stimulated a flow of pro-slavery literature.
Books and pamphlets, which offered a studied defence of the
institution, can be supplemented many times over by overt
assertions and implied assumptions in southern newspapers,

speeches, and private letters. The principal burden of all this argument was that Negroes were fit for slavery, that slavery was a justifiable (some said the best) system of labour for a civilised society, and that no other relationship between the races was possible. Within this general framework there were arguments over the religious instruction of slaves, the pros and cons of voluntary emancipation, the condition of free Negroes, the practicability of using slaves in industrial employment, and the vexed question of whether Negroes formed a separate species or descended with other men from Adam. There was generally silence in the South about four aspects of the slave system which drew most comment from abolitionist critics: the internal slave trade, the refusal to give legal recognition to slave marriages, miscegenation, and excessive punishment.

In addition to general, philosophic, theological and scientific discussions of slavery, there were a large number of discussions of the practical details of slave management. This included many discussions of Negro health, for though his hardy physique was one justification for his enslavement he was subject to many ailments, and a day sick was an unprofitable day for the master. In addition to the normal diseases there were some peculiar to the Negro race, including 'Drapetomania' or the disease causing Negroes to run away. One southern doctor diagnosed this as a psychological malady, and maintained that it could be minimised by sensible precautions:

> If treated kindly, well-fed and clothed, with fuel enough to keep a small fire burning all night—separated into families, each family having its own house—not permitted to run about at night to visit their neighbours, to receive visits, or to use intoxicating liquors, and not over-worked or exposed too much to the weather, they are easily governed—more so than any people in the world. When all this is done, if any one or more of them, at any time, are inclined to raise their heads to a level with their masters or overseer, humanity and their own good require that they shall be punished until they fall into that submissive state which it was intended for them to occupy in all after-time, when their progenitor received the name of Canaan or 'submissive knee bender'. They have only to be kept in

237

that state and treated like children, with care, kindness, attention, and humanity, to prevent and cure them from running away.[1]

Not every extract from pro-slavery literature can rival this one in naïvety, but like the majority it tells us more of the mind of the master than of the slave.

The private correspondence of planters and overseers is more revealing. Here at least one is away from generalities, spurious science or biblical appeals, and can gather information about tasks, management, health, clothing, food, and pastimes. Again it is the voice of the master-class, but one is dealing with people in real situations, and occasionally one can catch a glimpse of a slave personality. Few travellers in the South left any evidence of slavery worth preserving. Most of them came South with fixed ideas about slavery which they found supported by the evidence of their eyes. F. L. Olmstead was more detached than most, and penetrated deeper into the back country, but even he spoke directly to few slaves. He does give an occasional glimpse of slavery on the smaller plantations and farms (from which letters are rare). Even in private letters planters were usually reticent about the more vulnerable aspects of slavery. There is little about the slave trade, the break-up of slave families, the children of white men by slave mothers, or punishments of unusual severity. Apart from the daily round and routine of slave life, there is a good deal about fugitives, the misbehaviour of slaves belonging to other masters, and occasionally religion.

One class of information is particularly instructive. Helen Catterall has collected and edited a very large number of reports from the Federal and state courts dealing with slavery.[2] Many more examples probably lie buried in the records of county

---

[1] J. B. D. De Bow, *The Industrial Resources of the Southern and Western States* (New Orleans, 1852), i, 323. Quoting a Dr Cartwright, of New Orleans, who had published a treatise on Negro diseases. *The Industrial Resources* collected together numerous articles from *De Bow's Review*; the selected pieces on Negroes and Slavery (i, 196 ff.) provide an excellent compendium of pro-slavery argument.

[2] Helen T. Catterall, ed., *Judicial Cases Concerning American Slavery and the Negro*, 5 vols (Washington, 1926–37; reprint, 1969).

courts. Here one can find ample evidence of the seamy side of the system, for litigation dealt with ownership, sale and purchase, the break-up of estates and the inheritance of slave property, trespass and injury done by slaves and punishments illegally inflicted by men other than the owner. Some cases dealt with fugitives and the apprehension of slaves travelling around without passes. An interesting class of case dealt with Negroes, held as slaves, suing for freedom. The judges in the late eighteenth century applied the doctrine that a man was presumed free until proved to be a slave, and were prepared to accept hearsay and circumstantial evidence as proof that ancestors in the female line had been free. As the nineteenth century went on, the construction of the law stiffened; Negroes were presumed to be slaves unless they could produce positive evidence of freedom, hearsay evidence was excluded, and little would suffice save documentary evidence. However, the evidence of courts, like most other evidence bearing upon slavery, tells us more about the masters than the slaves.

So far then one has the scaffolding of slavery rather than its internal structure. The very considerable detail in which it is possible to reconstruct the details of the system on some of the larger plantations, still furnishes little evidence of what the Negroes thought and whether their attitudes evolved in the seventy-five years preceding Emancipation. Can these obstacles be overcome? What is the real prospect of 'black' history which is not dependent upon what white men said?

A standard collection of documents on Negro history by Herbert Apetheker demonstrates the problem.[1] One hundred and

---

[1] Herbert Apetheker, *A Documentary History of the Negro People in the United States* (New York, 1951). It would, of course, be foolish to suggest that all white evidence should be discredited. Mrs Willie Lee Rose writes of the sources used in her study of the Port Royal experiment that 'the letters and diaries of the missionaries constitute the single indispensable category of primary materials . . . The focus of many sympathetic and perceptive eyes, over a period of several years, upon the individual Negroes who were reborn in freedom during the turmoil of war sometimes gave these usually mute participants in the struggle a real dimension of personality.' *Rehearsal for Reconstruction* (Indianapolis, 1964), 409–10.

sixty-four extracts (some in two or three parts) cover the period from 1787 to 1860; of these only ten were written by slaves, eleven by free Negroes in the South, and six by slaves emancipated before the Civil War. Twenty extracts came from fugitive slaves, but of these, eleven were contributed by Frederick Douglass. This makes a total of thirty-seven individuals who had actually experienced slavery. All the other extracts in the collection covering these years came from northern Negroes. The narratives of fugitive slaves are fairly numerous. Many of them show signs of having been severely edited before publication, and this kind of literature was the stock-in-trade of abolitionist propaganda. Skilful use of slave autobiographies can however add a new dimension to knowledge of life among the slaves.[1]

Thus, until comparatively recent times the literature on slavery was dominated by evidence from the larger plantations, written by whites, and supplemented by accounts from fugitives. Moreover many fugitives had already undergone a partial process of selection when they were taken for training as craftsmen, industrial slavery, or employment in towns; and many in these categories were hired out by masters and lived on their own for long periods.[2] Fortunately it is now possible to write with much more confidence about other aspects of the slave system. Studies of slavery in the towns and of industrial slavery have enlarged knowledge of the system as a whole. This has also meant a much wider range of sources, even though the bulk of it remains of white origin. Thus Richard C. Wade, in his study of slavery in the cities, describes his primary sources:

Court records, police dockets, real-estate conveyances and tax and assessment books provided essential information about masters and

[1] John W. Blassinghame, *The Slave Community: Plantation Life in the Old South* (New York, 1972) is based mainly upon slave autobiographies; the 'Critical Essay on Sources' presents a convincing case for the use of this material.

[2] Richard C. Wade, *Slavery in the Cities* (New York, 1964), 221–25 (paperback edition). Many fugitives from rural areas found refuge in the Southern cities; some subsequently made their way to free soil. Many fugitives from the plantations of the Lower South escaped to remote, mountainous or swampy areas and remained unknown to abolitionist writers.

slaves as well as many glimpses into the working of the system. The minutes of the city councils, municipal ordinances, and the reports of special committees dealt often with slavery and the control of Negroes. Grand jury presentments proved especially useful because they sometimes became 'state of the city' messages viewing this question in relation to many others. State archives contained the enactments of the legislatures, messages by governors, reports of committees, and petitions by private citizens and municipalities which dealt with race and slavery.[1]

But, he adds, the story could not have been told without 'the voluminous files of early local newspapers'.

Robert S. Starobin's study of industrial slavery benefited from the fact that so many fugitives had had industrial experience, but his major sources were the records of industrial enterprises and the papers of slave-owning industrialists. Industrial labour occupied only a minority of the total slave population (approximately 5 per cent is suggested), but the development of southern industry (to about 15 per cent of the national capacity in 1860) was a matter of deep importance to slavery and the slaves themselves.[2] If, as a majority of southern planters continued to maintain, most slaves could only be used in low-grade agricultural employment, then there was a definite though distant horizon to its future; but if, as a minority insisted, slaves could be trained effectively for industrial employment, then there was no limit to the possibilities of future development.

The abundance of one-sided evidence about slavery causes one to ask whether the balance can be redressed by the use of less orthodox sources. Some years ago Stanley M. Elkins created an academic stir by applying analogies drawn from sociological studies in other fields.[3] The particular study chosen – of the behaviour of prisoners in German concentration camps—appeared bizarre to many critics. With all its faults, the slave system was not

[1] *Slavery in the Cities*, p. 285 (paperback edition).
[2] Robert S. Starobin, *Industrial Slavery in the Old South* (New York, 1970), p. 11 (paperback edition).
[3] Stanley M. Elkins, *Slavery: A Problem in American Institutional Life* (Chicago,

a concentration camp, and the prime object of most slave-owners was to keep their 'property' alive, healthy, and useful. Elkins was, however, not trying to suggest exact parallels but explanations for the apparent contrast between the well-attested 'Uncle Tom' type and evidence of brutality and smouldering resentment. Other sociological studies of authoritarian closed societies might be brought into play. Assuming some uniformity in behaviour patterns, one might, for instance, learn something about slavery by studying reactions to military or naval discipline; the soldier or sailor is not, like the slave, condemned to serve for life, but for a period he lives in a closed society under iron discipline. The variety of response and the existence of good soldiers along with bad ones, of the happy with the desperately unhappy, may provide some clues to the behavioural structure of slavery.

The consideration of the sources raises serious questions about the nature of slavery itself. Unfortunately many practitioners of black history will not stay for an answer. Their object is not to explain but to condemn, and to load the white race with the guilt of a great iniquity. As the influence of Ulrich B. Phillips wore off—with his gentle if not apologetic attitude towards slavery— the field was taken by historians who used the same evidence with very different preconceptions. Kenneth Stampp saw more of the sources than Phillips had ever done, he was able to profit from more than a generation of work done mainly by southern scholars, and his challenge to the judgment of the earlier scholar

1959). Especially Chapter III, *passim*. Curiously enough his argument has become a target for modern black historians. Elkins wrote, 'Is it possible to deal with "Sambo" as a type? The characteristics that have been claimed for the type come principally from southern lore—Sambo, the typical plantation slave, was docile but irresponsible, loyal but lazy, humble but chronically given to lying and stealing; his behaviour was full of infantile silliness and his talk inflated with childish exaggeration' (*op. cit.*, 82). His offence, in the eyes of modern radicals, lay in concluding that 'the picture has far too many circumstantial details, its hues have been stroked in by too many different brushes, for it to be denounced as counterfeit. Too much folk-knowledge, too much plantation literature, too much of the Negro's own lore, have gone into its making to entitle one in good conscience to condemn it as "conspiracy".' (*Ibid.*, 84.)

was accompanied by an enlargement of knowledge. Stanley Elkins stated that 'Not only has Phillips' moral position been overwhelmingly reversed, but even his scholarship . . . has been left in the shade by scholarship more painstaking still,' but went on to observe that both Phillips and Stampp assumed the problem of slavery could be answered in moral terms by studying plantation records. The difficulty remains that the study of slavery has tended to be the study of a social system rather than the study of the race which suffered from it. The approach by way of behavioural sciences which Elkins advocated can lead us a certain distance, but it can provide clues rather than solutions, new questions rather than new answers. In this impasse it is legitimate to look in yet another direction for aid.

Folk-lore and folk songs may provide the evidence which the more formal record cannot supply for they alone can reach down into the mind of the illiterate mass.[1] Joel Chandler Harris is not popular with modern students of black history, for the golden haze surrounding Uncle Remus is the very thing they wish to dispel. Nor has he a high standing amongst modern folklorists. Nevertheless, the inspiration of his stories was authentic, and even if accuracy sometimes gave ground to literary effect, he began with real tales, passed orally from generation to generation, and reaching back to dim African roots. Uncle Remus himself is not merely a feeble and docile old man; servility is there but so is paternalism, he is ignorant but full of shrewd wisdom, he displays a childish simplicity but usually as a foil to his own histrionic skill. Brer Rabbit lives in a hostile world from which he cannot escape; but he meets his difficulties with resilience. He is lazy, impertinent and cunning—on occasions he is a thief, a liar, and a cheat—the prototype of a modern anti-hero. He is lazy because

[1] Zora Neale Huston, a black folklorist, wrote, 'Folk-lore is not as easy to collect as it sounds. The best source is where there are the least outside influences and these people, being usually under-privileged, are the shyest. And the Negro, in spite of his open-faced laughter, his seeming acquiescence, is particularly evasive. You see we are a polite people and we do not say to our questioner, "Get out of here!" We smile and tell him or her something that satisfies the white person because, knowing so little about us, he doesn't know what he is missing.' *Mules and Men* (New York and London, 1936), 18.

there is no profit in working for other men, impertinent because this alone preserved self-respect, and cunning because this is the way of survival when oppression has law on its side. The famous story of the tar-baby is an allegory of slavery. Tar is the degradation awaiting the slave who shows independence, and the cringing supplication of Brer Rabbit symbolises humiliation when there is no remedy in justice or law. But the Fox is taken in by a favourite myth of the master-class that Negroes cannot survive in freedom; escape in the briar patch proves the contrary and Brer Rabbit, laughing at the Fox, and cleaning the tar out of his hair, is the epitome of the successful fugitive. The Rabbit is one of a family of mythical figures fathered by Jack or John who 'is the great human culture hero in Negro folk-lore. He is like Daniel in Jewish folk-lore, the wish-fulfilment of a race. The one who, nevertheless, or in spite of laughter, usually defeats Ole Massa, God and the Devil. Even when Massa seems to have him in a hopeless dilemma he wins out by a trick.'[1]

The serious and tragic side of slave life is epitomised in the 'spirituals': Christian imagery acquires new meaning with its endurance, compassion, and promise of a better life; Jordan becomes the great frontier, angels the messengers of hope, and betrayal of faith the one unforgivable sin. These are the songs of submission but not of despair, of the acceptance of evil but not of resignation to its sway, of present tears and eternal hope. The value of all this as a historical source will be disputed, and danger lies in the degree to which personal predilections can be read into the text. Folk tales and songs contain the dreams of a race enslaved, and the interpretation of dreams can hardly claim scientific accuracy; but they may reveal more than travellers' tales, account books, or modern calculations of profitability.

Free Negroes left little impact upon the record in the South. Some records of Negro Churches survive, and a good deal of hostile comment by white writers; but there is little real evidence of their lives and livelihood. In the North the evidence is more prolific, for although the majority were in low-grade menial

[1] Zora Huston, *op. cit.*, 305.

employment, a few acquired education and the ministers of Negro Churches provided an intellectual élite. Most northern Negroes tended, however, to remain in the status into which they had been born, and there was therefore a hereditary element in the Negro élite; families who had won modest business success in the eighteenth century (when the colour line was less strictly drawn) tended to hold on to this status in the nineteenth century, and ministers and teachers tended to run in families. To this extent the educated Negro was not typical of his race; but the severe discrimination practised against all Negroes gave them a sense of racial solidarity which might otherwise have been fragmented by economic and educational differences.[1]

Educated Negroes, mainly ministers of religion, who took an active part in the abolitionist movement, contributed more to the literary sources than any other group. Though their numbers in the movement as a whole were small, their influence was considerable. White abolitionists were keen to encourage them as examples of what the race could achieve once freed from the shackles of slavery, though they were often readier to encourage them from a distance than to welcome their appearance on platforms in negrophobe districts. For their part Negro abolitionists kept their white fellow-workers aware that the emphasis in their campaign should be upon injustice to a race rather than upon the harm done by slavery to white society. They also demonstrated— by conventions, petitioning movements, and local organisation— that Negroes were capable of independent action without white supervision. It is therefore no accident that the best evidence of free Negro life and thought in the first half of the nineteenth century comes from the black abolitionists. It is necessary to be on one's guard against accepting their comments on slavery; but on the intellectual heritage of Afro-Americans it is the best evidence we have, eloquent, and often moving.[2]

The Civil War opened a new era in Negro history. It brought not only Emancipation but a limited degree of social mobility

---

[1] Leon Litwack, *North of Slavery* (Chicago, 1961), Chap. VI *passim*.

[2] There was an outcrop of works by Negro leaders in the mid-nineteenth

in the South and a relaxation of discriminatory practices in the North.[1] There is also a flood of information about people whose lives had hitherto been hidden. The military records provide much information about fugitive slaves coming into Union lines, and subsequently the records of the Freedmen's Bureau (especially those of its district headquarters) throw light upon the whole spectrum of southern Negro life. It is true that the record was compiled by whites, but for the most part by whites who looked at the freedmen without the deeply ingrained prejudices of slavery. Some were genuinely convinced by the theory of racial equality, most believed that somehow freedom must be shown to work, and all had to persuade rather than punish. The result is that even in the records compiled by Army officers who were least sympathetic to Negro aspirations, one gets the sense of dealing with human beings and not with models made to play their part in a system. The controversy over the enlistment of Negro troops left a marked impact upon Congressional debates, the press, and the writings of Negroes themselves. So, too, did the controversies, mainly at state and municipal level, over discriminatory laws, education and voting rights. The early experiment in emancipation and free labour at Port Royal aroused much interest, and its history has been written with professional brilliance.[2]

---

century which aimed to establish the claim of Negroes to share in the achievements of civilisation. The best known include Martin Delany, *The Condition, Elevation, Emigration and Destiny of the Colored People of the United States* (1852); Henry Highland Garnett, *The Past and the Present Condition and Destiny of the Colored Race* (1848); and James T. Holly, *A Vindication of the Capacity of the Negro Race for Self-Government and Civilised Progress as Demonstrated by Historical Events of the Haitian Revolution* (1857), the latter of particular interest in view of the prominent place given to Haiti in pro-slavery propaganda.

[1] For the story and sources of attempts to end discrimination see James M. McPherson, *The Struggle for Equality: Abolitionists and the Negro in the Civil War and Reconstruction* (Princeton, 1964). The bibliographical essay which concludes this important book is comprehensive and authoritative; see especially his comments on the Abolitionist Press (437–40), Abolitionist publications (441–43), and contemporary memoirs (443–44).

[2] Willie Lee Rose, *Rehearsal for Reconstruction*. A special aspect of the black role during Reconstruction is amply documented from Federal and state sources in Otis A. Singletary, *Negro Militia and Reconstruction* (Austin, 1951).

Radical Reconstruction in the South presents unique problems in the analysis of evidence. For the first time there was Negro participation in public life, and the interest and bitterness occasioned by the experience produced a flood of literary evidence. But few of the Negro leaders themselves left much in the way of written evidence, and their speeches are buried away in long-forgotten convention debates or in the files of short-lived Republican newspapers. By far the greatest part of the evidence comes from white southerners who had the strongest possible reasons for discrediting the consequences of Emancipation and equal rights. Indeed the volume and the unanimity of the sources misled historians, and provide a striking example of the truth that historical understanding cannot end with the evidence alone. One must ask, at every step, why the written word was committed to paper and under what circumstances. Pseudo-scientific history can see only a mass of evidence pointing to one conclusion; this may appear convincing until one realises that the verdict preceded the evidence. The record of corruption and ignorance was finally consolidated in the several volumes of the 1876 Congressional Committee ordered and conducted by a Democratic majority.

It would be irresponsible to assume that nothing in the white southern record of Reconstruction is true, but it is equally wrong-headed to assume that it tells the whole truth. Historians of the present generation are trying to disentangle the story, but it requires skill and perseverance to run down the evidence which puts this episode of Negro history into better proportion. Unfortunately contemporary prejudice is as strongly disposed to see no wrong committed by politically active Negroes as were their predecessors to see no right.

The end of slavery wrought changes in the mood of northern Negro leaders. The end of the crusade, and the modest relaxation of racial discrimination, turned their thoughts away from agitation and into the normal channels of middle-class advancement. If they had once emphasised the wrongs suffered by their race, they now sought to establish themselves as acceptable Americans. The typical mode was to celebrate the material or professional success achieved by individual Negroes, and this replaced the former emphasis upon the collective wrongs of the race. Though the large majority of northern Negroes remained amongst the poorest paid and worst housed urban and industrial workers, educated Negroes played little or no part in radical or reform movements. Negro newspapers and magazines increased, and the records of Churches became fuller; but though the volume increases its interest declines. Writers such as Martin Delany and Edward Blyden, who showed some originality and whose racial doctrines earn the approbation of modern black writers, had little contemporary influence. The economic and social aspects of Negro history in the North became lost in the general stream of evidence about urban and industrial growth.

In the South the problem of evidence, after the subsidence of Radical Reconstruction, is somewhat different. Though few of the Negroes active in politics left extensive collections of papers, the social and economic aspects of Negro life are fully documented. State and county records have still much to yield in detail, but one is no longer dealing with people who can be seen only through the eyes of others. Even if the great majority left no personal records, some owned property, some appear on tax rolls, in the courts they could sue and be sued. A small but substantial number moved up the social ladder to modest prosperity. The record is not a pleasant one when contrasted with the high hopes which followed Emancipation; but the 1880s were not entirely a period of despondency. Indeed, between the bitterness of political Reconstruction and the advent of Ben Tillman and his like, it looked as though the southern Negro would slowly better himself. This was the atmosphere in which Booker T. Washington lived his formative years, and by 1890 he was ready to begin his remarkable career as the principal spokesman and strategist of Afro-Americans.

The central problem of Afro-American history remains the definition of its content. Is it the study of a race transplanted or the history of Americans who are of African descent? Should the present popularity of 'black history', with its emphasis upon separation and distinctiveness, be compared to the filio pietistic study of other ethnic minorities? Should it record the distinctiveness of black culture, or should it emphasise black contributions to the common store of American civilisation? Can the problems of a bi-racial society be settled by applying the time-honoured principles of equal rights, or should white segregationist and black militants agree that separation is the answer? The dilemmas are symbolised by an argument over nomenclature. Is it Negro History or Black History or Afro-American History? The early nineteenth century recognised three categories, white, slave, and 'free persons of color'. Colloquially they distinguished between Negro, Mulatto, Quadroon and Octoroon; they spoke of black, very black, brown, light-skinned, and 'high yellow'. Whatever its ethnic accuracy this classification recognised that men of African descent, like other Americans, were becoming a mixed race. Neither Frederick Douglass nor Booker T. Washington was 'black' in a literal sense.

Around the turn of the century some writers began to press for 'Negro' with a capital letter to express their contention that they formed a distinct racial group. Negro writers thus consciously embraced white usage which classed as 'Negro' everyone with recognisable African descent, even though some have lighter skins than many 'whites' of Mediterranean ancestry, and persons who are part white and part Indian are often accepted as 'white'. As Gunnar Myrdal observed 'The definition of the "Negro race" is thus a social and conventional, not a biological concept'.[1] Yet 'Negro' writers were ready to adopt this usage and to claim as Negroes all who were recognisably descended from African ancestors. Most historians who wrote under the influence of the Civil Rights movement of the 1950s wrote of 'Negroes' and imagined that they were thus putting 'Negro' on the same footing as 'English' or 'French', 'Caucasian' or 'Aryan'. Yet in the more militant mood of the 1960s many 'Negroes' became aware of the truth of Myrdal's statement that 'The "Negro race" is defined in America by the white people',[2] and rejected the word along with

[1] Gunnar Myrdal, *An American Dilemma: The Negro Problem and Modern Democracy* (New York, 1944), 115.

[2] *Ibid.*, 113. Otto Klineberg, editor of *Characteristics of the American Negro* (New York, 1944), which was an offshoot of Myrdal's comprehensive survey,

white law, white politics, and white morality. In future there would be a Black race with Black History studied in programmes of Black Studies.

'Black' is deliberately emphasised to erase the association, in European languages, of 'black' with evil or unclean. It is insisted that only black historians can write black history or black critics interpret black literature. There is some justification for this attitude if one uses 'black' to describe not a colour or a race but all people whose ancestors experienced servitude. The bond of union and the distinguishing characteristic of black people is the legacy of slavery and the experience of discrimination. Yet many 'black' writers go beyond this historical definition and speak of 'black' as a race with characteristics of its own. These black separatists present a mirror image of the old southern segregationists; just as anyone with remote though recognisable African descent was 'Negro' and for this reason denied equal status, it is now maintained that anyone with remote but recognizable African descent is 'black' and so qualified to understand other 'blacks'.[1]

---

summed up the attitude of his contributors as follows: 'No one of them makes use of the concept of a distinctive and inherited Negro mentality. No one of them makes the assumption that the physical distinctiveness of the Negro indicates an innate difference in intellect. On the contrary · . . they all agree that psychological differences between Negroes and whites, though they may exist, are temporary . . . What differences there are appear to depend on existing discrepancies in the opportunities offered to the two groups.' Unfortunately, a quarter century after these confident words were written, the case remains unproven; if fewer white writers now proclaim that blacks are psychologically different and inferior, more black writers assert that they are different and potentially superior.

[1] One unfortunate effect of this attitude is that it tends to discourage some of the more interesting consequences of bi-racial experience. As Melville J. Herskovits wrote in 1930, 'What is the effect of environment on human types? Does Man retain his different racial characteristics no matter where he may be transported? . . . There are the whole group of problems which centre about the question of the physical results of racial crossing. Is there a decrease of fertility with race mixture? What is the effect on the behavior of the crossed individuals when compared with pure breeds?' *The New World Negro*, ed.

Dissatisfied with this position some historians have adopted the hyphenated 'Afro-Americans'. This may be used merely as a neutral device for avoiding the semantic difficulty presented by 'black', but it can also have the more subtle implication that persons of African descent in America are a part of American civilisation and cannot be studied separately from it. In the same way as some historians of immigration react against the filio-patristic study of ethnic groups as isolated phenomenon, so some historians use 'Afro-American' to stress the hope of convergence rather than the fact of divergence. In this chapter 'Afro-American' is not used with any such preconception but merely as the most accurate way of describing the people with whom it is concerned.

It would be inappropriate, in a book on historical sources, to enter too deeply into these controversies; but they cannot be wholly avoided because they influence the way in which sources are used. If one takes the racialist view one can hardly be content with a situation in which one is dependent, for the greater part of what one knew, upon evidence accumulated by another race. White Americans would hardly be content with a history of the United States written entirely from British sources. If, however, one accepts Negroes as a component part of the American people, one can accept the fact that for a part of American history know-ledge derives mainly from another element in that society. In the history of most countries there is somewhere a silent group which may be composed of an ethnic minority, a depressed class, or an illiterate mass. One regrets these lacunae in the historical record, but once they have been recognised they can contribute to the picture of the past. It may often be as important to show what cannot be known as it is to gather all the facts which can be known. But if history deals with a chosen people these gaps, and this dependence upon evidence supplied by others, can hardly be tolerated. The Israelites would hardly have been content to derive all evidence of the Exodus from Egyptian authorities, nor all knowledge of the captivity from Babylonian sources. It would be

---

Frances S. Herskovits (Bloomington, 1966). Insistence upon the solidarity of 'black' people drives questions of this kind out of court.

unfair to suggest that black historians must resort to myths when the evidence is one-sided, but at least it can be said that they have strong motives for going beyond the sources and invoking the aid of sociology, anthropology, and folk-lore. These skills may not be harmful if they provide new insight into human behaviour, but honesty compels one to draw a line between hypothesis and evidence. This is essential when—as in the study of slavery in the South—experience suggests that the available evidence is almost exhausted, or that new evidence when found will be of the same type as the old.[1]

[1] Emphasis in this chapter has been upon the difficulty in writing 'black history' with 'white' evidence or with no evidence at all; many contemporary Americans are, of course, fully aware of this difficulty and there are considerable efforts being made to investigate and organise sources which may have been overlooked in the past. Monroe N. Work, *A Bibliography of the Negro in Africa and America* (New York, 1928), has been supplemented by Dorothy B. Porter, *A Selected List of Books by and about the Negro*. There is a useful *Guide to Documents in the National Archives for Negro Studies*, by Paul Lewinson (Washington, 1947), and more recently Earl Spangler, *Bibliography of Negro History* (Minneapolis, 1963), Erwin K. Welsch, *The Negro in the United States: a research guide* (Bloomington, 1965), and Erwin A. Salk, *A Layman's Guide to Negro History* (Chicago, 1966). The reader who is unable to consult these specialised works can gain much from the bibliography to John Hope Franklin, *From Slavery to Freedom*, 3rd edn. (New York, 1967).

CHAPTER 13

Immigrants

The sources for the history of immigration lie scattered over two continents and a dozen countries. The direction in which one seeks will depend largely upon the questions asked, for the study of immigration comprises several separate though overlapping fields. There are studies of specified ethnic groups in America, problems of assimilation to American culture, changes in society produced by immigration, responses to immigration in various forms of nativism, immigrants as a source of information about the United States, the forces and motives behind migration, and its economic consequences. Exclusive attention to the transatlantic migration and emigrant arrivals tells only half the story; for once the alien had landed he became part of a stream of movement which carried both old and new Americans from state to state, from East to West, from the towns to new agricultural land and from the country to industrial and urban areas.

Newspapers and census returns, church records and city directories, port books and the reports of foreign consuls, the archives of American states and of foreign governments, the letters of simple men and ponderous official reports: all these and other sources can be pressed into service. No other field of enquiry demands so wide a range or demonstrates so effectively that American history is a part of international history.

Possible defects in the statistical record were explained in Chapter 1, but the census figures are sufficient to trace the main course of immigration history.[1] Though the figures before 1820

[1] In Chapter 1 the failure to record immigration from British North America was noted, and also the lack of distinction between the permanent settlers and transient travellers. Recent studies suggest that (a) the number of people re-

are sporadic and incomplete one can say with confidence that there was substantial immigration in the years following Independence, a slackening of pace during the generation of European wars, and a sharply rising trend from 1815. In 1820 the recorded figure was 8,385; in 1854 it reached a pre-Civil War peak of 427,833. This was followed by a downward movement, and a very sharp drop at the beginning of the war; but it began to revive before the end of the conflict and by 1873 it was 459,803. The depression years saw a drop but by 1880 it was almost up to the previous peak with 457,257 and in 1882 reached the highest point of the nineteenth century at 788,992. A trough at 334,203 in 1886 was still remarkably high; from then a generally upward trend, with fluctuations, prepared the way for the spectacular record of the early twentieth century when, between 1900 and 1914, the figure topped a million in six separate years.

Another way of considering these figures is to give the number of immigrants per 10,000 of existing population.[1] This gives some measure of the impact as distinct from gross numbers. The figures on the opposite page show the peak years.

These figures relate immigration to the population of the whole United States, and are useful mainly for global calculations about the effect of immigration upon American growth. The regional distribution is very different. There were parts of the South where men lived through the whole century without ever meeting a person who had come directly from Europe and would probably meet only a few born outside the United States; but even in slack years the wharves of New York, Boston and Philadelphia were busy with incoming immigrants, and the back streets of these

---

turning home after a spell in the United States has been underestimated, and (b) that there were some international wanderers who crossed the Atlantic in both directions two or three times.

[1] This calculation is drawn from Brinley Thomas, *Migration and Economic Growth: A Study of Great Britain and the Atlantic Economy* (Cambridge, 1954), p. 327, Table 134. This work contains an invaluable collection of statistical data; the inferences drawn are not accepted without qualification by economic historians, but no one else has tackled the statistical aspects of migration on so large a scale or with such impressive results.

Immigrants

Year	Number of immigrants per 10,000 of population.
1837	55.2
1842	62.7
1854	178.9
1873	109.2
1882	156.8

The years of least impact were

1831	18.6
1838	28.5
1843	41.0
1858	50.0
1862	35.2
1878	29.2
1886	58.9

cities were filled with new arrivals for whom urban life was either a Mecca or a staging post on the way to find land of their own.

In 1790 the culture of the United States was overwhelmingly Anglo-Saxon and Protestant. There were sizeable German enclaves, notably in Pennsylvania, retaining the language and churches of their homeland; but they had little influence in public life outside the districts in which they had settled. The old Dutch families continued in New York; retaining some sense of separate identity but speaking English and, in some cases, playing a part in public life which was important but indistinguishable from their neighbours of British descent. The same was true of a few old Huguenot families in South Carolina. Some Catholic Irish were already settled on the eastern seaboard, but their numbers were insignificant. For the next fifty years immigration did little to change the character of the people; though immigration from Germany and Ireland increased, so did that from England, Scotland, Northern Ireland, and Wales. Then came the dramatic period when the numbers of Catholic Irish and mainly Catholic Germans soared; the peaks were 221,253 Irish in 1851 and 215,009 Germans in 1854. High as these figures appear they are probably underestimated significantly through failure to record immigrants entering from British North America. In the later years of the nineteenth century Germans continued to figure very prominently, though

255

in the 1880s there were large numbers of Scandinavians (most of whom headed for new land in Minnesota and the further North-West where they formed compact settlements).

A quantitative picture of immigration therefore requires a good deal more than round figures, for the impact was unevenly distributed by region, year, and ethnic background. The Federal census returns give the number in each county of foreign birth, and this information can be supplemented by state figures. A good deal of information was shown cartographically in the beautifully prepared *Statistical Atlas of the United States*.[1] It is particularly important to obtain this information for British immigrants who did not congregate in particular areas, and who were easily assimilated; without this check it is easy to forget that though immigrants from Great Britain never touched the spectacular peaks of the Irish and Germans they continued to come in large numbers. Over the whole century the immigrant whom the ordinary American was likely to meet, outside certain well-defined regions, would have been born in England, Scotland or Wales. This should be remembered when considering the continued ascendancy of Anglo-Saxon and Protestant culture.

The study of select immigrant groups in the United States draws upon materials which are diffuse but fairly easy to locate. As the historian of immigrants from Ulster writes,

> Primary sources for Scotch-Irish settlement and social life in America are almost inexhaustible. There are county records, with their details of wills, purchase of land, and the like; court records . . . tax rolls—these make dull reading, yet afford such raw material as specific dates of settlement in an area, size of farms, movement of families, marriages, and offences against order.[2]

Where settlement was on public land it may be necessary to pursue the chase to the Federal Department of the Interior. Groups which made strong efforts to maintain cultural links with their

[1] Henry Gannett (compiler), *Statistical Atlas of the United States* (Washington, 1898). Based on the 11th Census, but containing much historical information. A series of maps show the distribution of foreign-born population.

[2] James G. Leyburn, *The Scotch-Irish: a Social History* (Chapel Hill, 1962), p. 362. This is a scholarly work with an excellent bibliography.

country of origin were normally solicitous to record the movements and whereabouts of their members, and the Church was a natural clearing house for information; it would often fall to the lot of the minister to carry on correspondence with Church authorities and others in the former country. From this point the quest for evidence may take one to the former country itself to search for immigrant letters. One may carry the enquiry further back in time to investigate the original motives for migration, government policy, and shipping. Many ethnic groups formed their own historical societies early in this century, and their published proceedings contain a wealth of material, though this may often have to be sought amidst a mass of genealogical and antiquarian material which has little relevance for the more general problems of migration and settlement. There are also several historical societies formed by churches in which one ethnic element predominated. Finally, the foreign language press will always be a source of primary importance; in some cases immigrant communities were strong enough to maintain their own newspaper, in others a newspaper based on a city attempted to serve a region.[1]

It may be anticipated that this kind of research will be easier when immigrants formed communities in rural areas and formed small towns than when—at the two extremes—they scattered widely over frontier areas, joining a general stream of westward migrants—or congregated in the cities. In cities the records tend to be more numerous but also less accurate, while small groups found it more difficult to remain cohesive. With all the facilities of urban life around them there was less incentive for communal leadership and action. The study of immigrants in cities also spills over into all kinds of other urban problems: housing, sanitation, crime, public order and city government. Two examples illustrate

[1] Various lines of enquiry are suggested by Theodore C. Blegan, 'The Saga of the Immigrant', in John F. McDermott, ed., *Research Opportunities in American Cultural History* (Lexington, Ky, 1961), pp. 66 ff. A great deal of material was collected by Carl Wittke, *We Who Built America* (New York, 1939) and in other books and articles; for a bibliography of his works see Fritiof Ander (ed.), *In the Trek of the Immigrant: Essays presented to Carl Wittke* (Rock Island, 1964).

the range and character of these urban studies: Oscar Handlin's *Boston Immigrants*,[1] and Robert Ernst's *Immigrant Life in New York City 1825–1863*.[2] Handlin's 'Note on Sources' is an essay on the available materials with comments. The immigrant press was a major source, 'particularly valuable' and 'because the press was not yet a big business, every significant shade of opinion could afford an organ of expression'.[3] Foreign newspapers were not of great value except for occasional news of compatriots in America or published letters from immigrants. In addition to the Federal census, both the State of Massachusetts and the City of Boston compiled population records; indeed the example of Boston's 1845 census was responsible for several improvements in the Federal census of 1850. The state of Massachusetts also compiled four industrial censuses in 1837, 1845, 1855 and 1865. The Municipal Records are incomplete after 1822, but contain a good deal of information about government and health. The state archives furnished important material on Education, Alien Passengers, and crime. The state also ordered a number of special investigations into housing, health, and sanitation. The British consuls in Boston sent a good deal of information home, and their letters are now in the Foreign Office Archives of the Public Record Office. Many travellers visited Boston, and a few left accounts of conditions in the city. Immigrant guides were not very helpful, but there are large collections of pamphlets in Dublin and Boston, and published sermons often contained comments on social conditions. Finally there are city directories from 1789.

Robert Ernst used the manuscript schedules of both New York and Federal censuses. There were a large number of public documents published by the city and by the state, and he noted eleven city and ten state documents as being of special interest for his study. From the Federal government came Congressional reports on the immigration of foreign paupers into the United

---

[1] *Boston's Immigrants: a Study in Acculturation* (Boston, 1st ed., 1941, revised and enlarged ed., 1959). The information which follows is extracted from 'Note on Sources' 1959 ed., pp. 267 ff.

[2] *Immigrant Life in New York City 1825–1863* (New York, 1949).

[3] *Op. cit.*, p. 268.

States, in 1890 a statistical report on European emigration, and consular correspondence from five Irish, three German, two Italian, one English and one Cuban port. The Chamber of Commerce of the City of New York and private organisations interested in social conditions and sanitation published several reports; one from the Citizens Association of New York in 1865 was described as having excellent materials on slums, while the annual reports of the New York Association for Improving the Condition of the Poor were 'absolutely essential'. Reports of the German Society of New York were 'packed with detailed information on aid to newly arrived German immigrants'. There were a batch of directories, guidebooks, the New York Annual Register, reports on election frauds, and other miscellaneous publications. Church records, trade union records, private records, and a large selection of newspapers, including the foreign press, were used. An exceptionally long list of primary sources concludes with immigrant guides, travellers' accounts, and other contemporary writings.

These two examples give some idea of the range and opportunities in studying the history of immigrants in cities. All immigrant studies spill over into two other important fields—assimilation and nativism—but the urban story is more entwined with them than rural settlements. Assimilation can be considered under three main headings: the acceptance of American culture, the success of immigrants in achieving their goals, and the extent to which ethnic groups maintained a degree of separation from the society around them. The acceptance of culture was not only a matter of language and education; it often meant the acquisition of new patterns of behaviour and scales of value. Politics could be as important as schools, but one has to remember that immigrant groups had different responses, and understood aspects of American culture in different ways. There were interesting contrasts in political attitudes between German and Irish immigrants. The revolutionaries who left Germany after 1848 were a special brand of middle-class intellectual who responded eagerly to the opportunities for political participation in America. Carl Schurz left eloquent testimony to the enthusiasm and vigour with which some of them embraced the Republican party and the cause of Union.[1] But these were exceptions: the great mass of German immigrants had no tradition of political activity and were prepared to accept whatever they found. A modern scholar observes that 'the bulk of these arrivals had no incentive to change the national ideology or political institutions to accommodate themselves'.[2] They welcomed freedom from the exactions and petty impositions of noble landowners, and were natural but generally inactive recruits for the Democratic party. On the other hand the Irish had a tradition of intense dislike of a landlord class and of the government which supported it; but they 'were much less concerned with the character of government as such, than whether they controlled the particular one which was closest at hand'.[3] They became extremely active in local government, but as the Federal government did not bear upon them they were interested in it only so far as the patronage and influence of a national party enabled them to achieve local power.

There are other contrasts between immigrants in their acceptance of American culture. Language was no barrier to the Irish, but they clung tenaciously to their Church and their ancient hatred of Great Britain; there was little to treasure in folk memories of life at home, but a tremendous loyalty to Irish people. The Germans clung to their language, and treasured memories of traditional customs, including beer, Christmas trees, and a variety of sausages which they engrafted on to native American life. They were divided in religion, but the Lutheran majority found little difficulty in establishing good relations with American Protestant denominations, while German Catholicism had none of the fiercely nationalistic strain of the Irish.

The sources for these problems of cultural assimilation must clearly be drawn from the large body of material to which

[1] Carl Schurz, *Reminiscences* (New York, 1913), ii, 67. 'Thus the old cause of human freedom was to be fought for on the soil of the new world. The great final decision seemed to be pending.' (Writing of the 1865 election.)

[2] Walter O. Forster, 'The Immigrant and the American National Idea', in Fritiof Ander (ed.), *In the Trek of the Immigrant: Essays presented to Carl Wittke* (Rock Island, 1964), p. 166.

[3] Forster, *op. cit.*, p. 167.

reference has already been made. A problem for the historian is the extent to which he should draw upon the concepts of anthropologists or sociologists to explain the varying reactions, and the tensions involved. A historian must rely upon his sources, and there are a good many ways in which he can use them to measure even so indefinable a process as assimilation. The foreign language press can, for instance, yield information about the number and interests of its readers, the respective amounts of space devoted to the parent country and to 'American' news, and the type of advertisements inserted. On the other hand some indicators can be picked up from the English language press. The reports and investigations of boards of education should provide much evidence. The records of foreign language churches may help one to detect the watershed, when the church ceases to be a welcome haven in an alien world and begins a struggle to keep the allegiance of an American-born generation. A theory is no substitute for evidence, but it is worth remembering that anthropologists have much experience in recording cultural tensions, and that sociologists have much experience in tracing the movements of groups in society; this experience may well suggest new sources which should be investigated and new ways in which they should be used.

The counterpart to the study of assimilation is the effect of immigrants upon the society they entered. There can be no uniform rule, for at one extreme are the communities which succeeded both in keeping their separate identities and in dominating a district or a town, and at the other are the immigrants who sought to preserve no links with the old country and slipped unostentatiously into the main stream of American society. Between the two came immigrants such as the Irish who became self-conscious Americans while remoulding that part of American society which they took over. There is an obvious danger that the nature of the evidence may distort reality. The exceptional impact is far more likely to leave a record than quiet infiltration; but over a long period the latter may have a greater influence. In industrial labour, for instance, what attracted attention in the later years of the nineteenth century, was the recruitment of unskilled labour from Irish, Polish, Ukrainian and other East European people; but the smaller number of skilled British immigrants had a much greater influence upon the strategy of labour action.[1] In the sweated garment, cigar and similar trades, the Jewish immigrants exercised an influence out of proportion to their numbers.[2] It may often be difficult to disentangle the true story of immigrant influences from the mass of prejudiced information. Nativist attacks on immigrants are particularly untrustworthy because they not only magnify the influence of some groups but are highly selective in the influences singled out for attack.

Some aspects of nativism will be discussed in Chapter 17, when dealing with American nationalism, but in the present context the character and purpose of the literary evidence will be considered. Nativism always coupled hatred of alien races and religion with attempts to define the true essence of Americanism. From the earliest days it was therefore caught in a contradiction between the universal promises of the Revolutionary era and the belief that they were valid only for Protestants of North European (and preferably British) descent. The two ideas might be reconciled by an environmental theory which suggested that some experiences and some beliefs rendered men incapable of appreciating American blessings; but there remained a contradiction between the inherent strength of the American tradition and its vulnerability to comparatively small numbers of immigrants of different race and religion.

The old Federalist hostility which left a memorial in the Alien Act of 1798 was somewhat more consistent than later manifestations. At least they lived in a period when there was genuine doubt about the future of the new nation, and it could be argued (though not proved) that 'Jacobin' agitation was detrimental to the Union. Nevertheless it is symbolic that the first attempt to repulse the foreign threat to American culture should have had a

[1] Cf. Rowland T. Berthoff, *British Immigrants in Industrial America 1789–1950* (Cambridge, Mass., 1953).

[2] Cf. Henry Pelling, *American Labor* (Chicago, 1960), pp. 87–8, and Melech Epstein, *Jewish Labor in U.S.A. 1882–1914* (New York, 1950), *passim.*

decidedly conservative tone. Basically the Federalist case was that the people were deluded enough without the risk of exposing them to foreign propaganda. The debates and pamphlets generated by the controversy have, perhaps, been too little regarded by historians. As in later episodes it is assumed that the case against aliens was so obviously wrong-headed that its arguments do not merit serious consideration. Nativism in the 1840s and 1850s has tended to suffer in the same way from condemnation by neglect. Few care to ponder the arguments of Samuel F. B. Morse in his *Foreign Conspiracy against the Liberties of the United States* or of Lyman Beecher in his *Plea for the West*, and it is only in passing that the anti-Catholic activities of Elijah Lovejoy, the abolitionist martyr, are recalled. No historian has been moved to write sympathetically of the American or Know Nothing Party though, as Richard Hofstadter remarked, 'anti-Catholicism did become an enduring factor in American politics'. The motives which could have persuaded Millard Fillmore, a self-made Whig of impregnable respectability, to become a candidate for the party in 1856 are seldom given serious examination. An exception was Allan Nevins, whose dislike for the principles of the party was clear, but who also gave prominence to a sentence written by Orestes Brownson in his *Quarterly Review* in July 1854,

> We beg our naturalised citizens and foreign residents to bear in mind that the Native American sentiment is but the sentiment of American nationality, and that it is their duty as well as their interest to respect it, and not to ridicule and vituperate it.[1]

More recently another scholar has pointed out the reality of the questions raised by nativists, even though their remedies were violent and unattractive. If their fears for American culture were fictitious one faces a basic problem that either 'all immigrants shared the values of American society, or that American society had none, or that it did not matter whether it did or they did'.[2]

---

[1] Allan Nevins, *Ordeal of the Union*, ii, pp. 23–32. The quotation from Brownson is on 328.

[2] Forster, *op. cit.*, p. 171.

Without entering too far into the issues raised by this statement, it can be agreed that historians who ignore the evidence provided by nativist books, newspapers and speeches exclude from consideration an important source of evidence about the social problems of immigration.

Immigrants themselves contributed a great deal of information about the United States in their letters home. Some were written in the expectation that they would be published in the newspapers of their old homes. Others were written for parents, relatives, or friends alone; but their chance of survival was somewhat greater than that of a normal letter written by a person in humble circumstances. They would be treasured, shown to friends, and stood a good chance of preservation in the next generation. One study of letters written for publication and private consumption revealed the curious fact that the former were far more likely to be extreme in their praise or condemnation of the United States.[1] Other limitations upon the usefulness of immigrant letters is that they were written by men and women who were not trained observers, whose vision was limited, and who were often (like many of us) at a loss when it came to filling out a letter to someone who had shared none of the experiences. Banal comments and the weather were stand-bys.[2] Taken in all, letters home are an excellent

[1] Charlotte Erickson, 'Agrarian Myths of English Immigrants', in Ander, *op. cit.*, 59.

[2] A number of nineteenth-century collections of letters from British emigrants to America are available. Erickson cites G. Poulett Scrope, *Extracts from Letters from Poor Persons who emigrated last year to Canada and the United States* (London, 1831); Benjamin Mount (ed.), *Twenty Letters from Labourers in America to their friends in England* (London, 1829); *Letters from Sussex Emigrants . . . to Upper Canada* (Petworth, 2nd ed., 1833); *Counsel for Emigrants with Original Letters from Canada and the United States* (Aberdeen, 1834). Modern collections include Milo M. Quaife (ed.), 'An English Settler in Pioneer Wisconsin; the Letters of Edwin Bottomley, 1842–50', *Publications of the State Historical Society of Wisconsin Collections*, 25 (Madison, 1918); Alan Conway, *The Welsh in America: Letters from Immigrants* (Cardiff, 1961). The most recent addition to the list is Charlotte Erickson, *The Invisible Immigrant: the adaptation of English and Scottish immigrants in nineteenth-century America* (London, 1972): a collection of letters with Theodore Blegon (ed.), *The Land of Their Choice* (St Paul, 1955).

record of men's own reactions, and they enable one to build up a collective picture of life through immigrant eyes; but they should be used with caution as evidence of conditions in America. Newly arrived immigrants were unlikely to understand the complexities of American politics, and their judgment upon economic conditions was frequently poor. English immigrants with agricultural experience were likely to be scornful of American methods, but sometimes found that the tried expedients of closely cultivated English farms were unsuccessful in American forest clearings. On the other hand, English agriculturalists may sometimes have been more successful than Americans in the early days of prairie settlement.[1]

The private letter was supplemented by an increasing volume of promotional literature issued by states, land companies, and railroads. These suffer the obvious defects of any advertising campaign, and may reveal more about the intentions of the boosters than about actual conditions. For this very reason, however, promotional literature is a first-hand source of information about aspirations and methods in the economic development of the country. Immigrant guides are numerous but somewhat less helpful (with a few marked exceptions). The guides were normally written to make money for the author, were sold to men who had no check upon the information, and whose subsequent criticisms were unlikely to come home to roost. The writers had to demonstrate some familiarity with America, but

---

[1] Erickson, *Agrarian Myths of English Immigrants*, argues that the majority of British emigrants came from agricultural areas and went into farming. She uses the British census of 1841 to demonstrate that though the highest proportion of emigrants came from the West Riding of Yorkshire, the next highest (in order) were Sussex, Cornwall, Cumberland, Monmouth, Somerset, Devon and Hereford; except for Monmouth these were dominantly rural counties by 1840. But many rural counties were not in the seventeen counties supplying most emigrants, and the East Riding of Yorkshire, with the highest percentage of agricultural labour, was low in the list. Clearly more investigation of the social and economic background to British emigration is necessary. British Parliamentary debates and reports contain much information on the Poor Laws, assisted emigration and (before 1825) restraints upon the emigration of skilled artisans.

it was more important for them to write something than to ascertain the facts. It was too easy to present a guess or a piece of third-hand gossip as the truth. This does not mean that they are valueless as sources, but they are more likely to be evidence of what the migrant may have believed than of what actually existed.

Letters, promotional literature, and guides therefore tell us a great deal more about people than about things, and this is their great value. The letters of immigrants above all throw light upon the personal problems of the migrants, and raise a curtain-revealing experience in a stratum of society where little written evidence survives. The letters which found their way into print also help to build up a picture of the images and aspirations which persuaded so many thousands to cross the Atlantic.

From the human story distilled from this kind of evidence one can turn to the social and economic forces behind the great migration. Nineteenth-century Americans normally assumed that the primary motive which brought so many to their shores was a desire to escape from oppressive political and social systems. Modern scholars have been more inclined to stress the impersonal economic pressures at work in the Atlantic economy. 'What is needed,' writes one authority, 'is a concept of economic development which stresses the widening of markets, the dynamic of increasing returns, and the international mobility of labour and capital as a medium through which an international economy grows and changes its character. Viewed as an essential part of the process of economic expansion, migration not only induces but is itself partly determined by changes in the structure of the international community.'[1] In this light the Atlantic migration ceases to be a uniquely American experience and becomes part of the changing balance of production and labour in an advancing international economy. This involves not only the use of a different kind of source material but also emphasis upon the geographical origins of migration. A British scholar has observed that 'it was in the nature of things that American tradition and, when it came to recognise migration as a legitimate field of study,

[1] Brinley Thomas, *op. cit.*, 30.

American historical scholarship should assume the same point of view and, taking the migrant's departure very much for granted, should concentrate upon his destination'.[1] He went on to point out that 'the long cycle of mass migration from Europe was determined by the settlement of the great grass lands which colonised not only North America, Australia and Argentina, but also the Indus Valley, Siberia, Inner Mongolia and Manchukuo'.[2] So far as the United States were concerned the greatest volume of migration after 1870 was not to the grass lands but to industrial areas, and that even amongst native-born Americans there was a migration from the farms to the cities and industrial or mining districts, so that though one can argue that at one stage the dominant factor for most migrants was a desire to possess their own land, it later became the desire to escape from the depressed countryside to the higher rewards and wider opportunities of urban and industrial employment. 'The inner secrets of emigration are to be sought in the working of those two "revolutions" which are so inter-connected, the demographic and the industrial.'[3]

It is not, however, possible to place too much emphasis upon broad chronological divisions. If one can generalise by saying that before 1840 most migrants made for farmlands, and that after 1870 a majority went to towns, factories and mines, one must also remember that not only each ethnic group but often each locality or each occupation within an ethnic group, had its own pattern of migration. Studies of Welsh and Cornish migrants, of specialised groups such as potters, tin miners, and slate quarry workers, and of peasant communities in the Mediterranean and the West of Scotland, each reveal a distinctive pattern of migration but also strong associations with particular districts in the United States or elsewhere. This, in turn, can be explained either by the accident that early settlers had chosen a district to which their kith and kin were attracted, or by the existence of a particular kind of employment, or by a combination of both.

---

[1] Frank Thistlewaite, 'Migration from Europe Overseas in the Nineteenth and Twentieth Centuries,' in *Comité International des Sciences Historiques XI*ᵉ *Congrès International des Sciences Historiques 1960. Rapports*, v (Uppsala, 1960). 33–4.   [2] *Ibid.*, p. 49.   [3] *Ibid.*, p. 51.

It will be seen that as soon as one moves in the direction of statistical evidence for migration, one is drawn off again by questions which cannot be quantified. Indeed it may prove impossible to separate emotional, social, and economic factors. The Irish migrants did not dissociate their economic distress from English rule, the power of the landowners, and Protestant ascendancy; but they did not move in huge numbers until famine provided the spark which set off a desperate explosion. When this happened they overcame obstacles—such as poverty, poor communications, and shortage of shipping—which would have been sufficient to slow if not to halt other movements. It would be possible to cite other cases in which economic conditions seemed to favour migration and the obstacles were not formidable, but the will to do so did not exist.

In these conditions arguments over the respective force of the 'push' and the 'pull' in Atlantic migration become somewhat pointless. On the one hand there is a broad canvas, yet to be fully covered, on which are sketched out the shifts of population within an Atlantic economy; and this can be strengthened by statistical evidence of population increases, economic growth, business fluctuations, and employment opportunities. On the other hand one can move to the micro-studies of selected groups, both in America and in their homelands. The current trend is away from studies which concentrate exclusively upon ethnic groups in the United States, towards consideration of ethnic, occupational, and regional groups extending across the seas and lands of the nineteenth-century world. Nor need the study be confined chronologically or to the Atlantic; twentieth-century movements and Asiatic migration may well provide some clues to the behaviour of Rhinelanders in the 1850s or Norwegians in the 1880s.

It becomes clear that in the study of immigration, as in so many other fields, the problem is not shortage of materials but organising concepts. When we know the questions to ask we can say with some confidence that the evidence exists to provide at least partial answers. Somewhere between the comparatively simple task of reconstructing the experience of cohesive ethnic communities in rural America, and contemplation of the great swirling tides of international population movements, lies the point at which one can bring together personal decisions and impersonal pressures into a grand synthesis. But the road to the heights of speculative theory lies through the forests of individual and communal records up the stony slopes of verifiable statistics. There is no shorter road.[1]

[1] There are two excellent collections of source material edited by Edith Abbott: *Immigration: Select Documents and Case Records* (1924), and *Historical Aspects of the Immigration Problem* (1926). The experience of a particular category of immigrant is studied by Ray Boston in *British Chartists in America* (Manchester, 1971). Here the problem was to follow the careers of identifiable individuals not the fortunes of an ethnic group, and as many former Chartists maintained their transatlantic links there was much material in British newspapers, pamphlets and periodicals.

CHAPTER 14

People in Factories and Mines

It might seem that the field of labour history is clearly defined; yet there is a basic question, often unasked, which should determine not only the approach but also the sources to be used. Is it the history of labour leaders or of men who labour? Most labour historians have been primarily concerned with organisation, leadership, and the development of strategy for labour. The first serious historian to work in this field studies the labour 'movement'; the founder of the modern school of labour history wrote 'The History of Labour' but he and his colleagues devoted most of their time to organised labour; in 1929 an influential work was entitled *The Labor Movement in the United States*.[1] Thus scholars who worked during the formative period of modern professional history took organised labour as their principal theme. In this they were the children of their age. The ambitious and oecumenical objectives of the Knights of Labor formed the background, while the political rise of European socialist parties was in the foreground of their experience. Rightly they accused their predecessors and contemporaries of neglecting a significant aspect of American history. 'American historians,' wrote John R. Commons, 'until the last ten or fifteen years were wholly unconscious of the existence of a permanent labour question.'[2] Yet

[1] Richard T. Ely, *The Labor Movement in the United States* (Baltimore, 1886); John R. Commons et al., *History of Labor in the United States* (New York, ed., 1918); Norman J. Ware, *The Labor Movement in the United States 1860–1895* (New York, 1929). These comments, and those which follow, are not intended to denigrate the efforts of men who laid the foundations for the scholarly study of labour history, but to demonstrate that the quest for sources is often guided by current social attitudes, and that, once the sources to support these attitudes have been assembled, they tend to determine the direction of future study.

[2] John R. Commons et al., *History of Labor in the United States*, 2 vols, (New York, 1819), ii, 546.

organised labour never comprised more than a minority of the industrial labour force. The perspective has also changed. No one today would deny the importance of organised labour in American life, but they would hesitate to describe as a 'movement' a social phenomenon so deliberately void of ideological content. The 'movement' which the early labour historians studied had doubtful claims to represent more than a part of labour, and it has not developed the political or intellectual force which they anticipated. The importance of organised labour need not be denied, but it should not be the sole concern of labour history.

Preoccupation with organised labour determined the sources to be sought. Evidence of active combinations against employers; the formation and proceedings of associations, societies or unions by wage-earners; the countermoves by employers, officials, and the public—these were their major themes. Press comments and court cases were the staple diet for labour history in the first half of the nineteenth century. For this period Commons and his associates relied heavily upon the reports of labour conspiracy trials, and the comments of newspapers. After the Civil War the sources multiplied, throwing a stronger but still narrow beam upon labour history.

Even on this chosen ground the task of the historians was not easy. Nineteenth-century men were not likely to regard working-class activity as 'history', while labour organisations themselves were financially poor, lacked staff, and were far too preoccupied with immediate tactics to preserve their records for posterity. Archivists and librarians reflected these attitudes, and while much effort went into collecting records of the colonial and revolutionary past, little attention was given to the contemporary history of wage-earners. Dozens of newspapers, aimed at wage-earners in general or at particular trades, were launched between 1830 and 1860, but few copies survived and of some no complete files could be found. Pamphlet literature and the published proceedings of early unions had gone the same way to oblivion. Even reports of the labour conspiracy trials, which attracted wide interest and were published commercially, rarely survived, and such was the lack of interest in libraries that even when the reports had been entered in the catalogues they could not be located.[1] In the event 'some of the most important material . . . has', Commons recorded, 'not been found in libraries but has been obtained by searching dusty old bookshops in many cities, and by begging or buying personal collections from aged labour leaders'.[2]

Since that time the collection of material has gone steadily forward, but the emphasis is still heavily upon organisers, organisations, and the conflicts between them and employers. The men who figure in these sources are almost exclusively the skilled men, and those amongst them who became active. Thus 'labour history' really dealt with a minority of a minority, and though it was clearly worthwhile to recover the history of their efforts, there was a danger in substituting what was known of the few for what was not known of the mass. There was a temptation, for men who criticised their contemporaries for assuming that labour activity was not 'history', to fall into a similar error in assuming that only the vocal minority deserved the attention of historians.

If this was an error it was pardonable, for if contemporaries had taken little notice, save in crises of conflict, of organised labour, they had almost ignored the unorganised masses. This was especially true when the low-paid or unemployed were also of foreign birth and recently arrived in America. Of the Boston poor in the early nineteenth century it has been observed that

> Since . . . immigrants did not form an integral part of Boston's economy, it is difficult to know precisely how they managed to exist. They played no role in the usual accounts of her commercial and industrial life. Their contemporaries were aware that Europeans were there . . . but completely neglected them in describing the business of the city.[3]

There was a difference between American and British attitudes. In the older, hierarchical society it had always been assumed that the

[1] John R. Commons *et al.* (eds.), *Documentary History of Industrial Society in America*, 10 vols (Cleveland, 1910). Noted in the Preface to vol. iii (*Labor Conspiracy Cases*).

[2] *History of Labor in the United States*, ii, 543.

[3] Oscar Handlin, *Boston's Immigrants* (Cambridge, 1941), 55.

social edifice would rest upon a permanent labouring class; relieving the distresses of the poor—either officially through the rates or by private charity—was a constant topic of conversation and endeavour. In America it was assumed that no one was condemned to permanent poverty, and in an expanding society no one seriously considered that unemployment might be endemic. There was no need to talk about the poor, because the political and social conditions of America had a built-in remedy for poverty. Thus there was no need to investigate the causes of poverty, and in America, unlike Britain, there is no large volume of contemporary comment upon the condition of the poor. This assumption was shared even by the professed friends of labouring men. The Workingmen's Parties of the Jacksonian period, mainly composed of skilled craftsmen and small property owners, assumed that equal rights would open the gates of opportunity to all. Moral reformers believed that sober living and religious observance would dissolve the crime, vice and deprivation in the lower ranks of society; and, of course, the cities—where these evils were evident—formed only a small part of American society. Horace Greeley, who claimed with some justice that his New York *Tribune* was labour's most effective and sensitive champion, shared the American dream that the working man who displayed honesty and industry could make good, or at least live decently on his earnings. The skilled men who organised unions referred to the unskilled and recent immigrants only when alarmed by the possibility of blackleg intrusion into their preserves. Travellers, to quote Oscar Handlin again, 'frequently misled . . . by emphasising the curious rather than the commonplace'.[1] Thus the sources of information and informed comment on the lives of the unskilled poor are very meagre.

The British traveller James Silk Buckingham, whose radical opinions inclined to take a favourable view of American society and who visited the United States in 1837, commented upon 'the entire absence of those revolting scenes of drunkenness, prostitution, wretchedness, and misery which obtrude themselves on the eye in almost every part of the great towns of England', but

[1] *Op. cit.*, 56.

round, even in Philadelphia (which had the best record of any city for private philanthropy) 'suffering among even the sober and industrious classes of labourers . . . for want of adequate remuneration'.[1] In New York he saw 'destitution in its most abject state and . . . intemperance in its most fearful forms', and observed that 'the instances of death, from destitution and want, are much more numerous than I had thought possible in a country like this, where food of every kind is abundant and cheap; and where labour of every description is largely remunerated'.[2] In Baltimore 'the great bulk of the labouring classes' were 'Irish or German, originally imported as emigrants, with a union of Americans, and the descendants of all three'. They were 'in general uneducated, intemperate, and turbulent'. By contrast, however, the 'small shopkeepers, native mechanics, and tradesmen . . . appear to be better informed, more industrious, and in better condition as to circumstances than the same class of persons in England'.[3]

Other evidence could be adduced to demonstrate the existence, in American society in the first half of the nineteenth century, of a fairly sharp social line drawn between skilled workers and the mass of the unskilled; yet most of the sources for labour history in this period are concerned exclusively with the skilled. It seems impossible to obtain any quantitative check upon the observations of travellers such as Buckingham or upon the generalisations which may appear in the proceedings and publications of charitable societies. Not until the census of 1850 instituted the first systematic check upon occupations is it possible to describe accurately the anatomy of American industrial society.

This deficiency in the sources handicaps efforts to analyse the process broadly known as 'industrialisation'. In many branches of American industry the transition to factory production came much later than is commonly supposed, and there were a number of transitional stages. Masters and journeymen worked side by side although one employed the other, and both could, on occasion, recognise common interests against the merchants who bought

---

[1] J. S. Buckingham, *America: Historical, Statistical and Descriptive*, 3 vols (London, 1841), ii, 85.   [2] *Ibid.*, i, 151, 160.   [3] *Ibid.*, i, 455.

and distributed their products. This form of organisation had important consequences at a formative period in American labour activity for, as John R. Commons and Helen L. Sumner wrote,

> Whatever may have been its origin in other countries, the labor movement in America did not spring from factory conditions. It arose as a protest against the merchant capitalist system.[1]

As industrial operations enlarged, and the demand arose for more unskilled labour, some masters began to recruit—mainly from the immigrant population—and some came to specialise as labour contractors rather than as manufacturers—or men who had no original connection with the trade could insert themselves as bosses recruiting and controlling the supply of unskilled labour. Or in course of time some of the masters ceased to be intermediaries and would become capitalist manufacturers employing both skilled and unskilled under a single roof.[2] A still further stage was reached when machinery reduced the numbers of skilled operatives and increased the demand for unskilled labour (which could often consist mainly of women and children). The different conditions created different relationships, different tensions, and different psychological attitudes; but it is often difficult to determine, from the available evidence, the stage reached by a particular industrial operation. The Labor conspiracy trials are useful sources because the nature of the accusation demanded precise investigation into the conditions of an industry, but, as already noticed, these trials touched only a small portion of American industry.

The evolution of the old skilled trades from independent crafts

---

[1] *Documentary History of Industrial Society in America*, v, 23.

[2] The career of Henry Wilson, Vice-President of the United States from 1873 to 1877, is a good example of this career pattern. He was the son of a very poor agricultural day labourer, and from ten to twenty years old he was apprenticed to a neighbouring farmer and educated himself. He then hired himself to a shoemaker at Natick, and soon set up independently. After an interval, during which he used his savings to finance his further education, he set up as a 'manufacturer' on a very small capital. He built up his business until he employed over a hundred men, but his establishment was not a factory and his 'hands' were skilled craftsmen. The next stage would have been for him to acquire machinery and move towards large-scale factory production, but from 1840 onwards he devoted himself to politics and political journalism.

to factory production can be contrasted with the patterns adopted in new industries. The textile mills of New England provide familiar examples, and attracted much attention from visitors, but less noticed was the experience of the railroads. Here, from the outset, was the need for a highly skilled 'aristocracy' of labour, which had to accept responsibility to the public as well as to employers, while, at the same time, construction demanded large gangs of unskilled labourers under firm discipline. Individualism in skilled employment generated co-operative action to protect wages and conditions of work; collective employment left the unskilled mass without any machinery for mutual protection, This experience transmitted its legacy to the future, but the sources if not deficient, have yet to be fully explored.

Whether the Civil War did or did not accelerate 'industrialisation', it introduced an era in which the sources for the study of labour become far more abundant and wider in range. In the first place there evolved machinery for the collection of statistics which was far in advance of anything previously attempted, and eventually superior to that in most other industrial nations. A large number of investigations were undertaken in the various states, and much important material survives in their reports. At the end of the period, in 1888, the Federal government's share in responsibility for labour conditions was recognised in the establishment of the Department of Labor, though it was not given cabinet status and was for some years little more than a fact-finding bureau. As early as 1867 the body styling itself the National Labor Union, as its second convention, resolved that 'whereas there is no department of our government having for its sole object the care and protection of labor . . . and the elevation of those who labor', a Department of Labor should be established.[1] No action was taken by Congress, but in 1870 Massachusetts set up a Bureau of Statistics of Labor.

The first efforts of the Massachusetts bureau were unpopular and unsystematic, but in 1873 the state appointed as commissioner Caroll D. Wright, who was to make a career as one of the great

[1] Cited Ewan Clague, *The Bureau of Labor Statistics* (New York, 1968), 4.

public servants of the nineteenth century and to be honoured as a major strategist in modern statistical investigation. After consulting Francis A. Walker, who was Superintendent of the Census and President of the American Statistical Association, Wright produced the first reliable reports in American history on wages and prices. Other states followed the example of Massachusetts, and in 1884 fourteen were represented at a National Convention of Chiefs and Commissioners of Statistical Bureaux. In the same year Congress established a Federal Bureau of Labor Statistics, and after a delay—during which President Arthur first nominated a political opponent as commissioner, withdrew the nomination, and then allowed the post to remain vacant until almost the close of his term—Carroll D. Wright was appointed as its head. He would continue in office when, in 1888, the bureau was incorporated in the new Department of Labor, and serve, in all, for five consecutive four-year terms before being appointed Director of the Census.[1]

The formation of a labour statistical service—to which historians in search of quantitative evidence will turn with relief—was a by-product of more melodramatic events. The strikes and violence of the depression era, culminating in the tremendous events of 1877; the rise of the Knights of Labor; the unprecedented success of strikers in the mid-1880s; anarchist violence (especially the Haymarket affair) and the 'law and order' backlash—all made the actions of labouring men news for the public, anxiety for executives, and concern for legislators. Press comments upon labour accumulate, and though the judgment was markedly more hostile than it had been in anti-monopoly Jacksonian days, there is enough of it to piece together a great deal of information. During the same period the skilled trade unions continued with fluctuating fortunes, but with the strongest surviving with increased vigour.

[1] Wright wrote that: 'The positive policy of the Bureau of Labor is that this office makes its initial work that of pure fact, and any desire on the part of individuals or associations of individuals, whether of labor or capital, seeking more or less than this policy indicates, must be considered as wanting the work of the Bureau to conform to adopted theories or to be influenced to shaping special ends.' Cited Clague, *op. cit.*

Many of them established journals which had comparatively long histories of publication, and a few newspapers and periodicals appeared which aimed to serve a general working-class leadership.[1] In addition, several of the Unions held national conventions, with proceedings which survive, and there are voluminous records of the Knights of Labor. The interminable negotiations, and disputes over membership and responsibilities, between the Knights and the unions, make tedious reading, but from them the patient historian can recover many of the facts about industrial and labour organisation. Also, from this period, there survives a good deal of autobiographical material, or of biographical material written by authors who were in close personal touch with their subjects.[2]

Abundant as the evidence becomes, there are obvious grounds for caution in its use. On the one hand most official pronouncements, and the majority of press comments, were not only hostile to but also ignorant of industrial labour. In a period of growing class-consciousness a great many Americans were determined to turn a blind eye to its existence and to believe that conflict was an unnecessary departure from a normal harmony of interests. Attitudes were complicated by the fact that so many of the less-skilled labourers were recent immigrants of eastern European origin. The leaders of the older unions were often even more

[1] Norman J. Ware, writing in 1929 a history of 'the Labor movement' from 1860–95, provided a good example of the range of sources available to the labour historian of the period. Amongst labour journals he cited the *American Federationist*, *The Carpenter*, the *Cigar Maker's Official Journal*, *The Craftsman*, *The Furniture Workers' Journal*, *The Granite Cutters' Journal*, *The Iron Molders' Journal*, *John Swinton's Paper* (described as 'the least partisan labor paper of the period, and the best edited'), *Journal of United Labor*, *Journal of the Knights of Labor*, *Labor Enquirer*, *Labor Standard*, and the *National Labor Tribune*. *The Labor Movement in the United States* (New York, 1929), selected bibliography.

[2] The best known is Samuel Gompers, *Seventy Years of Life and Labor* (New York, 1925). This can be compared with the earlier work of T. V. Powderly, *Thirty Years of Labor* (1st ed., Columbus, 1889, 2nd ed., Philadelphia, 1890). Other works by less prominent leaders are Joseph R. Buchanan, *The Story of a Labor Agitator* (New York, 1903); Lucy Parsons, *Life of Albert R. Parsons* (Chicago, 1889); Richard T. Ely, *The Labor Movement in America* (Baltimore, 1886). Many of the early academic studies of labour history profited from conversations and correspondence with surviving labour leaders.

hostile than the general public to these 'foreign' working men and women. Side by side with generalisations based on misconceptions, which characterised public comment, was the narrowness and self-interest of much material issuing from the leaders of organised labour. Terence V. Powderly, leader of the Knights, has never been a favourite with labour historians, but at least it is refreshing to encounter a man with such wide if erratic vision. From both sides in most controversies the unorganised and unskilled had little to gain, and both were equally ready to denounce the tiny groups of Socialists or Anarchists who claimed to speak for the working class. The Anarchists, most of whom were mild German idealists who hoped for much in the utopian traditions of their adopted country, became the favourite stereotypes of vicious, unthinking violence. In moments of high tension, such as the reaction to the Haymarket affair of 1886, the normal sources become more useful as examples of national pathology than as evidence of fact.

The problem of violence plays a peculiar part in labour history. It is a part of modern American folk-lore that they are a violent people, and this is offered, almost with pride, as an explanation for many unhappy incidents. Men of the late nineteenth century did not take this view; rather they were struggling to recapture an imaginary condition of the past when law and personal restraint had been normal. There was thus a tendency to deplore with exaggerated emphasis the evidence of violent behaviour. Moreover, employers had good cause to magnify the existence of violence, in order to secure the aid of state militia or Federal troops to protect property; while labour leaders might sometimes use the threat of violence as a weapon in negotiation. It is therefore as well to scrutinise carefully any accounts of labour violence, and to accept as little as possible without corroborative evidence.[1] When this is done some examples of violence will stand unchallenged, but others may well resolve into threat and rumour. There is, however, a large problem to be faced in the enforcement of order. The state archives, Presidential papers, the records

[1] My attention was drawn to the difficulty of evaluating this kind of evidence by Dr R. Jeffreys-Jones of the University of Edinburgh.

of the Attorney-General and of the War Department should all provide valuable evidence. So, too, should business archives (where discretion has not led to the disappearance of the evidence), and the founder and leader of the Pinkerton detectives can speak for himself.[1] The problem is one which still lives and deserves historical investigation.

The statistical information for the later nineteenth century, together with the other sources, enables one to go much further than in an earlier period towards a history of labouring men (as distinct from leaders of labour). Much of the work that has been done concentrates upon the experience of immigrant groups, and (as argued in the preceding chapter) prominence has been given to letters from America written by men who had recently arrived. Some of the older unions had international affiliations (particularly with British unions), but it is not likely that their correspondence will yield much evidence of value.[2] There may be a good deal of information about industrial labour buried in the despatches of foreign consuls in the United States. It is also worth remembering that though most of the press was hostile or uninterested, there were areas in which organised labour was locally dominant and in some of these the newspapers should yield much information. However, it may well prove that county records, both administrative and judical, are the best sources for studying the history of labouring men. The task is worth contemplation for, in a democratic society, it is ultimately the wage-earners who determine drift of events.

[1] Alan Pinkerton, *Strikers, Communists, Tramps and Detectives* (New York, 1900).
[2] An interesting example was that of the Window Glass Workers (cf. Norman Ware, *op. cit.*, 191–2). This was a small union with probably no more than 1,700 members at its peak; but it controlled every factory in the United States. Its position was impregnable because it established close ties with glass workers in England, France and Belgium. In 1882 the Glass Manufacturers tried to import Belgian glass workers, but these were 'organised as fast as they arrived'. In 1884 the President of the Union went to Europe and organised an International Glass Workers' Association, and in 1885 a convention at Pittsburgh was attended by delegates from England, Belgium, France, Italy and Portugal.

PART IV

The American Mind

Introduction

The most influential work on economic theory, published in the twentieth century, concluded with the following statement:

> I am sure that the power of vested interests is vastly exaggerated compared with the gradual encroachment of ideas. Not, indeed, immediately, but after a certain interval; for in the field of economic and political philosophy there are not many who are influenced by new theories after they are twenty-five or thirty years of age, so that the ideas which civil servants and politicians and even agitators apply to current events are not likely to be the newest. But, soon or late, it is ideas, not vested interests, which are dangerous for good or evil.[1]

If this is true, or even partly true, it follows that the history of ideas is the key to an understanding of history. The suggestion may be unacceptable to historians who believe that what cannot be measured cannot be evaluated; but it cannot be dismissed without an answer.

The danger for historians who leave the ideas out of history is that they substitute their own assumptions for those of the past and end with an historical edifice which rests at every point upon verifiable evidence, but built to a design of the contemporary world and not of the men who lived in it. Having got to this point, and realised the need to recover thoughts as well as things, the historian is faced with the need to operate in a field where many techniques of historical research do not apply. Evidence exists in the form of writings which are supposed to have exerted influence; but the extent and reality of that influence may be impossible to ascertain, and it is easy to exaggerate the importance of writings which appear original but lay unread in their day. On the other hand, the historian may have to examine beliefs

[1] John Maynard Keynes, *General Theory of Employment, Interest, and Money* (London, 1936), 383-4.

which were so common that no one thought them worthy of special comment.

In politics Americans have been more prone than most peoples to proclaim and reiterate their basic beliefs; but the comparative fixity of their political system has made them less ready to scrutinise and explain their institutions. Where they have been articulate, they have frequently been so in emotive words which have lost precise significance. Thus fourth of July orations are valuable indicators of popular political attitudes, but weak contributions to political theory. Words such as 'freedom', 'Union', 'rights' and 'democracy' were the political deities invoked by rhetoric; 'monarchy', 'aristocracy', 'tyranny' or 'disunion' were devils in the play; each symbolised ideas which were once powerful and real, but seldom subjected to analytical examination.

These political ideas grew up with the nation, providing both its fundamental inspiration and its guidelines for development. The European origins of these concepts lie outside the range of this book; here it is a part of the 'data' from which the American mind is made. Other influences enter the stream of thought and it is sometimes difficult to reckon their impact or distinguish them from indigenous growths. The forces of religious revival played back and forth across the Atlantic; anti-slavery and other humanitarian reforms are sometimes British and sometimes American in their origin. Some ideas, such as economic laissez faire, are clearly of foreign origin, but found an environment favourable to growth in the United States. The later influence of Herbert Spencer is well-known, but his importance arose from the economic and intellectual environment of America. In other words, convenient categories of native and foreign influences are likely to mislead.

The historian of ideas moves from popularly accepted ideas to popular culture. Here the problem is a dual one; firstly, the sources must be identified and analysed, secondly, the significance of this study must be established. Popular culture is often fun, but it may become merely nostalgic fun. How important are the simple pleasures of the people? Is ephemeral literature worth the effort needed to disinter it? In reply the historian of popular culture might question the right of others to abstract the political man, the economic man, the religious man, or the man of culture from the whole man. In the intellectual environment in which seminal minds flourish the great majority are concerned with other things; nevertheless, just as popular culture may be affected by the new ideas generated in its midst, so the lonely thinker may not be entirely unaffected by the trivial things around him. The links may become easier to establish when one considers not great constructive thinkers but more normal leaders in politics, business, or intellectual activities. The relationship may be tenuous, but a political system cannot be divorced from the popular culture in which it exists.

There still remain some difficulties in deciding the place of popular culture in the broad spectrum of historical research. Is it the environmental stage upon which great events are played? Or is it illustrative detail produced when appropriate to remind us that men of the past had simple pleasures like ourselves? Can one build a theory of historical determinism out of what men played, read or enjoyed; or are these things mere incidentals?

In American history some questions are easily answered. In the early national period the course of history was settled by the men who made the Constitution, ran the early governments, and led the early parties. In the middle period it was dominated if not deflected by the men who argued over slavery, forged the instruments of sectional misunderstanding, and took the momentous decisions in secession, war and Reconstruction. In the later period individual decision may be somewhat less important, but the ideas about social evolution, government responsibility, currency, gold, railroads, trusts and political protest made modern America. In a country which made a fetish of individualism, weak government and decentralised authority, it was still the decisions of comparatively small groups of men which counted.

A primary task of intellectual history is to understand the influences which played upon the minds of these decision-makers. This does not mean a narrow focus upon the ideas of prominent individuals, but a study of the intellectual environment created by thinkers, preachers, teachers, and publicists. At one end of the spectrum are deep-rooted religious and philosophic assumptions; at the other end the ideas—some weighty and some ephemeral—which constitute 'informed opinion'. But for large masses of mankind, who do not make decisions but are affected by them and whose acquiescence may make them viable, popular culture may be the only road to understanding. Embodying traditions and fashions, affirmations of faith and aspirations for future improvement, compensation for social suffering and implied protest, popular culture may be of deep significance for the historian; but it is often necessary to use careful discrimination in distinguishing fundamental attitudes from trivial responses to passing fancies.

CHAPTER 15

Religion and Education

The culture of nineteenth-century America was impregnated by religion. For most people religion was an essential part of the social fabric, and even those without strong attachments to Christian faith believed in the existence of a moral order to which the Bible was the best—if not the only—guide. Indeed the language, imagery and teaching of the Bible are themselves essential sources if one is to understand the nineteenth-century American mind. Mission, purpose, destiny and providence became fundamental concepts in American thought about themselves; Christian belief was the strand by which Americans attached themselves to their European and ancient past, while transforming it into an American institution. Faith was universal and timeless, but the organisation of churches reflected the peculiar genius of the American people for self-government and voluntary action.

In spite of this distinctive position in American culture, religion plays a surprisingly small part in 'general history' as it has been written heretofore. From 1790 to 1830 it almost drops out of sight, though these were formative years in the history of several denominations. The most that one normally finds are references to the more bizarre aspects of revivalism. From 1830 to 1860 religion is mentioned only as an influence upon anti-slavery and nativism. In the period after the Civil War the reaction to evolutionary science and the challenge of social depravity brings religion nearer to the main stream; first for the defence of orthodoxy and then for its convergence with secular reform. One could read much 'general history' without realising the importance attached by so many Americans to religion or grasping the extent of religious activity. Talents, energy and funds were at the service of religion, but for a majority of the historians of nineteenth-century America it has remained in the wings.

To anyone familiar with Britain or Europe the diminutive part of religion in American historiography must appear strange. On the eastern shores of the Atlantic no one could doubt the political and social significance of religion; it entered into every controversy, attacked or defended established Churches and their privileged position, exercised special rights over education, and claimed to arbitrate in social controversy. Anti-clericalism was always an element, and often the principal theme, in European radicalism; and in England the chasm between Anglicanism and nonconformity stood at the head of two great political traditions.

In the second half of the eighteenth century there were signs in America that upper-class deism and popular anti-clericalism might become, as in England, driving forces in politics; but their battles were too easily won and the consequences too tame. When Jefferson, the 'atheist', became President, American religion continued its untroubled way without the terrible consequences foretold by conservative New England ministers. Controversies over religious instruction in schools did take place during the first half of the nineteenth century, but were conducted at the state level and despite a considerable body of literature made little impact upon national history. In spite of the Know-Nothing flurry, no politician built a national reputation upon religious prejudice. During the Civil War religion seemed to play only a peripheral part, though there was a natural tendency in the North to express the struggle in religious terms. For all these reasons it has been possible to write the history of the United States during the nineteenth century with a perfunctory mention of religion.[1]

The neglect of religious history by secular historians has meant that a great body of historical source material has been ignored or left to the historians of the various denominations. Indeed no other aspect of American life has left so much unexplored evidence. A bibliographer of Church history does not exaggerate in saying

[1] Henry F. May in 'The Recovery of American Religious History' (*American Historical Review* 70 [1964–5]) notes that in 1922 a volume of essays entitled *Civilization in the United States* included no article on religion because the editor (Harold Stearns) could find no one interested in the subject.

that 'the amount of unpublished manuscript source material, and of little used printed archives, is colossal'.[1] Printed materials include the proceedings of conventions, assemblies, and synods both national and regional. Sermons, either singly or in collections, never seemed to lack publishers or presumably readers. Pamphlets dealing with theological questions were almost as numerous, and specific issues (such as religious instruction in schools) turned the stream into a torrent. The religious periodicals were always the most numerous in every count of newspapers and magazines. A check made in a large theological library showed that members of one of the smaller national denominations, the American Episcopal Church, supported forty-eight general, thirty-one local and six diocesan periodicals between 1790 and 1890. In 1936 the same library held about 10,000 pamphlets dealing with the history of the Episcopal Church.[2] Few of the religious periodicals survived for long—of the eighty-five Episcopal magazines, only nineteen had a life of more than ten years—but in any year of the nineteenth century the total circulation of religious periodicals was far greater than the combined total of their secular contemporaries. Much of the literature in secular controversy utilised religious arguments and aimed at actively religious readers. In addition there were the publications of national associations, from the purely religious Bible and missionary societies to semi-religious anti-slavery and temperance literature. Many of these forgotten publications made tedious reading; but it is often a task of the historian to explain why today's tedium was yesterday's excitement.

The unpublished materials for religious history are also scattered in many different kinds of depository. The papers of public men often contain some correspondence on religious questions, and often there may be some surprises for the searcher. For instance

[1] Nelson R. Burr, *A Critical Bibliography of Religion in America* (vol. IV of *Religion in American Life*, ed. James Ward Smith and A. Leland Jamison, Princeton, 1961), Part I, p. 14.

[2] Charles Mampoteng, 'The Library [of the General Theological Seminary] and American Church History', *Historical Magazine of the Protestant Episcopal Church*, vol. 5, no 3, 1936.

Jefferson wrote a good deal, as might be expected, about disestablishment in Virginia, but also corresponded about the problems of church establishment in the New England states. The national and local headquarters of the denominations have their archives; many college, university, and seminary libraries possess extensive materials. Church leaders often observed little distinction between private and official correspondence, so that important materials for religious history may turn up in private hands or in the collections of state or local historical societies. Much of this voluminous material is uncatalogued or known only to students of single denominations in select regions. The Federal Writers Project, during the New Deal era, was responsible for preparing several inventories of the surviving archives of the Protestant denominations; unfortunately this plan was overtaken by the coming of World War II and comparatively few volumes were published. In addition to the records of the denominations, there are also those of the numerous religious societies—some preserved at national headquarters, some at regional or state headquarters, and others in private hands. Finally, the missionary societies have preserved records which bear witness to Christian activities overseas, fund-raising at home, the enthusiasm generated by religious enterprise, and the 'image' formed by nineteenth-century Americans of non-European societies.

The problem of handling the history of religion does not lie therefore in meagre sources, but in unresolved questions about the place of religion in national history. Everyone would admit its importance, but many who have drawn their inspiration from Jeffersonian springs would maintain that the constructive forces in American history have been secular. Religion entered into national history to combat the claims of an establishment and withdrew because it was essential to maintain the principle of the separation of Church and State; it became private and personal, not public and national; it provided the basic moral precepts for nineteenth-century America, but did so by reinforcing the national law rather than by doctrinal argument. Denominational history *per se* became unimportant on the broad canvas of national growth.

This state of affairs is readily explicable because freedom of worship and the denominational principle made the United States very unlike nations in which 'one State one Church' was an original and basic principle (however diluted in modern times). Church historians have themselves felt the need to supply a new explanation, and have tended to concentrate either upon the voluntary principle—with its diversification—or upon the unifying concept of a 'basic' religion which crosses denominational frontiers and underwrites the ethical consensus of the nation. The one tends to ecclesiastical biography and the quest for information about the separate history of congregations in different regions; the other becomes diffuse and rhetorical rather than exact. Whichever road the Church historian takes he seems to have little to contribute to the main stream of American activity; yet again one must emphasise that, in nineteenth-century America, religion absorbed more talents, stimulated more people, and (over the whole field) controlled more money than politics.

A leading Church historian, Sidney C. Mead, has taken a hard look at some of these problems and suggested a new approach. One has to begin with the fact that 'Church' in America has a different meaning to Europe.

A 'church' as 'church' has no legal existence in the United States, but is represented by a civil corporation in whose name the property is held and the necessary business transacted. Neither is the denomination a 'sect' in any traditional sense and certainly not in the most common sense of a dissenting body of relationship to an Established Church. It is rather a voluntary association of like-hearted and like-minded individuals who are united on the basis of common beliefs for the purpose of accomplishing tangible and defined objectives.[1]

From this follow certain consequences. A 'denomination' has a separate religious identity, and therefore claims to be, in some sense, the custodian of 'the truth'; but the religious character of American society as a whole depends upon the belief that there is a basic faith upon which all right-minded people can agree irrespective of their denominational affiliation. This would make the particular tenets of a denomination matters of personal concern, and irrelevant

[1] *Church History*, vol. 23 (1954), 291.

for the general welfare. The comparative ease with which a Protestant American can move from one denomination to another demonstrates the existence of this basic doctrine, but at the same time the leaders of a denomination have a duty to insist upon the virtue of loyalty and the special nature of their own 'truth'. This is made easier because the major differences are organisational rather than devotional; but the importance of organisational unity engenders impatience with doctrinal innovations which might create division. There is 'a kind of massive and stubborn stability, inertia and momentum of its own, deeply rooted in and broadly based on the voluntary commitment of the individuals composing it. Here is the real basis for the tremendous vitality of these denominations'.[1] Thus American Church history reveals a bewildering range of paradoxes: the virtues of separatism combined with an emphasis upon universality; voluntaryism combined with the duty of loyalty; the right to choose combined with an insistence upon conformity.

The same contradictions have been displayed in missionary activity. The customary restraint in criticising fellow-Protestants at home has not precluded vigorous competition in new fields. In the early national period most denominations concluded that future strength depended upon success in newly settled areas. This meant missionary work on 'the frontier' and in all parts of the United States where new communities were being established. Whenever the national or regional representatives of a Church were gathered together, some were sure to proclaim that 'the labourers are few' and to launch urgent appeals for help in the states and territories—old, new, and abroad. Sometimes it seemed that the spread of a Church was more important than conversion to Christianity but, typically, when faced with a formidable task, Church leaders brought out the oecumenical principle: the American Board of Foreign Missions became perhaps the supreme demonstration of the truth that all denominations could co-operate in propagating a basic Christianity.

This oscillation—between the narrow vision of a denomination, which seems to have little relevance for 'general history', and the

[1] *Ibid.*

wide appeal to everyman's ethics—helps to account for the neglect of religious history. The sources are abundant, but they seem to lead either to a cul-de-sac in a theological college or to the wide world of platitude. Yet it may well be that these contradictions are not irrelevant to American history, but very much a part of its substance and character.

One might expect that the two religions which deliberately stand apart would have some revealing comments to offer upon American culture. The Catholics with their claim to universality and their respect for authority, and the Jews with their faith in a separate mission, do offer some kind of challenge to Americanism; but their voices have been strangely muted. The Catholics, as a minority religion, have rejected the claims of Protestantism— whether in its particular form or as a generalised Protestant ethic —but have tended in consequence to support the separation of Church and State which their co-religionists in other countries denounced so vigorously. 'No other Church,' says a prominent Catholic historian, 'has sympathised more profoundly with the basic American distrust of ecclesiastical interference in public life.' Catholics have taken it as a virtue that they refused to participate in the debate over slavery, or in the arguments over racial equality in the post-war years.[1] Priests might claim that their duty was to all children of God who espoused the Catholic faith, but their pronouncements were suspiciously similar to those of Protestant leaders who avoided embarrassment by invoking the detachment of religion from politics. Thus Catholic historians have spent less time than might have been expected upon the struggle against Protestant bigotry and for a separate educational system, and have placed their emphasis upon the compatibility between Catholicism and Americanism.

[1] Monsignor Peter Guilday, the leading Catholic historian of the older generation, wrote: 'Perhaps the outstanding proof of the wisdom of our prelates lies in their silence over the slavery issue . . . No other Church in this land then as now has realised the supreme need of keeping itself free of political questions; and no other Church has sympathised more profoundly with the basic American distrust of ecclesiastical interference in public life.' *A History of the Council of Baltimore* (New York, 1932). Quoted David J. O'Brien, 'American Catholic Historiography', *Church History*, vol. 37 (1968), 80 ff.

The writing of Catholic history by Catholic historians has tended to be introspective, biographical, dominated by internal controversies, and mainly Irish-American in focus. The political implications of Catholicism have been ignored, though most political analysts would agree that Catholicism was always a major factor in Democratic electoral support. A few tentative attempts have been made to present the history of Catholicism as the dominant religion of urban America, but the documents are likely to be far less numerous than those of the prosperous Protestant congregations. If Catholic historians have declined to emphasise the distinctiveness of their own history, it is hardly surprising that the Protestants and Jeffersonian deists, who have been responsible for the writing of surveys and text-books, have tended to ignore Catholicism.[1] The modern American Catholic, conscious of wealth, numbers and influence in the present-day United States, may well resent the impression that his predecessors contributed little to the culture of a predominantly Protestant society; but Catholic historians have themselves done much to foster this illusion.

Rather similar observations can be made on the history of American Jews. In 1954 the Jews in America celebrated the three-hundredth anniversary of the arrival of the first permanent Jewish settlers. A Tercentenary Committee initiated various projects, and the weightiest outcome was *The Jews in the United States: A Documentary History, 1790–1840*, edited by Joseph L. Blau and Salo W. Baron, and published in 1963.[2] This was an admirable three-volume work which rescued from oblivion much unpublished and unknown source material. Chronologically the great immigration of Russian and East European Jews in the later nineteenth century was excluded, and the focus of the volume was on the constructive part played by individual Jews in the development of the United States. There was no attempt to demonstrate that being Jews had made Jews act differently in either social or moral attitudes from Protestant Americans; rather the emphasis

[1] David J. O'Brien, *op. cit.*, 81. 'A survey of some widely used text books reveals that American Catholicism receives little treatment in the history of the country.'   [2] New York, 1963.

was upon the acceptance of Judaism in the colonial, revolutionary and early national periods. The editors set the tone when they observed that,

> In a sense, one can say that there was no Jewish life in the United States but only life in the United States as lived by Jews. It is this unique situation that has—thus far, at least—made the dialectic of Homeland and Exile a purely theoretical exercise among many Jews of the United States.

They have not sat down by the waters of Babylon and wept, but have found themselves at home in a land of opportunity.

In the later years of the nineteenth century the emergence of the 'social gospel' attracts interest, and, for the first time since independence, religious influences are credited with a positive and distinctive effect upon American history. There are several reasons for this. The 'social gospel' tends to be more social than religious; it is a reform movement cast in the typical American mould. It is an exploration of underlying ethical attitudes underlying American life, and a plea for their application to social problems. Moreover, the leading advocates of the social gospel were educated and articulate; many of them left autobiographical accounts, many were noted preachers, and their activities can be traced through secular sources.[1] It also throws important light upon the origins of Progressivism, which has been a major preoccupation with recent historians.

In 1964 Henry F. May welcomed a revival of interest in American religious history with the statement,

> For the study of understanding of American culture, the recovery of American religious history may well be the most important achievement of the last thirty years. A vast and crucial area of American experience has been rescued from neglect and misunderstanding.[2]

May's advocacy was welcomed by Church historians, but no

[1] The best-known social gospel writers were Josiah Strong, Washington Gladden, William Jewett Tucker, W. S. Rainsford and Samuel L. Loomis. The movement was also well represented in periodical literature.

[2] The Recovery of American Religious History', *American Historical Review*, vol. 70 (1964–5), 79.

religious interpretation of American history has yet emerged. It is arguable that, in the last analysis, religion has been more important than 'the frontier'—or the agrarian versus capitalist thesis—in explaining the American past; but the interpretation awaits its Turner or Beard.

Indeed Church historians have not agreed amongst themselves. For Sidney E. Mead denominationalism was 'the shape of Protestantism in America',[1] but in 1964 Peter G. Mode, introducing a *Source Book and Bibliographical Guide for American Church History*, wrote that in his selection of material he had been

> guided by the principle of choosing only such documents as most significantly set forth the contribution that the Church has made to the progress of American society, and the manner in which from time to time she has adjusted herself to her new and changing environment. Denominationalism, therefore, has been relegated to the background.[2]

This is the present dilemma of religious history. Voluntaryism, the proliferation of denominations, and the consequent pattern of behaviour are themes which can be presented as both unique and as prototypes of American culture in many other aspects. Alternatively the function of religion in providing a framework of ethical teaching, largely divorced from denominational peculiarities, can be seen as the constructive role of religion in American history. It will not be easy to construct a religious 'interpretation' of American history until a synthesis between these views has been achieved.

The history of education in all countries has been closely entwined with that of religion; but in America the focus of debate was very different from Europe. There was no national Church with exclusive educational rights to defend and a strong tradition of public support for primary instruction; the large number of denominations made particularism in education diffi-

---

[1] The title of an article in *Church History*, vol. 23 (1954), 291 ff.

[2] Boston, 1964. Separate chapters were included on Unitarianism and Universalism, Catholicism, Mormons, and Jews; but the major Protestant denominations were not given separate treatment.

cult and most nineteenth-century Protestants were able to agree that 'common Christianity' could be taught without reference to the tenets of the different Churches. Controversies there were, but most were argued at the local level and were resolved in the middle years of the century. The major exception is found in the sustained fight of the Catholics against the compulsory reading of the English Bible and for public assistance to their own parochial schools.[1] In consequence the sources for educational history are to be sought in the states and counties, and in the papers of prominent educators, rather than Federal archives or the records of national Churches.

In most European countries the problem of public support for secondary education was a major national issue; in most American states it came about as the result of a quiet revolution when educators and superintendents of schools discovered that the state laws placed no limit upon the number of grades for which taxpayers were responsible. The evolution of higher education went forward with similar lack of major controversy. Whereas in England and Scotland the exclusive privileges of the established Churches, in the ancient universities, became major items of political controversy, the founding of new universities (according to secular and denominational needs) became so normal a part of American life that their inauguration occasioned only local comment. It was also unfortunately true that laissez-faire in higher education allowed wide variations in standards and some very odd experiments in College education; but few can doubt that the opportunities offered to young men greatly enriched American society.

As with religious history, and for very similar reasons, education is given short measure in 'general history'. Few historians would fail to pay tribute to the achievements of American education, but the statements are usually general and the lack of national controversy leads to a bland and uninformative treatment. Every American student knows of the Abolitionists, but how many could describe with any precision the ideas and achievements of

[1] See E. R. Norman, *The Conscience of the State* (Cambridge, 1967). Ch. 4, *passim.*

the men who so vastly improved American education during these years? Ask any educated American about William Lloyd Garrison and he will give a picture which may be vigorously unfair or partisan, but will display some knowledge; but how many recall Horace Mann?[1]

Educational questions appear on the national scene briefly during the debates over Land Grant colleges, and more extensively after the Civil War in the lengthy and abortive discussions over a national education bureau. For the great part of educational history it will, however, be necessary to delve into state and county archives. It was in the latter particularly (or in other comparable local units) that the most intense battles were fought, and the real progress was made. By the middle of the century there were elected school boards in a majority of counties, though local options and reconciliation between new and older authorities produced a complex pattern in New England. For instance, in New Haven county prior to 1909, some towns had boards of school visitors (elected for each district), some had a consolidated system under a town school committee, and others had one large district operating under a board of education.[2] But almost everywhere the pattern had moved towards the supervision of education by locally elected officials, while competition between districts for good schooling held in check the natural parsimony of local residents. It is an apt comment upon American educational history that today, in many small towns, the school buildings are the largest and architecturally the most attractive to be seen.

There is obviously much history to be written in recording the rise, progress and development of the American schools system. The sources are there, but the would-be historian must either be content with a piecemeal study or with selection to build up a composite picture.[3] Educational histories have been written largely

[1] For Mann, and for educational problems in general, see *Life of Horace Mann*, by His Wife (Boston, 1865), which reprints many letters by Mann and others. Two further volumes reprint his most important reports and public papers.

[2] National Works Progress Administration, *Inventory of the Town and City Archives of Connecticut*, No. 5, *New Haven County*, p. 33.

[3] See William W. Brickman, *Guide to Research in Educational History* (New York, 1944).

to provide teachers in training with an elementary knowledge of the way in which the organisation and curriculum of schools has evolved and there has been little attempt to bring education into the orbit of professional social history. Thus one of the more important contributions of the United States to civilisation receives brief treatment in general surveys while more informative treatment of educational history usually fails to satisfy professional historians or their students.

On the plane of higher education the picture is very different. Most colleges and universities have their histories, and though some have strayed into hagiography others are first-rate productions by professional historians (tempered by the need to produce a work which the alumni will find readable). In the nature of things, the man commissioned to write a university history is likely to be a man of wide experience and good academic judgment; if devotion to his alma mater may sometimes blunt the edge of criticism, he is almost certain to show himself aware of the social and intellectual forces which have shaped the fortunes of his institution. There are thus a large number of histories of this type which can be used in confidence that they are soundly based upon the available sources.

In 1857 the National Education Association was born; the health of the infant remained precarious for several years, but it survived to become the principal professional association for teachers and a pressure group with a remarkable record of success behind it. The records of the association provide the best source for the history of education through the eyes of teachers and their representatives.[1] As with similar organisations in other fields, it has often been more concerned with winning status for its members than with the content of their work, but its annual meetings became the principal forum in which educational ideas were discussed. As in other conferences the most important discussions were initiated informally and thus left few traces for the record.

Two special educational problems gave rise to a great deal of discussion (and consequently of available sources): the education of Negroes after the Civil War and of immigrant children in the cities.

[1] Edgar B. Wesley, *NEA: The First Hundred Years* (New York, 1957).

The public discussion of both issues was in general terms and throws little light on the actual problems of instruction, school building and school attendance. The records of the Freedmen's Bureau contain, however, a mass of material on the detailed problems of education in the South during the period of Reconstruction, and the papers of Senator George F. Hoar, the principal sponsor of a National Education Bill, contain much on the general principles involved in accepting national responsibility for education.[1] The natural place to seek for information about the educational problems of immigrant children will be in the records of state, county and city education boards or commissions. The public debate emphasised the importance of training for citizenship, and throws light upon the fundamental function of an educational system in teaching the assumptions which underlie national life. There is an interesting chapter in the history of public education about the Catholic fight to keep the Protestant Bible out of tax-supported schools, and thus to protect Catholic children from the consequences of secular education. There may also be a minor but interesting study to be made in the history of saluting the flag as a part of the daily routine in schools.

Religious history and educational history both illustrate the curious phenomena of activities fundamental to American society, with abundant and easily located sources, which have attracted little attention from general historians. Their histories have been left largely to specialists who have sought to enlighten special groups of persons—ministers, priests, or teachers—rather than to communicate the importance of the subject to a wider public. Recent years have seen signs of a new mood, and secular historians have shown an awareness of religious experience in American history. The problems of higher education and academic freedom have attracted the attention of some distinguished scholars, but much remains to be done; and the reason for the previous neglect remains an important and intriguing question in the history of American historiography.

[1] The principal collection of Hoar's papers is with the Massachusetts Historical Society.

CHAPTER 16

Ideas and Actions

In nineteenth-century Britain a study of political and social ideas can be organised around three concepts: the establishment, reformers, and movements.[1] The Church, with its domination over higher education, the great country houses, with their influence over politics and culture, and the ancient universities are the features of 'the establishment', though its doors were open to men of wit and talent and its circle was constantly enlarged. The London clubs, transformed from places where men went to gamble into places where they could relax in congenial company, became typical institutions of the mid-Victorian establishment. An intellectual continuum linked public men and upper civil servants with the more fashionable Colleges of Oxford and Cambridge, the higher clergy, and the landed aristocracy and gentry. Within the establishment there were controversies, but the participants accepted the same social conventions and had shared the same kind of education. In terms of status and education many reformers differed little from the establishment, but they deliberately allied themselves with social and intellectual 'out-groups'. Reform covered a wide spectrum—from aristocratic Whigs to the more radical kinds of Nonconformity—but its essential characteristic was detachment from the establishment in order to bring about social and political change. Reform was not confined to radical politics—there was a tradition of Tory reform which honoured

[1] In order to avoid misconception it should be stated at the outset that the purpose of this chapter is not to describe or analyse the sources for American intellectual history. It is rather to survey the means available to the historian for estimating the effect of ideas, argument and conventional wisdom upon action. It is hoped by these means to bring out some of the important differences in approach, emphasis, and attitude to source material between American and European historiography.

Pitt, Canning, Huskisson and Peel, and nurtured Gladstone—but most reformers gravitated towards the Whig and later the Liberal party. Thus one of the major political organisations in the country was committed to change in the ancient institutions, diminishing privilege, and rational analysis of social needs.

A movement was an association (usually loosely organised) of like-minded men to bring about specific and perhaps fundamental changes. It operated on a narrower front than reform, but had a stronger ideological commitment. Nineteenth-century British history abounds in 'movements': the Evangelical movement, the Anti-Slavery movement, the Romantic movement, the Utilitarian movement, the Oxford movement, the socialist movement, and the labour movement. Men who became interested in specific reforms, without accepting a more general ideological commitment, became associated in movements for the abolition of slavery, for factory reform, for civil service reform, for free and compulsory education, and for improvements in public health.

These introductory remarks underline some of the difficulties encountered in organising material for the study of intellectual influences in American society. There was no national establishment, nor was there a national capital which concentrated political, cultural and economic life as did London or Paris. There was an 'establishment' in New England, and Emerson may have been the first to use the word in its modern meaning when recalling the New England culture of his youth.[1] There was also a New York, a Philadelphia, and a Baltimore social establishment, but these did not serve and hardly influenced a national constituency. In the old South there was something akin to the country house culture of England, and in the great days of Jefferson it had welcomed speculation and opened its doors to the intellectual currents of the Atlantic world; but by the middle of the nineteenth century obsession with slavery and agricultural profits had narrowed the vision and fostered an aggressive provincialism.

[1] There are always two parties, the Party of the Past and the Party of the Future; the Establishment and the Movement.' 'Historic Notes of Life and Letters in New England,' *Complete Works* (Riverside Edition), vol. X (Boston, 1886), 307.

In a limited sense there was a national political establishment. Senators, Representatives, and a few high-ranking executive officers formed the nucleus of a political society; though it lacked the sense of continuity which was the distinguishing characteristic of the British establishment. Between the more powerful political magnates at Washington there had to exist a web of understanding and conventions governing the conduct of business. Even political rivals joined in tacit agreement that there were limits to obstruction and harassment. When new men intruded into this inner circle—as did the Jacksonians in the first days of their triumph and the Republicans during Buchanan's administration—there was bound to be dislocation which might have serious consequences for the transaction of government business. It is not possible to describe this 'establishment' save in impressionistic terms; it may be possible to analyse the assumptions upon which it operated, but the exercise will not describe the beliefs of a particular group but summarise American political attitudes. The intellectual quintessence was the conviction that government ought to work as most Americans expected it to work.

In other countries it is sometimes possible to describe the political climate by organising the explanation around certain traditions—utilitarian, Catholic, anti-clerical, radical, socialist, and so on—but in America it is necessary to grasp ideas which were amorphous yet powerful, universally accepted yet difficult to identify. The Americans were, above all, a political people, and a body of political beliefs were the focus for national loyalty; yet this is like saying that a medieval European society was Christian, for while the ideas were pervasive they cannot be summarised and no one has yet devised a scale for quantifying the influence of commonly held beliefs. The problem is made more difficult because once the tremendous burst of constructive political thought in the eighteenth century was exhausted Americans contributed little to political philosophy so that one cannot approach the problem through the writings of influential theorists.

Similar comments could be made about American economic thinking. Although an expanding economy is a major determinant in American history, and although business absorbed much energy and talent, Americans in the nineteenth century made no original contributions to economic thought. Henry Carey is a possible exception, but he was too diffuse and not sufficiently systematic to make an impact beyond his immediate usefulness in providing protectionists with theoretical arguments.[1] In the later years Henry George is sometimes claimed (though seldom accepted) as a major economic theorist, but his ideas were indignantly rejected alike by academic economists, businessmen and orthodox moralists. Joseph Dorfman surveyed American economic thought and was able to fill many pages with lucid summaries of long-forgotten works of economic argument; but the overall impression of his work is the derivative character of American economic thinking.[2] For the historian this emphasises the difficulty of reckoning the imponderable weight of British ideas.

The difficulty in analysing the influence of ideas makes the concept of 'ideology' attractive: a few powerful ideas can be seen as magnets drawing into their orbit a host of associated themes. Studied individually the popular ideas may seem platitudinuous, and it is difficult to explain their appeal; but seen collectively, as part of a single ideological system, their force can be understood. This way of approaching the material borrows from twentieth-century experience but may help historians to escape from over-emphasis upon single themes or crude attempts to ascribe political actions exclusively to economic interest. The technique can be best applied at the point where powerful new forces are injected into American life. The Jacksonian period has proved particularly attractive, and there are new possibilities being explored in anti-slavery and the impact of the Civil War. Treatment on these lines might also throw new light upon the great battle between the Federalists and the Jeffersonian Republicans,

[1] Henry Carey has attracted little attention from modern scholars, but there is a useful study by Arnold W. Green, *Henry Charles Carey: Nineteenth Century Sociologist* (Philadelphia, 1951), which includes a bibliography of Carey's works and of writings about him.

[2] Joseph Dorfman, *The Economic Mind in American Civilisation*, 3 vols (New York, 1946–49).

and upon the character of late nineteenth-century American civilisation.[1]

These speculations may seem to have led a long way from consideration of the sources of history; yet systems of belief lie at the very heart of the questions that historians must ask. If they cannot be answered from the sources we are at the mercy of false prophets looking backwards, and this is therefore a field in which the burden of duty lies heavily upon professional historians. The sources for this kind of enquiry do not and cannot lend themselves to ready description; unlike census figures or economic statistics they do not form orderly series in which it is comparatively easy to spot the deficiencies or discover with confidence the firm ground. It is possible to deal only with evidence accumulated from many different sources. Public speeches, newspaper comments, forgotten works which may have had a reputation in their day, sermons and school text-books as well as weighty discussions, eulogies and polemics, popular orations and judicial opinions: these are the kind of sources from which systems of belief can be studied, and, paradoxically, the more evidence a historian has accumulated the more one depends upon his skill

---

[1] A number of historians have used 'ideology' as a conceptual framework. For the Jacksonian period see Edwin C. Rozwenc, ed., *Ideology and Power in the Age of Jackson* (New York, 1964). This collection groups together extracts from contemporary writers to make a collective portrait of Jacksonian ideology. Some of the writers represented (e.g., Gouge, Mann, Finney, and Leggett) are not easily found elsewhere. The Jacksonian period lends itself to this kind of treatment and it has been employed by earlier writers without using the word 'ideology'. See especially Arthur Schlesinger, jr, *The Age of Jackson* (New York, 1946), John W. Ward. *Andrew Jackson — Symbol for an Age* (New York, 1953), and Marvin Meyers, *The Jacksonian Persuasion* (Stanford, 1957; New York, 1960). A recent work upon the early Republican party makes deliberate use of the concept: Eric Foner, *Free Soil, Free Labor, Free Men: the ideology of the Republican Party before the Civil War* (New York, 1970). George M. Frederickson's excellent *The Inner Civil War: Northern Intellectuals and the Crisis of the Union* (New York, 1965) describes the formation of a new current in American ideology as intellectuals rationalised the meaning and implication of the conflict. In the first chapter of *The American Mind* (New York and London, 1950) Henry Steele Commager gives an impressionistic picture of the late-nineteenth century American.

and integrity in selection, in emphasis, and in weaving together the whole into a coherent pattern.

The nearest approach to an American 'establishment' has been the legal profession. Most public men have been lawyers, Americans have been proud to claim that theirs is a government of laws, not men, and that legal rights enshrined in the first eight amendments are the bulworks of liberty. These facts may suggest that ideas derived from the law have been more continuous than any others in their effects upon American life and action. In his unfinished *The Life of the Mind in America* Perry Miller devoted seven brilliant chapters to 'The Legal Mentality' in which he discussed the place of the law and of legal ideas in early nineteenth-century America.[1] Willard Hurst has made notable contributions to studying the social environment of law; but legal theory remains in the hinterland of most general histories.[2] Clearly the writings of the great lawyers and law teachers must provide the backbone for a study of the effect of law upon action. Kent and Story are obvious starting-points (after one has grasped the inheritance of English Common Law and the teaching of Blackstone); but there are a host of others, eminent in their day though now largely forgotten, who include David Hoffman of

[1] Perry Miller, *The Life of the Mind in America* (Cambridge, Mass., 1966).

[2] In 1960 James Willard Hurst, who has done more than any other scholar to bring legal history into the main stream of American historiography, observed that 'If laymen draw less understanding than they might from legal materials, they may properly say that they have had little guidance from law men to do better . . . Anglo-American law men are by tradition and training biased toward equating law with what judges do, to the neglect not only of legislative, executive, and administrative activity, but also to the neglect even of the out-of-court impact of the work of lawyers, let alone the additions or subtractions made to legal order by lay attitudes and practices affecting legal norms.' He added that though there were several excellent treatises on the Constitution and the Supreme Court, 'we lack a single first-rate modern work on the history of constitutional doctrine as it has been formed in the Congress.' 'The Law in United States History', *Proceedings of the American Philosophical Society*, vol. 104 (1960), 520, 522. For examples of Willard Hurst's own approach to socio-legal history see his *Law and the Conditions of Freedom in the Nineteenth Century United States* (Madison, 1956) and *Law and the Social Process* (Ann Arbor, 1960).

Maryland, John Anthon of Philadelphia, St. George Tucker of Virginia, Peter de Ponceau (an expatriate Frenchman) and Horace Binney of Philadelphia. In this field at least it is possible to say that American writers equalled if they did not surpass their English contemporaries; indeed the challenge of assimilating or adapting law to a new country, a new constitution, republican government and democratic society stimulated more penetration and greater originality than was found amongst English legal writers since Blackstone.

There is an obvious gulf fixed between the distinguished commentaries, which penetrated deep into the principle of juris-prudence, and the law as practised in simple county courts. Yet there are also obvious links, for the pressure of the times forced the great lawyers to stress the correspondence between common law, natural justice, the moral foundations of society and the needs of an expanding economy. The backwoods colleges or country attorneys' offices, where so many Americans learnt the principles of law and legal practice, were hardly centres of elegant learning; but somewhere along the line the law as handled by small lawyers and obscure judges had to meet the test imposed by men with minds trained by the great commentators. The result was to produce lawyers whose range of knowledge might be narrow but who grasped a few principles with great firmness. The effect of this upon political argument leads one into the realms of speculation; but it can be asserted without fear of contradiction that Lincoln would not have discussed political questions as he did if he had not been trained in American law. Nor would most other men upon whom the burden of political decision rested.

The conditions of rapid social and economic growth meant that American lawyers were peculiarly sensitive to the need for reconciling principles with altered circumstances. There was always a hidden but important dialogue between the lawyers and the men who presented new problems for legal solution. This is true of any legal system, but it played a particularly important part in America where it was necessary to interpret written constitutions in the light of changing circumstances. But the process could also breed the 'legalistic' attitude which is usually taken to mean the substitution of legal niceties for common sense solutions. The defect was seen at its worst when men imagined that the ideological differences between the sections would be healed by constitutional logic. These wide-ranging propositions raise still further questions, but for the present it is enough to say that they open a field of enquiry in which the sources are many but the methods perplexing.

After the Civil War Thomas M. Cooley was the pre-eminent name amongst American legal commentators. His major work, the *Treatise on Constitutional Limitations*, published in 1868, was not, as is sometimes implied, special pleading for laissez-faire, but a sustained and acute argument on the distinction between actions which the law should restrain and those which it should protect.[1] If Cooley believed that there were areas which should be immune from legislative control, and where the judges should be left free to apply the law and the Constitution, he was not a simple advocate of unrestrained economic freedom. The author of *Constitutional Limitations* was also the first chairman of the Interstate Commerce Commission.

The example of Cooley suggests that there is still much to explore in the legal ideas and arguments of the late nineteenth century. In his day he was ranked next to Story, yet he is lucky to get a footnote in a modern text-book. The legal theories of the age are known to the present generation through passages from the opinions of the Supreme Court selected in the first instance by men who were unconsciously but powerfully influenced by the need to justify the Progressives and F. D. Roosevelt. A new look at the sources might suggest a more sympathetic assessment of the way in which distinguished jurists grappled with the emerging problems of modern society. Whatever the conclusions it

[1] Thomas M. Cooley (1824–98) published *A Treatise on the Constitutional Limitations which Rest upon the Legislative Power of the States of the American Union* in 1868; it went through many subsequent editions. Amongst his other publications were *General Principle of Constitutional Law* (1880) which was widely used as a College text and (probably but anonymously) the early reports of the Interstate Commerce Commission.

may be agreed that general historians should pay more attention to the sources of legal opinion. Too often they have struggled along like men trying to explain the Reformation without reference to theology.

While Cooley was making his massive contributions to the formal literature of the law other men, not practising lawyers but strongly influenced by concepts of the law, were attempting to reconcile the traditional ideas of a Federal society with growth in national authority. Francis Lieber, who emigrated from Germany and became a teacher of history and jurisprudence in South Carolina and then at Columbia University, wrote his most influential works before the Civil War but they were regarded as authoritative texts in late-nineteenth-century colleges.[1] A re-examination of his writings may not do a great deal to restore his reputation as a political thinker but should supply some clues to the way in which the minds of educated men were moulded. Two other theorists, John C. Hurd and Elisha Mulford, were also strongly influenced by the German idealists, but unlike Cooley and Lieber their books were not widely read or used in higher education.[2] Hurd and Mulford are worth re-discovery, but rather as examples of the impact of the Civil War upon unusual minds than as guides to conventional attitudes. Of more direct influence was John W. Burgess, whose nationalism owed something to

[1] Francis Lieber (1800–72) came to America in 1827. His major works were the *Manual of Political Ethics*, 2 vols (1838–39) and *On Civil Liberty and Self-Government*, 2 vols (1853); the latter was much used as a College text.

[2] John C. Hurd (1816–92) made his reputation with *The Law of Freedom and Bondage*, 2 vols (1858, 1862), which is still regarded as an authoritative work on the law of slavery. After many years' reading and reflection he published (1881) *The Theory of Our National Existence*. In this he claimed to base a new theory of national existence on historical facts rather than constitutional abstractions; unfortunately his writing—which is of great intrinsic interest—is extremely difficult to follow. Elisha Mulford (1833–85) was an Episcopal clergyman who was deeply influenced by German philosophy. His major work was *The Nation*, published in 1870. According to his biographer in the *Dictionary of American Biography* (Daniel D. Addison), his theme was that: 'The nation is an organism, a personality responding in its total life to ethical ideals, and cannot perform its function of progress and helpfulness without an ever-living ethical consciousness, fulfilling a divine purpose.'

German influences and something to his own background in Tennessee Unionism.[1]

Early nineteenth-century critics of democracy lamented the fact that educated opinion and calm judgment were being swamped by the cult of popularity. Calhoun's attack on the power of the numerical majority was less concerned with quality than with the representation of interests, but he assumed implicitly that leadership in a small political society would be wiser and less swayed by emotion than in a national representative assembly. The deference which Americans continued to pay to the Senate also implied the belief that indirect election produced men of better calibre than the Representatives who had to render account directly to the voters every two years. This point of view has been accepted by many modern historians who stress the decline in the quality of public men and civil servants from the early days when men of breeding and intellect ruled the Republic.

This kind of thesis is extremely difficult to document because it depends largely upon the subjective impressions of contemporaries who felt themselves aggrieved by neglect or unwelcome measures. It was inevitable that this kind of criticism should reach a crescendo during the Jacksonian period, and that respect for the judgment of democratically elected men declined still further during the fifteen years preceding the Civil War. It is unquestionably true that no political leader after 1828 displayed the analytical vigour of Hamilton, the wide-ranging humanism of Jefferson, or the theoretical equipment of John Adams—nor indeed the strong will and massive common sense of George Washington—but the qualities displayed by the earlier generation of public men were exceptional by the standards of any political system. It would,

[1] John William Burgess (1844–1931) was for many years a dominant personality at Columbia University. He was the founder of the *Political Science Quarterly*. Charles E. Merriam says that: 'The nation he viewed as the highest product of political development. He exalted it, gave it a broad world mission, and held that it solved the problem of international organisation by avoiding world empire.' (*Dictionary of American Biography*.)

for instance, be difficult to maintain that the statesmanship of American public men, from 1830 to 1860, chosen by democratic processes, was inferior to that of French leaders from 1750 to 1789. Indeed, if one looks not at the terrible problem of sectional controversy, but at the way in which all the other problems of a growing society were handled, one might draw conclusions which are as favourable to the Americans as their radical European admirers believed.

One line of approach to the problem is biographical. The information exists to construct potted biographies of all men in Congress, holders of high executive office, many of those in the second and third ranks of public service, and others who were in public life in their states. It would not be right to anticipate the results of such an enquiry, but sampling suggests that some of the stock generalisations may have to be revised. The ignorant, and partly illiterate politician existed, but he was exceptional; the majority of men who rose high on the political ladder had received some kind of higher education (though its quality was often dubious), and most of them were trained lawyers. There were some self-made politicians, but their experience of public life was long and thorough. The United States was not governed by raw backwoodsmen but by men who had served in state legislatures, presided in courts as judges, learned the art of politics the hard way, and acquired a wide knowledge of public affairs. Speeches in Congress confirm this impression. If the modern reader finds them tedious, it is not because they were crude or ignorant, but because the conventions of the day demanded a florid style of oratory and a display of knowledge which tended to make every major speech a historical résumé of events for the preceding thirty years. But men in Congress understood all this and each other, so that business was organised by 'old hand' and new but powerful local leaders.

Thus biographical sources and public debate may suggest that there was, after all, a political 'establishment'. The effect of ideas upon action may therefore be focused upon the relationship between this political 'establishment' and the men of books and ideas; but here one is near the limit of what the sources can reveal, for the weight of educated opinion is imponderable. It has already been suggested that the pervasive influence of religion has been greatly underestimated by secular historians and that there is much evidence to show that religious activity and religious literature affected the lives of very large numbers of Americans. It is far harder to document the effect of literary culture, because one has the additional problem of separating indigenous from English influences.

There was, in the first half of the nineteenth century, a 'republic of letters'; that is a community of literary men, scattered about the nation though concentrated mainly in New England and on the Atlantic seaboard, who corresponded with each other, received each other's books, and contributed to the same periodicals. But this 'republic of letters' was far weaker in the United States than in Great Britain or France. Its members were less numerous; they had no common experience in university, salon or club; they had not the same intimate connections with the political establishment. Their correspondence therefore tends to confirm the thesis that men of education and literary culture were becoming alienated from public life.

If one takes a more comprehensive view of the reading public, and of those who were likely to exert influence upon it, one gets a rather different picture. The United States was already, in the early nineteenth century, an important market for books. The fight by British authors, led by Dickens, to protect their copyright is fully documented and indicates the importance of the American book trade in crude monetary terms. The avidity with which Americans produced and read newspapers, magazines, and pamphlets has already been stressed; and lecture tours were already, by 1840, an important source of income for transatlantic travellers. If high culture seemed weak and dispersed, America was nevertheless the most literate nation in the world, and the one in which the novel attitudes of the nineteenth century were likely to be most widely diffused. There is therefore a large field for investigation which need not be short of documentary evidence. It may be that, at the end of the enquiry, one will have to make some guesses about the effect of this popular literary culture upon public life; but at least the material exists on which to make some guesses which will be well-informed.

As one passes the Civil War the picture of the 'alienated intellectual' is apparently sustained. Mark Twain's *Gilded Age* has provided a name for the epoch, Henry Adams' *Education* and his novel *Democracy* have spread wide the impression that public life in the late nineteenth century had no place for men of cultured taste and sophisticated education. The two principal activities of the American male—politics and business—were equally distasteful, and with Henry's brother, Brooks Adams, this became a fully fledged philosophy of degradation and decline. Another example is that of E. L. Godkin, the English-born editor of the *Nation*, whose transit from Radical Republican enthusiasm to a conservative distrust of democracy is well-known.

This concept of the 'alienated intellectual' demands rigorous examination. An alternative view may suggest that there never had been a time when the prestige of preachers, scholars and writers stood higher, or when the influence of educated opinion had been stronger. The history of universities during the period is one of expansion, experiment, and scholarly achievement. By 1890 professional History, professional Economics, and professional Political Science were well established, with their professional associations and journals. Nor is it true that all this weight of opinion was ignored by the politicians. A recent study of the currency controversies after the Civil War suggests that a deciding influence in pushing the United States back on to the gold standard was not political calculation or economic interest but deference to the moralistic arguments of ministers, editors and educators.[1] There was also an increasing volume of writing about public questions by men with trained minds, and many of them were recruited temporarily into the public service to serve on railroad commissions, investigating committees, boards of education, or in advisory capacities. University presidents became men of power, literary oracles were listened to, editors were great public figures. The reception of Herbert Spencer in America has attracted

[1] Irwin Unger, *The Greenback Era: a Social and Political History of American Finance* (Princeton, 1964), 24–8, 121–44.

derisory comment; but it is significant that a man of books and theory should have been so extravagantly praised. All this suggests that too much attention has been paid to Henry Adams, with his record of disgusted retreat from public life, and too little to the facts of life as lived by educators, ministers of religion, literary men and others who claimed to represent the consensus of educated and honest opinion. Even Andrew Carnegie was not content with industrial wealth and aimed to make a reputation as a social philosopher and as a patron of learning and cultural activities. Abundant materials exist to recreate the 'mind' of the educated middle class, and to document its influence, but much remains to be done. For too long late-nineteenth-century America has been peopled by 'robber barons', 'spoilsmen', and 'corrupt bosses' on the one side, and voices of reform in the wilderness on the other. The press, the books, and the rhetoric of the day should correct the picture, and enable one to see these years in their correct perspective as the formative period in a civilisation which includes not only great corporations but splendid libraries and museums, great universities, and a highly sophisticated intelligentsia. Properly used, the sources will suggest that the massive weight of educated opinion is the unacknowledged colossus of late-nineteenth-century America.

The lack of an establishment, against which critics could launch their attacks, and the almost universal acceptance of common basic assumptions about the nature and purpose of American life, precluded the existence of a reform tradition. There was no place for men who believed in a continual process of change or advocated fundamental alterations in society. Even in the late nineteenth century critics tended to appeal back to the first principles of American society and to disclaim the role of innovators. There was however a succession of what may be called 'improvers' who advocated moral betterment within the existing framework. Borrowing from the pulpit (and many of them were ministers of religion) most 'improvers' preached personal redemption and charity rather than institutional change. Only on occasions, and then usually by implication, would they criticise political or economic leadership. The literature of improvement is vast, much of it is tedious reading, and heavily moralistic in tone; nevertheless, between the lines there is a great deal of information about social conditions. Vice and crime are the obvious targets; ignorance and drunkenness attracted continuous attention; there is a great deal of information about penitentiaries and prison reform. Pleas for the improvement of conditions in factories are comparatively rare; so are pleas from southerners for the humane treatment of slaves, though there is some interesting discussion of their religious instruction and worship. So far as these pleas called for legislative action they were directed to the state legislatures, and their practical effects must be sought in the executive and legislative records of the states.

The sources for these activities are numerous and diverse. If, like temperance, the cause was sufficiently popular to support a national organisation, there may be surviving records. Bible societies, home missions, campaigns for public education and church building flourished principally at the local level; their records or the papers of individuals involved may have found their way to the local historical society. For many such activities the only record will be in the local press or the occasional pamphlets which may survive. A great deal of the propaganda was never written down but was delivered in lectures, sermons and addresses.

Nineteenth-century Americans were devotees of the spoken word. They listened to orations, sermons, and lectures. Many of these rhetorical efforts are lost for ever, or preserved in abridged form in newspapers; but some were printed locally, others aimed at a national audience in book form, and some eventually appeared in volumes of collected works, but a lecture was part of an author's or public man's stock-in-trade, and he expected to deliver it several times and to be paid a fee on each occasion; once printed its value as a source of income was at an end. The published versions were therefore often printed either at the end of a career, when the subject had ceased to be topical, or when the lecturer needed to reinforce his public reputation by 'collected works'. The form and content of a successful lecture might change over the years. Emerson originally wrote his lectures out on single sheets and then had them bound loosely together. As time went on some parts of the original lecture were deleted and new or amended versions inserted on new sheets. He also made new lectures by piecing together passages from old lectures with new material. Late in life he got a young friend to sort out the now disorderly mass, and to put his stock of lectures together in new bindings. In this form most of them were eventually printed.[1] The printed version of a lecture may therefore have a very different form from the original. This need be of no great significance unless one is using phrases in the printed version as evidence for the presentation of views at an earlier date, but scholarship demands a considerable exercise in textual criticism (including research on the original notebooks), if the authentic text of a lecture at any given date is to be ascertained.

It is impossible to evaluate the influence of the spoken word. At best it may be possible—with sufficient knowledge of the environment and circumstances—to estimate the extent to which the speaker was formulating opinion or expressing commonly held beliefs. Impressions conveyed face to face remained when memories of the arguments had faded, a lecture could persuade where the printed word might barely have been understood, and an address by a distinguished public man would be a major experience in the lives of many citizens. Though nineteenth-century Americans seem, in retrospect, to have swum in a sea of oratory, the opportunities for many individuals to hear well-known men were severely limited; in small country towns the visit of a famous author or political figure of wide reputation might be the event of a decade. At the other end of the scale, the weekly sermon of even an indifferent preacher might have a pervasive and cumulative effect. So both the temporary exposure to a 'great man', and a regular diet of the spoken word provided by familiar figures, might affect opinion, but this can hardly be guessed and is certainly impossible to quantify.

[1] Stephen E. Wicker and Robert E. Spiller, eds., *The Early Lectures of Ralph Waldo Emerson*, 2 vols (Cambridge, Mass., 1959), i, Introd., xxiii–xxiv. A different style of public speaking can be sampled in Waldo W. Braden, ed. *Oratory in the Old South, 1828–1860* (Baton Rouge, 1970).

One index of a lecture's influence is the author's own estimate of its success. If, like Emerson, he kept some lectures for year after year, one can be fairly certain that he himself was pleased with their reception. But it hardly needs saying that some of the most successful lectures were the most platitudinous. Emerson's orations on John Brown and on Civil War questions—most of them delivered once only—probably had a greater influence (because of their topical relevance) than his oft-repeated lectures on moral, historical and literary themes.

So far this chapter has dealt with two concepts, 'establishment' and 'reform'; the third—'movements'—can be dealt with more briefly. Indeed there is only one development within this period which can be described in the same way as European 'movements': this is, of course, the anti-slavery movement. It was a 'movement' in the European sense because it concentrated upon a single theme while demanding, by implication, radical changes in the system as a whole; because its nucleus was formed by a dedicated minority who deliberately adopted propaganda and agitation as modes of action; and because it won support from a widening circle of men who disapproved of its method but accepted its basic premises. Finally the anti-slavery movement is comparable to the successful 'movements' of European history because it entered into politics, inspired a major party, and altered the course of history. It is also typical in that, on the road to eventual success, it developed all kinds of internal disputes and factions.

Each aspect of the anti-slavery movement has been studied intensively, but over the years emphasis and the judgment has altered. In an earlier generation most historians were hostile to the abolitionists and only slightly less hostile to the politicians who adopted anti-slavery as a cause. In recent years the pendulum has swung far in the other direction; abolitionists became the heroes of modern radical historians, though there is an increasing tendency to emphasise the racist and negrophobic influences upon men who came into anti-slavery by way of Free Soil rather than Abolitionism.

The sources for the anti-slavery movement are the papers of

317

anti-slavery societies, the correspondence of the leaders, and the great volume of pamphlet or other printed material.[1] *The Liberator* is the principal source for the views of William Lloyd Garrison, though one must remember that Garrison believed in exaggeration, and that the man himself was more reasonable and more human than the pages of his newspaper might suggest. The *National Era*, edited from Washington by Gamaliel Bailey, was the organ of the Liberty party; its range is wider, its outlook more tolerant, and its writing less vigorous than *The Liberator*. The papers of many abolitionist leaders survive in important collections, notably those of Lewis Tappan, Gerritt Smith, James G. Birney, William Lloyd Garrison, and Wendell Phillips. Several abolitionists published memoirs or reminiscent articles in their later years. In addition to the writings of avowed abolitionists, there were important arguments against slavery by William Ellery Channing and John Quincy Adams. After the imposition of the 'gag' Act discussion of slavery was smothered in Congress, but it flared out in 1842 with the ill-judged moves to censure John Quincy Adams and Joshua Giddings. After 1846 the principles of the Wilmot proviso became a staple topic in political controversy, and the pages of the Congressional *Globe* throw more and more light upon the anti-slavery movement.

There is, however, a good deal of scope for work on the source materials at the local level. The abolitionists planned a self-generating movement: agitation would breed local anti-slavery action and organisation (the physical assaults upon abolitionist speakers were particularly effective in promoting local anti-slavery activity); local organisation would then create more pressure for national action (as well as providing much-needed funds). Local churches almost inevitably became involved in a controversy phrased largely in religious terms, and the

[1] The best guide to the literature of Anti-Slavery is Dwight L. Dumond, *A Bibliography of Antislavery in America* (New York, 1965); there is an annotated bibliography in Louis Filler, *The Crusade Against Slavery* (New York, 1960). There is a brief 'Bibliographical Note' in Benjamin Quarles, *Black Abolitionists* (New York, 1969), but the notes to the separate chapter provide a more useful guide to the sources.

anti-slavery 'take over' of local congregations led to splitting the national denominations into Northern and Southern branches. An analysis of local activity may also throw more light upon the social background of anti-slavery. The sources for the local study of the anti-slavery movement should not be hard to find in state and county archives, in the collections of state historical societies, in the archives of the churches, and in the letters and papers of individuals.

The anti-slavery movement was also international. A good deal of exploratory work has already been done in tracing the relationship between the American and British anti-slavery movements. There is much correspondence in British collections relating to America, and American abolitionists hoped that their British friends would assist them with money and by using their influence with a government which was officially committed to an anti-slavery posture. They were more successful in attaining the former than the latter objective, but the international aspects of anti-slavery do lead one into the diplomatic archives of both American and British governments.[1]

The later stages of anti-slavery, when Free Soil rather than Abolition becomes the dominant motif, are harder to grasp and more difficult to evaluate. Like ripples on a pool the impact of anti-slavery spread outwards, and the movement which had once been compact now becomes diffuse and, though less powerful in its central thrust, affected the lives and thoughts of more and more people. Indeed, the records of the original abolitionist

[1] Some idea of the ramifications of international anti-slavery can be grasped from a survey of entries in B. R. Crick and M. Alman, compilers. *A Guide to Manuscript Relating to America in Great Britain and Ireland* (London, 1961). Important collections of correspondence between British and American anti-slavery men are located in the headquarters of the Anti-Slavery Society; Dr Williams's Library, London; Rhodes House Library, Oxford; John Rylands Library, Manchester; and the Mitchell Library, Glasgow. Some of the papers in Rhodes House (and apparently others now lost) were used in A. H. Abel and F. J. Klingberg, eds., *A Sidelight on Anglo-American Relations* (Lancaster, Pa, 1927), which prints correspondence between Lewis Tappan and the British and Foreign Anti-Slavery Society. Another aspect of international relations can be studied in Warren S. Howard. *American Slavers and the Federal Law* (Berkeley and Los Angeles, 1963).

societies, and the files of the anti-slavery newspapers, become less important as the conflict between North and South moves towards the crisis. Conversely the correspondence and speeches of Republican leaders, and their newspapers (above all the New York *Tribune*) become more important. Indeed, as one approaches 1860, the character of anti-slavery is likely to be dimmed, and it may be necessary to recall that one is dealing with the outcome of a 'movement', originally built around a single central idea, and gradually developing a complete ideology which could find room for the half-hearted and the deviationists as well as for the true believers.

These characteristics distinguish the anti-slavery movement sharply from the various essays in radical criticism in the nineteenth century. Some of them aimed to develop a similar pattern of growth, but conspicuously failed to do so; others aimed at limited objectives and tended to break up once these had been achieved; others were the work of individuals whose hopes outran their influence and achievement. Nevertheless these radical critics and prophets have considerable interest for twentieth-century students, and deserve further consideration.

The lack of a party of reform has not prevented individual Americans from speculating upon an 'alternative society'. Indeed the American environment spontaneously generated all kinds of experiment and encouraged individuals to seek remedies for the ills of the world. From the eighteenth century onwards an empty continent beckoned those who hoped to establish utopian communities. Many were inspired by the variety of Christian sects to establish communities, set up congregations, and indulge in active missionary work. Withdrawal from the world and the urge to convert the world can equally be illustrated from American experience. The temperance movement was the most active and successful, and its aims necessarily brought abstainers into politics. The early nineteenth century has become famous for the enormous number of causes embraced by a wide range of societies, and each of the 'isms' which aroused the scorn of contemporaries can be fully documented.

There is, indeed, no lack of material for the study of utopian and radical activity in the United States. The major problem of judgment is the place which these topics should be given in general history. Would it be appropriate to regard them as the by-ways and dead-ends of history, or should one see these attempts to define and popularise an alternative society as tributaries flowing into a mainstream of late twentieth-century radicalism? This is not the kind of question which can be answered with demonstrable proof, but the fact that it can be asked suggests that the rising generation of American historians may feel impelled to look at the hopes and failures of nineteenth-century reformers in a new light. In time they may be lifted from footnotes or passing references to more prominent positions in general text-books. The danger may be that exaggeration will then replace neglect.

Many of the religious and utopian communities of the late eighteenth and early nineteenth centuries left copious records, and in several cases these have been carefully preserved by modern historical societies. As one might expect, much of this work has been hagiographic rather than objective, but this is true of other classes of historical evidence. The original buildings of some communities have been preserved, others have been carefully restored, and often a museum has been established. The history of communitarian socialist communities has been surveyed with expert and sympathetic skill by Arthur C. Bestor in his *Backwoods Utopias* and the bibliographical essay which concludes the book is the best guide to the printed and manuscript sources.[1] Most of the communities, whether inspired by religious or secular creeds, were part of some larger movement, so that the quest for information about a 'backwoods utopia' may take one to the national or international headquarters of a sect or society, and sources may be widely dispersed. The best-documented community is Robert Owen's New Harmony, and Bestor's search for information about this short-lived social experiment took him to manuscripts in the library of the Co-operative Union in Manchester, the British Museum, and the Robert Owen Memorial Museum

[1] Arthur E. Bestor, jr, *Backwoods Utopias* (Philadelphia, 1950), Bibliographical Essay, 245–68.

at Newtown in Wales, as well as to papers on the spot at the Workingmen's Institute in New Harmony. There were also relevant papers in the collections of the Indiana Historical Society, the American Philosophical Society, the Historical Society of Pennsylvania, the Illinois State Historical Society, Yale University, Purdue University, Indiana University, the University of Michigan, the Chicago Historical Society, and the archives of Posey County, Indiana. In addition there were important papers in private hands at Pittsburgh, Bryn Mawr, and Carlow in Ireland. As well as these manuscripts sources, there are a very large number of contemporary periodicals, pamphlets, and other descriptive or polemical writings. The activities of Robert Owen are unusually well documented, and the volume of material for the study of New Harmony is probably greater than that for any other community; nevertheless the example indicates the range of enquiry which may be necessary to establish the facts and understand the motives of a handful of people in what was then a remote part of the United States. In addition to the history of the community itself, the movement which fostered it has to be explored, while the biographies of members throw further light upon the kind of men inspired by these ideals.

It is difficult to estimate the influence of these experimental communities upon American society as a whole, but it was probably slight. The history of human endeavour is never unrewarding, but nineteenth-century utopianism did not affect society in the way that medieval monasticism had done. The sources, which can be abundant so long as one is dealing with the life history of a community, become exhausted as soon as one tries to pursue the ripples set moving by this small experiment in social organisation.

A similar observation could be made about the socialist and Marxist intellectuals in the middle and later years of the century. The revolutionary thinkers, mainly German, made wide claims to understand the forces of the age, but were almost deliberately exclusive in their attitudes to others. Indeed the purity of their creed served these German émigrés much as adhesion to the Church of the homeland served their more conservative compatriots.[1] Most of the scanty evidence of their ideas and activity is in German. In 1870 the International Workingmen's Association established a committee in New York, and in 1872 the general council of the International was moved to New York but it had a tenuous existence and the International was formally dissolved in 1876. In the same year a fusion of socialist groups established the Workingmen's Party of the United States and in the following year it adopted the name of Socialist Labor Party. This was the progenitor of the modern American socialist parties, but its immediate influence was minimal. Better known because of its advocacy of violence was the International Working People's Association, the Black International, organised in 1881 and fathering the Revolutionary Socialist Party. The records of these associations and parties contribute evidence to the emergence of the idea of an 'alternative society', but their theories were purely derivative and no American made any distinctive contribution to socialist arguments.[2] The public reactions were often hysterical, but the records of the courts, of the state law enforcement officers, and of the Federal Attorney-General provide serious evidence upon a basic problem of modern society: the rights and duties of governments when faced with subversion.

The 1880s formed, however, a period of bewilderment and re-appraisal for a great many Americans who were unaffected by socialism, but dimly aware of its existence.[3] The disquiets of

[1] Stow Persons observes, of these mid-century socialists, that 'it would be difficult to say whether their Marxism functioned primarily as an expression of their aspirations for the working class or as a means of sustaining their ethnic and cultural identity in an alien world'. Introduction to Laurence Gronlund. *The Cooperative Commonwealth* (Belknap Press Edition, Cambridge, Mass., 1965).

[2] A possible exception is Laurence Gronlund, whose *Cooperative Commonwealth* was published in 1884 and in a revised edition in 1890 (cf. Stow Persons, *op. cit.*). Gronlund attempted to adapt Marxism to American conditions and traditions; he claimed to have had a major influence on Edward Bellamy and may therefore provide a bridge between European communism and native American idealism.

[3] The other Henry Adams, Henry Carter Adams, who became statistical director of statistics for the Interstate Commerce Commission in 1887 and was a perceptive commentator on economic problems, wrote in *The Relation of the*

the period are epitomised in the work of three major figures: Henry George, Edward Bellamy, and Henry Demarest Lloyd. They came from very different backgrounds. Henry George was a footloose youth, a working journalist, a passionate reformer whose opinions and methods were moulded by the harsh realities of economic conflict under California sun, and an active radical. Bellamy came from a conventional New England background and, before the publication of *Looking Backward* in 1888, had been described as 'a little known . . . journalist and author of pale romances'.[1] Lloyd was 'a successful literary man living in the style of a millionaire'[2]; he had been successively financial editor and a general editorial writer for the *Tribune*, before retiring (with the support of his wife's ample income) to prepare *Wealth against Commonwealth* (published in 1894) with the help of research assistants and secretaries. The influence of all three men belongs to the subsequent period of American history, but their works and papers are important sources for the social and intellectual history of their times. Of the three, George was the most theoretical and the most penetrating in his criticism of economic orthodoxy; Bellamy was the most impressionistic in his treatment of existing conditions but the most powerful in his utopian vision; Lloyd was the most fully documented in his indictment of prevailing business ethics.[3] All three were distinctively American in rejecting Marxian materialism and making a case which was primarily

---

State to Industrial Action (Publications of the American Economic Association, vol. I, 1887), 14: 'We are now passing through a period of interregnum in the authoritative control of economic and governmental principles. This is indeed cause for grave solicitude, for never were men so poorly equipped for the accomplishment of such a task as those upon whom these questions are being forced.'

[1] John L. Thomas in his introduction to an edition of *Looking Backward* (Cambridge, Mass., 1967).

[2] T. C. Cochran, Introduction (p. 6) to Spectrum Books ed. of *Wealth versus Commonwealth* (Englewood Cliffs, N.J., 1963).

[3] Lloyd has sometimes been accused of unfairness in his selection and use of evidence; but modern studies are inclined to vindicate the accuracy of his information (Cochran, *op. cit.*, 2–3).

ethical.[1] Each diagnosed false ethics as the basic defect in American society, and each owed his influence largely to this emphasis.

The works of these three major figures cannot be studied in isolation. They were the product of a society in which moral affirmations were a part of the common currency of debate, and if each of them produced highly original contributions, each was nourished upon traditions which went far back in American history. They also existed in an environment in which intellectuals were more likely to influence action than ever before. The passion of the reformers, and their repudiation of conventional wisdom, sometimes blind one to the fact that, the late nineteenth century was, for good as well as ill, the formative epoch in modern American civilisation. Because it was closer to our own age than that of ante-bellum America it is in some ways harder to understand and certainly more difficult to see in perspective. There is perhaps no period in which a return to the sources is more likely to result in profitable reconstruction.

[1] 'The ethical factors which the Marxists relegated to the scrap-heap of bourgeois illusions figured as independent determinants for Bellamy, Lloyd and George, and it was just their preoccupation with the ethical dimension of capitalism that gave a catastrophic cast to their thought and a moral stridency to their tone.' John L. Thomas, *op. cit.*, 33.

CHAPTER 17

Nationalism and Comparative History

The core of a nation's history is what the people imagine themselves to be. The single word 'nationalism' embraces a complex mixture of past traditions, ritual observances, conventional ethics, ideals, and hopes for the future.[1] Ideas of what the nation is cannot be constant, and even within a single nation there may be two or more contrasting versions of national character. Before the Civil War many Americans avoided the word 'nation' because they could not bring themselves to describe a Federal republic in the same way as a centralised European monarchy; but for some Americans the word 'Union' came to have the same emotive force. During the Civil War the word 'nation' came to be used in a 'strong' sense, and national authority was invoked to deny the legality of secession and later to impose equal rights.

Even this new emphasis upon nationalism left the definition of the American nation obscure. In the early days of the Republic Americans had claimed to speak for all mankind and had not, like later revolutionary societies, justified aggression by the need to extend revolutionary principles. Even as late as 1846 many Americans conscientiously opposed the war with Mexico because they could not believe that force was necessary to extend universal American principles. The universalism of the revolution could, however, be linked with the earlier and powerful idea of a chosen people, and once the need to act as a weak power was passed, manifest destiny could take command. At the same time the men

---

[1] A large number of works approach the problem of American nationalism obliquely. Two important books focus on the subject: Merle Curti, *The Roots of American Loyalty* (New York, 1946), and Hans Kohn, *American Nationalism; an interpretative essay* (New York, 1957). Merle Curti's book has a valuable bibliographical essay.

who were most easily attracted to this new and expansive nationalism were often those most opposed to national consolidation in the political and economic sense. This was an issue—perhaps the principal issue of the Civil War—and one of its results was to join the vision of a chosen people to the idea of Union and the facts of national power.

It would be easy to make an anthology of what Americans have said about themselves, for, from the earliest times Americans have speculated about the unique character of their political society and sought to identify the new men whom it was expected to produce. The writings of Jefferson, Hamilton, the two Adamses, and Madison would furnish many examples; Washington's Farewell Address is a classic exposition, while Philip Freneau's patriotic verse emphasises a strong sense of the young nation's purpose, while demonstrating the links between American pride and European romanticism. The debates preceding the War of 1812 furnish many examples of American pride, self-consciousness, and sense of destiny. Webster's reply to Hayne was a classic invocation of Union as the key to greatness, and the popular oratory of the Jacksonian period echoed every fourth of July the sentiments of their leaders. Foreign visitors complained of the American assumption that they were a fortunate people, living under a special providence, and enjoying the envy of the world.[1]

Nationalism is not, however, merely a matter of rhetoric and response; it is the culture of a people and the way in which it comes to have form and coherence. The relationship to other countries, the degree of independence claimed, and the merits emphasised are all part of the national image; so that the study of nationalism extends from popular prejudice to literature and from demagoguery to diplomacy. For Americans in the first half-century of their national existence the relationship with England was crucial to the evolution of their own future. The United

[1] Because nationalism is powerful yet diffuse in its operation its sources must go beyond the normal range of political history. Merle Curti writes of his *Roots of American Loyalty*: 'The main source for this study has been a body of material hitherto little exploited: the occasional sermon, the Fourth of July oration, and the academic address.'

States were deluged with British literature, and, despite the complaints of such eminent figures as Noah Webster and J. Fenimore Cooper, English novels, poetry and reviews continued to dominate the American mind. Political economy was learned from Adam Smith, Ricardo and John Stuart Mill; science from Lyell, Faraday and later from Darwin; even the history of the pre-revolutionary era had to be acquired from English books. Many Americans resented this dependence and Fenimore Cooper complained that an American writer could not even made a reputation in his own country without winning the approval of British critics; yet there was another side to the picture for, to many Americans, the essential mission of America was to perpetuate the principles of freedom and law which had been forged by England. The American who tried to be more English than the English was not, in his own view, abandoning the interest of his own country but carrying on the mission which divine ordinance had entrusted to the Anglo-Americans. This dualism was not merely a matter for the literary conscience, for it also entered into everyday transactions: America was economically dependent upon British supplies, markets and capital, yet the development of American strength meant both accepting and rejecting the supports which the more advanced country was prepared to offer. In foreign affairs Great Britain was the ancient enemy whose every move raised the deepest suspicion; yet it was the country with the greatest power to help the United States and also the country whose interests reinforced those of America in so many areas.

Thus the study of nationalism—which may, at first sight, amount to no more than the collection of patriotic sentiments—becomes a complex problem in the analysis of strains and forces which worked in different directions. Americans have tended to assume that there was something inevitable about their own brand of nationalism, and whether they approve or deplore the outcome they have taken its character for granted; yet the twist given to the national image often resulted from fortuitous events. If the United States had given active support to France in 1793, the character of America as a revolutionary power would have been imprinted upon history, and the mission to protect and establish republican constitutions would have become a part of the American mission. Even bolder speculation springs from the thought that President Grant wished to intervene in Cuba on the side of revolution, but was dissuaded from doing so. If war had been avoided in 1812 it would have been eloquent proof of the sincerity and wisdom of Jefferson's policy of avoiding war while protecting national interests through economic coercion; it is difficult to imagine the effect upon the American self-image, but one can say with certainty that 'The Star-Spangled Banner' would not have been written. Opposition to war in 1846 might, and California might have been won by diplomacy and ready cash. These 'contrafacts' demonstrate that one cannot write the history of national character without looking closely at the events which have influenced the direction of its growth. Historians who stick to their sources too often stop short when they come within range of an amorphous concept such as nationalism; historians who deal in images and concepts too rarely bring the evidence of what happened into their vision.

The collective understanding of how men should act, which is an essential ingredient of nationalism, affects all political and social decisions. Attitudes towards immigrants, radicals and reformers; self-sacrifice, idealism, and the prosaic questions of business behaviour; hard-headed calculations of national interest and romantic love of one's country are amongst its products. Indeed this study is precisely at the opposite end of the historical spectrum to the statistical framework with which this book opened. In statistical studies we usually know what we are looking for, and even if we fail to find it, we recognise the gap and decide what informed guesses are permissible. In the study of nationalism, which exists in the mind and is moulded by events, we are never likely to lack information, but we can never say with certainty that our facts answer the right question, that other facts would not suggest a different answer, or that the same facts cannot lead to different conclusions. There is ample scope for speculation, but a study of this kind must also depend upon pure empiricism; for whereas the compilation of statistics is guided by questions which we have decided to ask and made possible by questions which men of the past wished to satisfy, satisfactory conclusions on nationalism can be reached only by the patient accumulation of information about what men said in hundreds of different situations when they were not answering questions but trying to state convictions. Of course the study of nationalism—and of similar large concepts —too often begins with a preconception and seeks only for evidence to defend or prosecute. This is not, however, the way that it should be. There is, indeed, no field in which it is more apposite to quote a comment from *The American Archivist* made by a scholar with very different material in mind.

> The historian must collect the bits and pieces of man's culture, fitting them together as the medieval artisan assembled myriad-colored shining shapes to bring a stained-glass window to dazzling perfection.[1]

The facts with which the discriminating historian of nationalism deals are all 'true' even though some are demonstrably false. It is 'true' that in the controversies between 1790 and 1800 some men believed in the existence of a conspiracy to restore monarchy and to subject America once more to Great Britain; it is 'true' that others believed that religion would not be safe if Jefferson became President. It is 'true' that in the early nineteenth century most Americans believed that British North America would eventually join the United States, and it is 'true' that in 1844 and 1845 the conviction that Great Britain intended to intervene in Texas persuaded many Americans to support immediate annexation. In a still greater crisis it is 'true' that few northerners expected secession to succeed in the South, and that few southerners expected the North to fight for the Union. All these inferences were false, but we cannot understand the past without recognising that they were held to be true. The contrafacts of history may be a luxury for econometricians, but they are necessities for students of nationalism; for without them their subject might have assumed a very different shape.

[1] Philip D. Jordan, 'The Scholar and the Archivist,' *The American Archivist*, 31 (1968), 64.

Historians are themselves a part of the history of their times, and nineteenth-century historiography throws an illuminating light upon the problems of nationalism. In history, more than in any other branch of literature or learning, Americans achieved international reputations. Prescott, Motley, Bancroft and Parkman were read throughout the English-speaking world and beyond, while the foundation in 1884 of the American Historical Association witnessed the emergence of a new school of professional history which combined German standards of scholarship with Anglo-American literary traditions. This achievement was the outcome of American circumstances. From the days of the Revolution it was accepted that history had a special role of explanation and justification to play; it was national history even when the subject was the Spanish conquest of Mexico or the rise of the Dutch Republic, because each threw light upon the destiny which America had come to fulfil.

The historian who uses historical writing as a source can do so at three different but overlapping levels; he can diagnose underlying assumptions about the character of the American nation, study the way in which particular incidents were handled, and explore the lessons which men distilled from the past.[1] Americans who emerged from the revolutionary era were conscious of having lived through historic events and of the need to preserve the record before it had faded from memory. The first incentive for many writers was to concentrate upon their own states, but simple and material calculations forced them to write of the United States as a whole—the English market was poor for revolutionary epics and the citizens of other states had little interest in the internal history of others. In 1787 David Ramsay, who had already published a history of South Carolina, produced his *History of the American Revolution* which set the pattern for many subsequent national histories; Union inevitably emerged as the safeguard of republican liberty and—as most early writers came from well-to-do professional classes—the establishment of order under wise

[1] This and the following paragraphs rely principally upon David D. Van Tassel, *Recording America's Past: An Interpretation of the Development of Historical Studies in America 1607–1884* (Chicago, 1960).

leadership was presented as the happy outcome of revolutionary up-heaval. A key to early historiography was its acceptance of a cyclic view of history in which peoples raised themselves to a plateau of greatness; from this they would inevitably decline, but wise leadership could arrest the process. Thus the early historians tended to be national and conservative in temper, and it was not until after the turn of the century that Jefferson tried to encourage the writing of 'republican' history.

The writing of national history for the larger public did not kill the interest of enthusiastic amateurs in local history. Jeremy Belknap, founder of the Massachusetts Historical Society, was following the example of the Society of Antiquaries of Scotland, founded in 1782, to recover relics of the Scottish past before they were submerged in the generalised history of the United Kingdom. Though Belknap's interest was focused upon Massachusetts, his society also collected materials relating to the other states of New England and most of the histories of New England towns written between 1792 and 1815 were published in the collections of the Massachusetts Historical Society. In 1804 the New York Historical Society was chartered by the legislature and received several grants of public money in subsequent years. In 1815 the American Philosophical Society of Philadelphia set up a Historical Committee which became the Pennsylvania State Historical Society in 1824. Other state historical societies were established during the same period, and enjoyed varying degrees of public patronage. This cultivation of local history was not incompatible with national history, for it encouraged scholars to establish the claims of their own states for recognition in the story of American achievement. Belknap planned, but did not execute, an association of state historical societies under Massachusetts leadership and scholarship would thus accept the primacy of the Old Bay State in preserving freedom and making the Union.

This was the background to the most notable of all the nine-teenth-century national histories by George Bancroft. He was learned, achieved an unrivalled mastery of colonial and revolu-tionary sources, and was not unaware of the contribution of the South and particularly of Virginia; but almost unconciously the true merit of the South was seen in its acceptance of the principles advocated by New England. This was combined with an abandonment of the cyclic theory. Deeply influenced by German Hegelianism, Bancroft saw the idea of democratic freedom working itself out in American history; thesis and antithesis had been presented by Puritanism and by southern materialism, by the self-government of the town meeting and by the rule of the southern upper class; the synthesis was achieved in the Revolution, and democratic freedom became the dominant theme. Thus Bancroft wrenched national history away from its conservative anchor and aligned himself intellectually and politically with Jacksonian democracy. His northern bias did not pass unchallenged and southern critics complained that he had done insufficient justice to their past. More than local pride was at stake, for the true issue was whether one should see the essence of the new nation in the driving force of one great universal spirit or seek it in local autonomy, variety, and rights. A later generation of professional historians would be inclined to endorse contemporary criticism rather than to applaud Bancroft's love of universals, his emphasis upon the force of great ideas, and his invocation of a mystical spirit of democracy and nationalism; but an appreciation of Bancroft is essential for an understanding of American nationalism as it emerged in the first half of the nineteenth century.

The experience of war led to an outpouring of historical writing in the North. Most of the authors assumed the previous existence of a nation with power to suppress rebellion, and ignored the southern counter-claim that the right to secede was implied in the very existence of a Federal society. The development of this national historiography has been analysed by Thomas J. Pressly. In 1880 the appearance of the first volume of James Schouler's *History of the United States of America under the Constitution* indicated a new maturity in the national outlook. Schouler did not disguise his dislike of slavery and of southern extremists, but he saw sectional conflict as a clash between ideas and institutions, as a tragedy for which individuals could not be blamed and which did not permanently damage the achievement of the great experiment. In general Schouler, and after him James Ford Rhodes,

333

reflected the views of pre-war nationalist Whigs of the Clay tradition; nationalism of the war period, with its romantic view of American destiny and its insistence upon the right of the nation to subdue its internal enemies, was succeeded by a nationalism in which compromise and stability were keys to success. It would be possible to document the mood from other sources and to demonstrate that the historians reflected the national views of their generation. It was entirely in keeping with the nationalism of the late nineteenth century that the most widely read history of the time, John Fiske's *Critical Period in American History*, emphasised the achievement of the Constitution-makers in saving the United States from anarchy and ineffectiveness.

Americans of the nineteenth century made little attempt to compare their history with that of other nations except to infer the superiority of their own political system. Nationalist history was introspective history and it did not occur to most Americans that the experience of others could throw light upon their own except by revealing the darkness of the alien shade.

With rare exceptions the nationalism of the pre-war period was unselfconscious. Americans assumed that their society was superior and did not need to say so in print. Between 1870 and the end of the century a number of lines converged to make patriotism the cultivation and preservation of certain characteristics despite the assumption that American ideas would triumph in a free market. The literary evidence of nationalism tends to accumulate while its expression shows increasing confusion of mind. The various strands were fear of the effect of 'alien' immigration, suspicion of European radicalism, the efforts of old families to assert their services to the nation by stressing genealogy and hereditary virtue; there was a need to define the nation which had been preserved in the fight of the Union and a quest for basic American precepts upon which all could agree. Nationalism expressed as hostility to unwelcome immigrants was reinforced by Social Darwinism, so that feelings which had been associated with prejudice and ignorance in the past were now voiced by men of science, while organised labour was equally hostile to the incoming flood of easily exploited workers.[1]

The best-known example of intellectual nativism was Josiah Strong's *Our Country*, published in 1885. Its influence was greatest because Strong was primarily interested in the moral condition of the country and introduced his attack upon immigration only as an example of an evil which contributed much to the prevalence of crime, immorality and political corruption; but 'what made the words urgent and significant was a conviction that in each of these respects the foreign influx was hastening the onset of a terrible upheaval in American society'.[2] In a sense, therefore, Strong was continuing the tradition of the old Whigs who had allied with the Know Nothings in the 1850s; they, too, had seen disaster coming and sought to avert it by an insistence upon preserving certain vaguely defined American principles. The literature related to all these arguments has been studied mainly to document the origins of the movement to restrict immigration; but it is probable that further analysis with different questions in mind will throw more light upon the character of American nationalism. Books, pamphlets and newspapers link the eastern intellectuals, the social gospellers, the American Federation of Labour, and Farmer Radicals.

The second major strand in post-war nationalism was the emergence of hereditary societies. The historian of these movements examined the records of twenty-four, including such well-known societies as the Daughters of the American Revolution, the Colonial Dames of America, and the Society of Mayflower Descendants. For the most part these were harmless exercises in family pride, but they were also symptoms of reaction against equalitarian democracy and of an attempt to rediscover the historical principles of American national spirit. Far more influential and widely based were the veterans organisations led by the Grand Army of the Republic and societies preserving the memories of the Armies of the Potomac, Cumberland and Tennessee. Their

[1] A fully documented study is John Higham, *Strangers in the Land: Patterns of American Nativism 1860–1925* (New Brunswick, N.J., 1955).

[2] Higham, *op. cit.*, 39.

primary intention was to preserve the fraternal spirit of the fighting troops, but they became vigorously concerned with honouring the memory of fallen comrades, pressing for pensions and benefits for the survivors and widows, and seeing that the rising generation was correctly informed about the aims and achievements of the Union cause. The Grand Army introduced Memorial Day, pressed states to recognise it as a public holiday, and when successful deplored the tendency of the public to use it for pleasure, recreation, and intemperance. They also pressed to have Lincoln's birthday recognised as a holiday, and were foremost in promoting the cult of the Flag as the symbol of virtue, patriotism and unity. A significant development was the passage of laws in many states requiring that American history should be taught in public schools, and this led in turn to anxiety over the content of textbooks. All this activity left a legacy of proceedings, reports, magazines, legislative debates and enactments, public letters, and evidence of pressure behind the scenes.

It can be seen that the sources for the study of American nationalism lead one into extended fields; from Federalist reactions to the French Revolution to Manifest Destiny, from the War of 1812 to Know Nothings, and from popular oratory to the work of serious historians. The Civil War was, in a sense, a quarrel over the character of the nation, and the victors sought to define the nation in a new dimension of national power. The post-war years lead one to patriotic societies and attempts to discover and exalt the basic principles of Americanism. The definition of American nationalism presents the historian with a task of unusual difficulty; the outcome is so obvious and so important, but analysis of its evolution involves selection and a subtle blend of strands from all levels and all aspects of society. Though few historians have directed themselves immediately to this task, a great many have been unconsciously inspired by the need to explain 'this new man, this American'. Though American nationalism has not engaged the attention like Italian or German nationalism it has nevertheless been a major preoccupation of American historians. Today it becomes necessary to insist that much of American historiography has been too introspective, and too little aware of America's relationship to other societies in the developing civilisation of the nineteenth century.

Historians who wish to enlarge the international horizons of American history are confronted at the outset by a strategic problem. Is the best approach to compare American with other institutions and ideas? Or is it to trace the developments which America shared with other societies. Analogies drawn from the experience of other nations can help one to understand; contrasts can explain essential differences between American and other civilisations; but unifying concepts may help one to place American developments in perspective.

All the great changes through which historic civilisations have passed have involved most or all of certain characteristics, and a list may be as informative as a philosophic analysis.

> An increase in population.
> Shifts in population from occupation to occupation and from region to region.
> Technological innovations.
> Improvements in production and communication.
> New methods of organising economic life.
> Increased social mobility.
> The emergence of new men of power.
> Changes in political ideas and institutions.
> The decline of old-established authority.
> Adjustments in law.
> Changes in philosophy and religion.
> Scientific advances.
> A new morality.
> Internal conflicts caused by dislocation and social aspirations.
> International conflicts caused by changes in the balance of power and competition for a share in expanding resources.

This list is not exhaustive, and others might think of additions or amendments. Nor are the items presented in any order of priority, for a major feature of modern times has been the concurrence of all these changes without anyone presenting a convincing case

337

for one as the prime mover or trigger. The list may, however, provide a framework for analysis. Each of the factors is international in its operation, but the character of each can be understood only when one has studied local variations on a comparative basis.

The preceding chapters have surveyed the sources for studying the American aspect of most of these factors; but American events did not stand alone. Only superhuman vision and industry could embrace the whole in one synthesis, but no one should lose sight of the international context of his particular study. It may be possible to study some operations, particularly in the economic field where business activity overflowed national barriers, as single historical problems. It may be more appropriate to study some on a comparative basis, and this may be especially true of political institutions and social structure. There are other developments, such as industrialisation and urbanisation, which appear to have separate origins but which converge towards similar patterns of behaviour.[1]

If one is to avoid the flabby generalisations of courses in 'world history' the only road is the hard one of finding, using and interpreting the sources. A review of some of the topics covered in this volume may suggest possibilities. Demographers have already made investigations in some problems of population growth, including the age structure of the population, the age of marriage, and expectations of life. This is a field in which the sources are

[1] A group of distinguished scholars contributed to C. Vann Woodward, ed., *A Comparative Approach to American History* (New York, 1968) with varying results. The origin of the papers in talks given under the auspices of the Voice of America meant that the primary purpose was to explain American history by reference to similar or contrasting experiences elsewhere. The structure of the book was therefore determined by events and problems in American history rather than by international developments in which America shared. Some of the authors put American events firmly into an international framework: others gave a conventional account of the American topic assigned to them with occasional references to Europa. Nevertheless the volume did something to fulfil the promise implied by the editor when he wrote, 'To limit the subject of historical study within national boundaries is always to invite the charge of narrow perspective and historical nationalism. Historians of all nations have in some measure incurred that risk, but Americans have been accused of more than the normal share of this type of parochialism.'

numerous, comparatively accurate, and easily accessible. Problems of economic growth can be studied either from comparative econometrics or from the records of the economic institutions engaged in international business; in both approaches the sources are numerous, though in the first historians are dependent upon the accuracy and comprehensiveness of early statistics, and in the second upon the chance survival of materials relating to affairs which were often shrouded in secrecy. It seems that there are many opportunities both in the comparative study of economic behaviour and in the quest for the economic forces which span oceans and dissolve frontiers; but so far general historians have barely ventured into this field. More elusive are the influences which regulate the transformation of social life; some attention has been given to the impact of war—though mainly upon national communities—and there has been one essay in comparative technological change; but clearly the international dimension for many phases of modern evolution has yet to be defined.

Early commentators were fascinated by the political contrasts between Europe and America, and whether they approached from the conservative or radical side they were convinced that political innovation was America's claim to a character distinct from that of older nations. At a later date several of the first generation of American professional historians sought unifying concepts in an 'Anglo-Saxon' civilisation by going back to medieval times to find the roots of the American system. The popularity of economic interpretation in the early twentieth century, and the waning enthusiasm of intellectuals (until the New Deal) for political activity, pushed these studies into the background, and despite some perceptive work on Revolutionary constitutional history little was done, and many American historians were content to repeat Alexis de Tocqueville's generalisations as a substitute for new questions about the American political experience. Yet even if one confines the study of political evolution to the United States, Great Britain and Canada, there is a tremendous opportunity. A British scholar has shown how one can travel from the study of colonial poll books to large generalisations about theories of representative government, but most historians have been content to accept American political institutions as a part of the 'data' of history and to study national history without standing back to view its scaffolding. The alternative does not demand a plunge into 'megahistory', for the most revealing conclusions may be suggested by the microcosm of local society.

Some aspects of social history lend themselves readily to international treatment. Religion is, perhaps, the most revealing in illustrating both the strength of unifying concepts and the force of local variations in Church organisation. In urban history there are shared themes, significant local variations, and in most countries an abundance of evidence. There has already been some important work on the international aspects of slavery and race relations; but much remains to be done. The warning notes which were sounded in the chapter on Afro-Americans are even more relevant in international studies, where not only are the sources biased but have also been used by men unfamiliar with the more general environment of the country from which they are taken. The history of industrial workers offers similar opportunities for comparative treatment; for years Europeans have been asking 'Why did socialism not receive more support in the United States?' or 'Why has there been no labour movement?'—but no one has a satisfactory answer. The questions imply a comparison with countries where socialism became popular and labour became politically active; but the groundwork for making the comparison has not been laid.

Most difficult of all are problems of international intellectual history which demand a distinction between the original and the derivative, an explanation of the rapid diffusion of some ideas in some countries and their turgid development in others, and an examination of the profound influence of uninteresting ideas. It may not be too difficult to trace through important themes from distinguished writer to distinguished writer; it is much more difficult to explain 'climates of opinion' and still more difficult to give this elusive concept an international dimension. Yet it is impossible to ignore the tides of opinion which have beaten upon society and altered its character, and movements of this magnitude have left their traces in every crevice of the historical record.

These prospects may dismay working historians, who know their own limitations and have found mastery of the sources in one branch of national history sufficient to occupy a professional lifetime. But the great chain which connects the fragment of local history with the larger patterns of modern society cannot be broken; the detail becomes significant when it is related to the whole; and the horizons are constantly widening. Sources cannot be understood unless they are placed in the landscape of general history, but the visible terrain rests upon strata upon strata of source material.

Further Investigation

The number of guides, bibliographies, check-lists, and inventories covering the sources for this period are very numerous. The suggestions which follow are intended to help the student begin his own investigations. The first section contains general guides and aids to research, the second notes some books on the techniques of historians, and the third lists works which describe or classify materials in various fields.

I. GENERAL GUIDES AND AIDS

Oscar Handlin *et al.* *The Harvard Guide to American History* (Cambridge, Mass., 1954, 1960) contains invaluable chapters on many aspects of historical study. There are lists of specialised bibliographies, of principal periodicals, newspapers, diaries, memoirs and autobiographies. Reading lists for select topics include references to the standard collections of printed sources.

O. Lawrence Burnette, Jr. *Beneath the Footnote: A Guide to the Use and Preservation of American Historical Sources* (Madison, the State Historical Society of Wisconsin, 1969) contains a mass of information about the history and use of American archives; the bibliography runs to 58 pages and includes all the major guides to source materials and a large number of books and articles about their custody, classification, and problems of use. The presentation is more lively than this summary might suggest.

John Brown Mason. *Research Resources: Annotated Guide to the Social Sciences*, 2 vols (Santa Barbara, Calif., 1971), lists (in the first volume) indexes, abstracts and periodicals; the second volume contains official publications since 1789 and statistical sources.

Eugene R. Fingerhut, *The Fingerhut Guide: Sources in American History* (Santa Barbara, Calif., 1973), provides an extremely useful classified list of bibliographies, works of reference, and guides to sources.

Philip M. Hamer (ed.), *A Guide to Archives and Manuscripts in the United States* (New Haven, 1961) is invaluable for the location of source materials; it can be used in conjunction with the multi-volume *National Union Catalogue of Manuscripts in the United States* which lists and indexes many thousands of manuscripts in hundreds of repositories. The *Union Catalogue* is intended for experienced researchers who have a good idea of what they are looking for; it can be bewildering for the student who merely wishes to survey the sources for a particular period or topic.

Historical Statistics of the United States: Colonial Times to 1957 (Washington D.C., 1960—revised to 1960, 1962) gives over 8,200 statistical series, and in addition to demographic and economic materials includes data on government, civil service, elections, federal and state finance. The introductions to the sections contain much useful information and comment on statistical sources. The student who wishes for guidance in the use of statistical evidence can consult *The Historian's Guide to Statistics* by Charles M. Dollar (New York, 1971).

II. *THE HISTORIANS' CRAFT*

There are a number of works which deal with the general problems of historical study. The examples and references are often drawn from European or British history, but are used to illustrate precepts of interest to all interested in the nature and use of sources. Amongst the best of a growing class of literature are Jacques Barzun and Henry Graaf, *The Modern Researcher* (New York, 1957); Louis Gottschalk, *Understanding History: a primer of historical method* (New York, 1950); G. Kitson Clark, *The Critical Historian* (London, 1967); G. R. Elton, *The Practice of History* and *Political History* (London, 1967, 1970). Arthur Marwick, *The Nature of History* (London, 1970) has a good bibliography of works on historical scholarship and methods. Marc Bloch in *The Craft of History* deals mainly with problems of interpretation and use in periods remote from nineteenth-century America but it is worth reading as an account of his work by a master-historian. The value of computers in political studies is demonstrated in *Sectional Stress and Party Strength: 1830–1860* by Thomas B. Alexander (Nashville, 1967). A vigorous attack on modern historiography was made by Samuel Eliot Morison in his presidential address to the American Historical Association in 1954 (*American Historical Review*, Vol. LIX). A critique of the arguments and assumptions used by historians (which touches upon their use of sources at many points) is *Historians' Fallacies: Toward a Logic of Historical Thought* by David H. Fischer (New York, 1970). In *A Behavioral Approach to Historical Analysis* (New York, 1969) Robert F. Berkhofer argues that historians often use behavioral theory without saying or realising that they are doing it; his plea for sound theory can be contrasted with the plea (in several of the preceding chapters) for an understanding of the sources.

This brief review has brought the argument to the brink of the Philosophy of History; over that verge it is not intended to step.

III. *GUIDES TO VARIOUS CLASSES OF MATERIAL*

(a) *OFFICIAL PUBLICATIONS:*

Laurence F. Schmeckebier and Roy B. Eastin, *Government Publications and their Use* (Washington, Brookings Institution, 2nd ed., 1969) is not a catalogue or check-list but 'an aid to the acquisition and utilisation of the publications'. This makes it a most useful work for anyone who is trying to understand the range and variety of government publications. The defects of Ben Perley Poore's *Descriptive Catalogue of the Government Publications of the United States* (Washington, 1885, Johnson repr. 1962) are examined in Schmeckebier and Eastin (pp. 6–11), but for much of the material covered it remains the only catalogue and index; it was continued in John Griffith Ames' *Comprehensive Index of the Publications of the United States 1881–1893*, 2 vols (Washington,

1905, Edwards repr. 1953). *United States Government Publications* by Anne Morris Boyd and Rae E. Rips (New York, 1952) is a useful classified list. There is also the *Checklist of United States Public Documents 1789-1909* (Washington, 1905, Kraus repr. 1962) and Adelaide R. Hasse, *Index to the United States Documents Relating to Foreign Affairs 1828-1861*, 3 vols (Washington, 1914-1921).

Federal Archives relating to the Civil War by Kenneth W. Munden and Henry P. Beers (Washington, 1962) can be used as a general guide to archival material for the mid-nineteenth century. In *American State Archives* (Chicago, 1964) Ernst Posner deals mainly with archival problems and is of limited use as a guide to the character of materials. The *Inventories* of county archives, sponsored by the Works Progress Administration, contain masses of material (see Chapter VII above) but unfortunately only a few of published volumes contained editorial analyses of the sources surveyed. A check-list of State official documents would be a vast undertaking but would be worth the labour so far as scholars are concerned.

(b) *MISCELLANEOUS MATERIALS*:

Reference has already been made to the huge *National Union Catalogue of Manuscript Collections*, 7 vols to date (Ann Arbor and Washington 1962–   ). The sources for American history in the British Isles are listed and briefly described in B. R. Crick and M. Alman in *A Guide to the Manuscripts relating to America in Great Britain and Ireland* (London, 1961); this was a pioneer work (supplementing the earlier work by C. M. Andrews up to 1789) and a good deal of material (especially in business and law archives) remains to be investigated. *A Guide to the Principal Sources for American Civilization, 1800-1900, in the City of New York* by Henry J. Carman and Arthur W. Thompson (New York, 1960, 1962) is not only a guide to the New York collections but also a case study in the great extent and variety of the sources for nineteenth-century history. Very different in concept and execution is the *Guide to the Diplomatic History of the United States* (Washington, 1935, Peter Smith repr. 1959) by Samuel Flagg Bemis and Grace Gardner Griffin. This is intended as a guide for research and is, in many ways, a model of its kind; the text is intended not only to indicate what materials exist but also their value and limitations. Henrietta M. Larson broke new ground with her *Guide to Business History: Materials and their Use* (Cambridge, Mass., 1948) and a new survey of this field, in the light of so much recent work, is overdue. Some materials still await analysis, classification, and authoritative survey; there is, for instance, no comprehensive guide to the sources for black history or for urban history. The former, when compiled, must go beyond such sources as slave narratives and indicate where to seek the evidence from folk-lore or religion. The bibliography of Oscar Handlin and John Burchard's *The Historian and the City* (Cambridge, Mass., 1963) lists the major urban histories at the time of publication, and these in turn will often indicate the sources used; but the new dimensions of urban sources can best be grasped by studying the bibliography of *The Private City: Philadelphia in Three Periods of its Growth* by Sam B. Warner (Philadelphia, 1969). Many other specialist guides to sources are listed in the invaluable *Fingerhut Guide* noted above. For education consult William W. Brickman, *Research in Educational History* (Norwood, Pa., 1973).

Index